VOCABULARY

OF

GERMAN MILITARY TERMS

AND

ABBREVIATIONS.

(SECOND EDITION.)

GENERAL STAFF (INTELLIGENCE),
GENERAL HEADQUARTERS.

July, 1918.

The Naval & Military Press Ltd

Published by

The Naval & Military Press Ltd
Unit 10 Ridgewood Industrial Park,
Uckfield, East Sussex,
TN22 5QE England

Tel: +44 (0) 1825 749494
Fax: +44 (0) 1825 765701

www.naval-military-press.com
www.nmarchive.com

In reprinting in facsimile from the original, any imperfections are inevitably reproduced and the quality may fall short of modern type and cartographic standards.

A.

Abänderung	alteration.
A-Bataillon	battalion in front line.
Abbauen	to dismantle (*e.g., a wireless station*).
Abbeförderung	evacuation (*of sick and wounded*).
Abbinden	to set (*concrete*).
Abblenden	to screen (*a light*).
Abbrechen	to break off; change from line formation to column formation.
abbrechen, das Schiessen	to cease fire.
zur Kolonne abbrechen	to break into column.
Lager abbrechen	to strike camp.
Abdachen	to slope away (*of ground*).
Abdämmung	blocking (*a trench*).
Abdanken	to discharge, dismiss from the service; to abdicate.
Abdecken	to uncover (*sometimes wrongly used* = to cover).
Abdeckerei	knacker's yard.
Abdichtungsring	expanding washer (e.g., *for hermetically closing receptacles in food carriers*).
Abdrift	leeway (*aeroplane, etc.*).
Abdruck	copy; impress.
Abdrücken	to press the trigger.
Abendmeldung	evening report.
Abfall	slope of a hill; waste, refuse.
Abfangen	to catch, capture.
Abfangen (ein Telegram)	to intercept a telegram.
Abfeuern	to discharge, fire off.
kernrecht abfeuern	to fire point blank.
Abflauen	to decrease, to abate (*artillery fire*).
Abflugstelle	pigeon station.
Abfrage-Apparat	exchange operator's instrument (*telephone*).
Abgabe	discharge (*light signals, &c.*).
Abgang (zur Truppe, &c.)	discharge (from hospital, &c.).
Abgang	departure.
Abgangsfehler	error due to "jump" (*gun, rifle, &c.*).
Abgangsrichtung	line of departure (*of a shot*).
Abgangswinkel	angle of departure (*of a shot*).
Abgase	exhaust gases (*of a motor*).
Abgeben	to give, to deliver; to transfer (*of soldiers*).
Abgehen	to start off.

(B 11413)

Abgegangen ...	dispatched.
Abgesessen ! ...	Dismount !
Abgespalten ...	isolated, detached.
Abgespaltenes Maschinengewehr	detached machine gun.
Abgezweigt (-e Kompagnie) ...	detached (company).
Abhalten ...	to hold off, restrain, check.
einen Appell abhalten	to call the roll.
Abhang ...	slope ; hill side.
Abholzen ...	to denude (of timber), to cut down the trees.
Abhören ...	to intercept.
eine Unterhaltung abhören	to intercept a conversation.
eine Telegraphenleitung abhören	to tap a telegraph line.
Abhören ...	listening, tapping (*a message*).
Abhörnetz ...	listening system.
Abhörstation ...	listening set station.
Abhörstromlauf ...	listening *or* tapping circuit.
Abhörtätigkeit ...	} listening, tapping.
Abhörverfahren ...	
Abkochen ...	to cook.
unterwegs abkochen	to cook on the march.
Abkommandieren ...	to detach, detail.
Abkrümmen ...	to fire off (*rifle*).
Abkürzen ...	to abbreviate.
Abladen ...	to unload ; unloading.
Abladekommando ...	unloading party.
Ablegen (Gepäck) ...	to take off (packs).
Ableitung ...	lead (*electric*), short circuit.
Ablenken ...	to divert (*attention*).
Ablösen ...	to relieve.
Ablösung ...	relief.
die Ablösung geht vor	the relief is in progress.
Ablösungstruppen ...	relieving troops.
Abmarsch ...	marching off.
Abmarschiert ! ...	fired ! (*colloquial* = "*abgefeuert*").
Abmarschpunkt ...	starting-point.
Abnahmebeschuss ...	proof-firing, trials (*of a gun, previous to delivery*).
Abnahmestelle...	issue depôt.
Abneigung ...	a turning aside, divergence ; alteration (*in range, elevation*).
Abort ...	latrine.
Abprallen ...	to ricochet.
Abpraller ...	ricochet.
Abprallweite ...	length of ricochet.

Abprotzen	to unlimber.
Abrechnen	to deduct, subtract.
50 Meter abrechnen	to shorten range 50 metres.
Abrede	agreement.
in Abrede stellen	to deny.
Abreissschnur	" pull-out " string.
Abreissvorrichtung	firing device.
Abreisszünder	friction lighter, friction tube.
Abriegeln	to block.
Abriegelungsfeuer	defensive barrage (*if on the defensive*); back barrage (*if attacking*).
Abrücken	to move off.
Abrufen	to recall; *sometimes* to repea verbally.
Abrüsten	to disarm, demobilize.
Abrüstung	demobilization; disarmament.
Abrutschen nach der Innenseite der Kurve	to side-slip (*aeroplane*).
Abrutschen nach der Aussenseite der Kurve	to skid (*aeroplane*).
Absacken, befindlich im	stalling (*aeroplane*).
Absatteln	to unsaddle, " off-saddle."
Abschätzung	estimate.
Abschied	departure.
seinen Abschied erbitten	to ask to be placed on the retired list.
seinen Abschied nehmen	to resign one's commission, to quit the service.
Abschiessen	to fire off.
Abschlagen	to repulse.
Abschluss	*sometimes* joint (*as in " gasdichter Abschluss " = gas-tight joint*).
Abschlussplatte	protecting plate (*of breech action of field gun*).
Abschneiden	to cut off (*retreat, &c.*); *sometimes* to coincide.
Abschnitt	sector.
Abschnittskommandeur	sector commander.
Abschnittsweise	by sectors.
Abschrift	copy.
Abschub	evacuation (*of inhabitants*), repatriation.
Abschwenken	to wheel (*to right or left*).
Absender	sender (*of a letter, postcard, &c.*).
Absendestelle	dispatching point.

Absetzen (das Gewehr)	to bring the rifle to the "ready" (*after firing*).
Absetzen (Seitengewehre)	to unfix (bayonets).
Absicht...	intention, view.
Absitzen	to dismount.
Abspannen	to unhook (*horses*).
Absperrung	barricade, blocking.
Abspielen (sich)	to take place, to develop.
Abspriessen	to strut (*engineering*).
Abstand	distance.
Abstecken	to mark out ; to undo, unfasten.
Absteckpfahl	iron peg.
Absteifung	strutting (*engineering*).
Absteigen	to descend, go down ; to dismount.
Abstellen (Motor)	to shut off (a motor).
Abstellgleise	siding.
Abstocken	to prop, strut.
Abstreuen	to scatter, sprinkle.
mit Schrapnel abstreuen	to sweep with shrapnel.
Abstufen	to form steps, graduate.
Abstürzen	to crash (*referring to aeroplanes*).
Absuchen, Gelände	to search ground (*for wounded, &c.*).
Abstützen	to prop, strut.
Abteilung	detachment, flight, &c., section (of War Ministry, General Staff, &c.) ; (*not translated if it refers to field artillery, when it is a group of 3 batteries*).
Abteilungsbefehl	order of artillery "Abteilung."
Abteilung für Licht und Kraft	electrician detachment.
Abteilungskommandeur (artl.)	"Abteilung" commander(*artillery*).
Abtransport (im)	on the move (from).
Abtreppen (nach)	to form steps (down to) (*when excavating*).
Abwarten	to wait for ; to attend to *or* groom (*horses*).
Abwässerungsanlagen	drainage system.
Abwehr	defence.
Abwehren	to repel, ward off.
Abwehrfeuer	defensive fire.
Abwehrgeschütz	anti-aircraft gun ; gun for repelling the assault.
Abwehrgraben...	support *or* reserve trench.
Abwehrschlacht	defensive battle.
Abweichen	to branch off ; to deviate from.
Abweichung	departure from (*orders*) ; deflection, deviation.

Abweisen	to repulse, beat back.
Abweiser	arm-guard (*light field howitzer carriage*).
Abwurfapparat	bomb release gear.
Abwurftasche	message bag (*dropped by aeroplanes*).
Abzäumen	to take off the bridle.
Abzeichen	badge, distinguishing mark.
Abzeichentuch	cloth used for badges.
Abziehen	to take off; to divert; to evacuate.
ein Gewehr abziehen	to pull the trigger.
von der Wache abziehen	to come off guard.
Abzug	retreat; outlet; trigger.
Abzugsbügel	trigger guard.
Abzugsfeder	trigger spring.
Abzugsgraben	drainage trench.
Abzugsgriff	trigger.
Abzugsschleife	string loop (*on band of hand grenade*).
Abzugsvorrichtung	trigger device.
Abzweig	point of bifurcation (*e.g., of two galleries in mining*).
Abzweigstollen	branch gallery (*mining*).
Achsband	axle clip.
Achsbandhalter	axle guard.
Achse	axle tree.
Achsel	shoulder.
Achselband	aiguillette.
Achselklappe	shoulder strap (*N.C.Os. and men*).
Achselschuppen	metal epaulettes.
Achselstück	shoulder strap (*officers*).
Achsenbruch	breaking of an axle tree.
Achsenzahl	number of axles (*in a train*).
Achsenschmierbüchse	tin of axle grease.
Achssitz	axle tree seat (*gun carriage*).
Achteck	octagon.
Achtung!	Attention! Look out!
Achtung! Gas!	Look out! gas!
Adjutant	adjutant.
Flügel-Adjutant	} Aide-de-Camp to the Emperor.
General-Adjutant	
Adjutantur	Administrative staff (*not translated—retain*).
Aferna (Armee-Fernsprech-Abteilung)	Army telephone detachment.
Affe	pack (*slang*).
Afl (Artillerie-Flieger)	artillery aeroplane.
Afla (Artillerie-Flieger-Abteilung)	artillery reconnaissance flight (*aviation unit*).

Afunka (Armee-Funker-Abteilung)	Army wireless detachment.
A-Gelände	zone of the battalion in line.
Agent	agent, spy.
Agru (Arendt-Gruppe)	listening set section.
Aka (Artillerie-Kampf-Artillerie)	counter-battery artillery.
Akkordarbeit	piece-work.
Akkumulator-Ladestelle	accumulator charging station (*wireless, &c.*).
Akofern (Armee-Fernsprech-Kommando *or* Kommandeur)	Army Telephone H.Q., *or* Commander.
Akofunk (Armee-Funker-Kommando *or* Kommandeur)	Army Wireless H.Q. *or* Commander.
Akonach (Armee-Nachrichten-Kommandeur)	Army Signal Commander.
Aktenkasten	despatch-box.
Aktiv	regular, Active (*as opposed to Reserve, &c.*).
Alarm	alarm.
Alarm blasen	to sound the alarm.
Alarmbereitschaft (erhöhte)	(increased) readiness for action.
Alarmbestimmungen	alarm orders.
Alarmpatrone	signal rocket.
Alarmplatz	alarm post, alarm station.
Alarmposten	sentry to give the alarm.
Alarmquartier	alarm station.
Alarmsammelplatz	assembly post, assembly station.
Alarm schlagen	} to sound the alarm.
Alarmsignal geben	
Alarmsignale (geblasene)	bugle calls, whistles, &c.
Alarmstellung	support line.
Alarmvorrichtung	appliance, device for giving the alarm.
Alarmzustand	"Stand to."
Alarmzustand (aufheben)	(to give) "Stand down."
Albatros	"Albatros" (*a type of aeroplane*).
Alder-B-Munition	"Alder B" ammunition (*explosive bullet for anti-aircraft purposes*).
Allerhöchste Kabinettsordre...	Order of His Majesty in Council.
Allerschwerst	heaviest (*e.g., gun*).
Allgemeine Wehrpflicht	universal military service.
Allgemeines Aufgebot	levy *en masse*.
Älter	senior.
Älterer Unteroffizier	senior N.C.O.

Altmessing	brass scrap.
Altmetall	metal scrap.
Amboss (der Zündglocke) ...	detonator cap (*literally, anvil*).
Ambossklotz	anvil block.
Ammonal	ammonal.
Ampulle	lamp (*electric*).
Amt	office.
Ana (Nachrichtenmittel- Abteilung des Artillerie-Regiments)	artillery regimental signalling detachment.
Anbinden	to tie to.
mit jemandem anbinden ...	to put in communication (*telephonic*) with someone.
Anbrechen	to break, dawn.
Anfall	attack.
Anfangsgeschwindigkeit ...	initial *or* muzzle velocity.
Anfassen	to take hold of, pick up (*arms*).
Anfertigen	to make, manufacture, construct, prepare.
Anfordern	to demand, request.
Anführen	to lead.
Anfuhr	supply.
Angabe	statement.
Angaben, beglaubigte ...	statements (verified).
Angängig	feasible.
Angeldraht	trip wire.
Angelehnt	in touch with, supported by.
Angezeigt	indicated, advisable, expedient; announced, reported.
Angreifen	to attack.
Angriff	attack.
Ablenkungsangriff ...	feint attack, diversion.
einen Angriff liefern ...	to deliver an attack.
Entlastungsangriff... ...	attack to relieve pressure elsewhere.
Gegenangriff	counter-attack.
Hauptangriff	main attack.
Luftangriff	aerial attack.
Scheinangriff	feint attack.
Angriffsabteilung	assaulting party.
Angriffsart	method of attack.
Angriffsbefehl	order to attack, attack orders.
Angriffserfahrungen	experiences in attack (*e.g., of an army*).
Angriffsfeld	zone of attack.
Angriffsfront	front of attack.
Angriffshandlung	conduct of the attack.
Angriffskrieg	offensive war.
Angriffslücke	gap formed to facilitate the attack

Angriffsplan	plan of attack.
Angriffsstelle	point of attack.
Angriffsstreifen	sector of attack.
Angriffstempo (in Einklang gebrachtes)	(pre-arranged) time-table of the attack, *literally*—pace of the attack.
Angriffsverfahren, planmässiges	methodical attack.
Anhalt	guide (*e.g., to construction, conduct, &c.*).
Anhaltspunkte	instructions.
Anhängewagen	trailer.
Anheimstellen	to leave (it) to.
Anhöhe...	high ground, hill, slope.
Ankergrund	anchorage.
Ankerrödel	anchor line belaying pin (*bridging*).
Ankerstellung...	anchorage.
Ankertau	cable, anchor line.
Anklammerungspunkt ...	a "holding on" point, strong point.
Ankündigungskommando ...	cautionary part of a word of command.
Anlage	emplacement, position, arrangement; appendix (*orders, documents, &c.*).
Bahnanlage	railway buildings, &c.
Festungsanlage	fortifications.
Scheinanlage	dummy trench *or* work.
Anlasser	down airshaft (*of mining galleries or dug-outs*).
Anlauf	rush, advance.
beim ersten Anlauf... ...	at the first onset.
Anlegen	to take aim; to plan; to construct.
ein Manöver anlegen ...	to suggest a scheme for manœuvres.
Anleitung	instruction.
Anmarsch	approach.
Anmarschieren	to approach.
Anmarschlinie	line of approach.
Anmarschrichtung	direction of advance.
Anmarschweg	approach, communication trench.
Anmelden, sich	to report one's arrival.
Anmeldung	report, notice.
Anmerkung	remarks.
Annähern, sich	to approach.
Annäherungsgraben ... ... ⎫ Annäherungsweg ... ... ⎭	communication trench, approach trench.
Annäherungsmassstab ...	approximate scale.
Anordnen	to arrange, order.

Anordnungen	arrangements, dispositions; instructions.
Anpassen	to fit on, fasten; to adapt.
Anpassen, sich, dem Gelände	to adapt oneself to the ground.
Anrichten	to produce, cause; to regulate.
Anrücken	to march up, advance (against).
Anruf	telephone call; challenge (*of a sentry*; call signal (*wireless*).
Anrufen	to challenge, hail; to call up (*telephone*).
Ansagen	to announce, notify.
Ansammlung	concentration (*of troops*).
Anschaffen	to provide, procure.
Anschalter	separator (*mining*).
Anschaltvorrichtung	tapping device (*electrical*).
Anschauen	to inspect; to observe (*a position*).
Anschirren	to harness.
Anschlag	firing position, the " present."
Anschlag	attempt to damage (*a railway, &c.*).
Anschlagbock	buffer stop (*gun carriage*).
Anschlagshöhe	height over which a man can fire.
Anschleichen, sich	to creep up to.
Anschliessen, sich	to join up with.
Anschluss	connection, junction (*e.g., with other troops*); enclosure, annexe.
geben Sie mir Anschluss mit	" Put me through to " (*telephone*).
Anschluss-Batterie	adjoining battery.
Anschluss-Kompagnie (-Zug)	flank company (platoon); directing company (platoon).
Anschlussmann	connecting file.
Anschlusspunkt	point of contact; junction.
Anschneiden	to cut; to make intersections; to obtain a bearing on (*e.g., gun flashes*).
durch Anschneiden feststellen	to locate by intersection.
Anschnitt	bearing.
Ansetzen	to launch (*e.g., an attack*).
Ansetzer	rammer (*artillery*).
Anspannen	to stretch, strain; to hook in horses.
Anspornen	to stimulate.
Anstalt	establishment.
Ansteckmagazin	detachable magazine.
Anstellung	appointment.
Anstrich	colouring.
Anstromkante	leading edge (*plane of aeroplane*).
Ansturm	assault.

Antenne	the "aerial" (*wireless*); wireless station.
Antransport (im)	on the move to.
Antreiben	to drive, urge on, set going.
Antreten	to begin; to fall in (*parade*).
wir wollen zum Sturm antreten	we are about to attack.
den Dienst antreten	to assume duties.
Anweisen	to direct, point out.
Anweisung	instructions.
Anzeige	notice, announcement.
Anzeigen	to give notice; to report; to proclaim.
Anzeiger	marker.
Anzug	suit, dress.
feldmarschmässiger Anzug	marching order.
Apotheker	pharmacist, chemist.
Apparat	apparatus, instrument.
Appell	roll call; the "assembly" (*cavalry*).
Appell abhalten	to call the roll.
beim Appell fehlen	to be absent from roll call.
Appellplatz	parade ground.
Arbeit	work, labour.
Arbeitende Mannschaft	working parties.
Arbeiterbataillon	labour battalion.
Arbeitsabteilung	fatigue party.
Arbeitsanzug	fatigue dress.
Arbeitsdienst	fatigue duty.
Arbeitskommando	fatigue party.
Arbeitskompagnie	labour company.
Arbeitsplan	working plan.
Arbeitssoldat	**soldier** of a disciplinary corps.
Arbeitstrupp	work squad.
Arbeitsverwendungsfähig	fit for labour employment.
Arendt-Abteilung	} listening set section.
Arendt-Gruppe	
Arko	*see* "Artillerie-Kommandeur."
Arm	branch gallery (*mining*).
Armauflage	elbow rest.
Armbinde	armband, brassard; sling.
Armee-Abteilung	Army Detachment (*equivalent to an Army*).
Armee-Arzt	Director of Medical Services (*of an Army*).
Armee-Befehl	Army Order.
Armee-Bekleidungs-Depot	Army Clothing Depôt.

Armee-Bericht	Army report, bulletin, despatch.
Armee-Fernsprech-Abteilung	Army telephone detachment.
Armee-Fernsprech-Kommando (Kommandeur)	Army Telephone H.Q. (Commander).
Armee-Fernsprech-Park ...	Army telephone park.
Armee-Flug-Park	Army aircraft park.
Armee-Funker-Abteilung ...	Army wireless detachment.
Armee - Funker-Kommando (Kommandeur)	Army Wireless H.Q. (Commander).
Armee-Funker-Park... ...	Army wireless park.
Armee - Fussartillerie-Kraft-zug-Park	Army foot artillery tractor park.
Armeegruppe	Group (*equivalent to a Corps*).
Armeehauptquartier	Army Headquarters.
Armeekabel	insulated cable (*telephone*).
Armeekorps	Army Corps, Corps.
Armee-Kraftwagenkolonne ...	Army M.T. column.
Armee-Kraftwagenpark ...	Army M.T. park.
Armeelastzug	army mechanical transport train.
Armeelieferant	army contractor.
Armee-Minenwerferschule ...	Army trench-mortar school.
Armee-Musik-Meister ...	Inspector of Military Bands.
Armee-Oberkommando ...	Army Headquarters (*Staff*).
Armee-Post-Direktor ...	Director of Army Postal Service.
Armee-Post-Inspektor ...	Army Postal Inspector.
Armee-Telegraphen-Abteilung	Army telegraph detachment (*obsolete*).
Armeeverordnungsblatt ...	Army Orders.
Armeeverwaltungs - Departement	Army Administration Department.
Armeezahlmeister	Army paymaster.
Ärmelaufschlag	cuff (*of tunic, &c.*).
Ärmelpatten	sleeve patches.
Armierung	armament (*fortress, &c.*).
Armierungsbataillon	labour battalion.
Armierungskabel	armoured cable.
Armstütze	tackle bracket (*bridging*).
Arrest	arrest.
Mittelarrest	light field punishment.
strenger Arrest	close arrest.
Arrestant	man undergoing confinement.
Arrest-Kasten	place of confinement, cell.
Arrest-Lokal	guard room.
Arreststrafe	confinement.
Arrest-Zelle	place of confinement, cell.
Arriere-Garde	rear guard (*obsolete*).
Art	pattern (*e.g., alter Art, neuer Art!*).
Artillerie	artillery.

Artillerie-Anschneidetrupp ...	artillery survey section.
Artillerie-Depot	ordnance depôt; artillery park.
Artillerie-Entwicklung ...	deployment of artillery.
Artillerie des Feldheeres, schwere	heavy artillery of the Field Army.
Artillerie-Fernsprechverbindung	artillery telephone communication.
Artillerie-Feuer	artillery fire, bombardment.
Artillerie-Feuer (flankierendes)	enfilade artillery fire.
Artillerie-Flieger	artillery aeroplane.
Artillerie-Flieger-Abteilung ...	artillery flight (*aviation unit*).
Artillerie-Funkerzug	artillery wireless section (of divisional wireless detachment).
Artillerie-Geschoss	shell, projectile.
Artillerie-Kampf	artillery duel.
Artillerie-Kampf-Artillerie ...	counter-battery-artillery.
Artillerie-Kommandeur (Arko)	artillery commander (*usually* Divisional Artillery Commander).
Artillerie-Kommando... ...	Divisional Artillery Headquarters.
Artillerie-Konstruktionsbureau	Artillery Technical Section (of Technical Institute).
Artillerie-Messtrupp	artillery survey section, observation group.
Artillerie - Munitions - Depot (— Lager)	artillery ammunition depôt.
Artillerie-Munitions-Kolonne	artillery ammunition column (heavy) (*obsolete*).
Artillerie-Nachrichten-Sammelstelle	artillery information centre.
Artillerie-Offizier vom Platz...	Fortress Artillery Officer.
Artillerie-Prüfungs-Kommission	Ordnance Committee.
Artillerie-Schiessplatz ...	artillery range.
Artillerie-Schiess-Schule ...	School of Gunnery.
Artillerie-Schutzstellung ...	artillery protective line.
Artillerie-Tätigkeit	artillery activity.
Artillerie-Unterstützung ...	artillery support.
Artillerie-Verbindungs-Offizier	artillery liaison officer.
Artillerie-Vergeltung	artillery retaliation.
Artillerie-Werkstatt	artillery workshop.
Arzneikasten	medicine chest.
Arzt	medical officer (*for ranks of medical officers, see under " Generalstabsarzt "*).
Aspirant	(*usually not translated*), Aspirant, candidate.
Assistenzarzt	Second-lieutenant (*medical*).
A-Station (Abhörstation) ...	listening set station.
A tgabel	rest (*e.g., for a rifle*).

Asto	listening set.
Astverhau	abatis.
Ata (Armee-Telegraphen-Abteilung)	Army telegraph detachment.
Atemeinsatz	breathing drum (*of gas mask*).
Atemfilter	breath filter (*of gas mask*).
Atemsack	respiratory bag.
Atemschützer	respirator (*gas*).
Atemwiderstand	breathing resistance (*gas mask*).
Atemwiderstandsfeldprüfer	resistance gauge for breathing drums (*gas*).
Atmungsschlauch	breathing tube (*oxygen apparatus*).
Attacke	charge (*cavalry*).
Attila	hussar tunic.
Auditeur } Auditor }	Judge-Advocate.
Auditoriat	Judge-Advocate's officials.
Aufbau	erection, construction; arrangement, disposition (*e.g., of a company in readiness for the attack*).
Aufbewahrung	storage.
Aufbrechen	to strike camp: to start.
Aufenthalt	stop, stay; beat (*of a sentry*).
Auffahren	to come into action (*of artillery*).
Auffangen	to intercept.
Aufflug	ascent (*aeroplane*).
Auffordern	to summon, challenge.
Aufforderung	request, order, demand.
Aufforderung zum Schuss	request for fire to be opened.
Auffüllung der Gräben mit Truppen	massing troops in the trenches, assembly.
Aufgabe	duty, task (*e.g., Aufgabe einer Batterie*).
Aufgebäumt	stalled (*of an aeroplane*).
Aufgebot	ban (*of Landsturm or Landwehr*), calling out of troops.
Aufgebot, allgemeines	levy *en masse*.
Aufhängeriemen	brace.
Aufhau	breaking out (*mining*).
Aufheben	to pick up; to withdraw an order.
Aufheben einen Posten	to capture a post.
Aufklärer	scout.
Aufklärung	clearing up, reconnaissance.
Aufklärungspatrouille	reconnoitring patrol.
Auflager	support (*for field gun in travelling position*).
Aufleuchten	flash (*of a gun*).
Auflösung	disbanding; scattering.

Aufmarsch	forming up, assembly, deployment, approach march.
Aufmerksamkeit (erhöhte)	(a sharp) look out.
Aufnahme	photograph.
Aufnahme der Fühlung	establishing contact with.
Aufnahme des Geländes	survey *or* mapping; aeroplane photograph.
Aufnahmestellung	rallying position.
Aufpflanzen (Seitengewehre)	to fix (bayonets).
Aufprotzen	to limber up.
Aufräumen	to clear (*trench, dug-out, &c.*).
Aufräumungsarbeit	salvage work, re-opening work.
Aufräumungswelle	wave of infantry attack detailed as clearing up parties.
Aufrechterhaltung	maintenance.
Aufreiben	to annihilate; to rub open.
Aufreibende Märsche	exhausting marches.
Aufrichten	to erect; to drive forward horizontally from bottom of an incline (*mining*).
Aufrollen	to clear *or* work along (*a trench, &c.*).
Aufsatz	gun sight.
Fernrohraufsatz	telescopic sight.
Libellenaufsatz	clinometer sight.
Aufsatzträger	sight bracket.
Aufschlag	burst on impact.
Aufschläge	facings.
Aufschlagen	to strike (*projectile, &c.*).
Aufschlagen, ein Zelt	to pitch a tent.
Aufschlagsgeschwindigkeit	striking velocity.
Aufschlagspunkt	point of impact.
Aufschlagzünder (Az.)	percussion fuze.
Aufschliessen	to close up.
Aufschneideverfahren	"flash spotting," (*obtaining intersections on the bursts of shells or flashes of guns*).
Aufschrift	address (*on a letter, &c.*).
Aufsichtshabender	officer or man in charge.
Aufsitzen	to mount (*horse*).
das Ziel aufsitzen lassen	to aim at 6 o'clock on the target.
Aufstapeln	to pile up; heap up, stack.
Aufstiegstelle (Ballon-)	balloon bed.
Aufstellen	to form up, take up a position; to site (*a gun*); to post (*a sentry*).
Aufstellung	order of battle *or* forming up, parade.
Auftrag	duty, order, commission.
Auftrag (im)	"By order," "Signed for" (*above a signature on a document*).

Auftreffsgeschwindigkeit	striking velocity.
Auftreffsstelle	point of impact.
Auftreffsschicht	bursting course (*roof of dug-out, &c.*).
Auftreffswinkel	angle of impact.
Auftreten	to appear.
Auftrieb	lift (*aeroplane, balloon*).
Auftriebsmittelpunkt	centre of buoyancy (*aeroplane, &c.*).
Auftritt	fire step.
Aufwurf	parapet, mound.
Aufzeichnung	sketch.
Aufzugbrücke	drawbridge.
Augen-angreifender Reizstoff	lachrymator.
Augenblicksziel	fleeting target.
Augen links !	Eyes left !
Augen rechts !	Eyes right !
Augenmerk zu richten	to take care, direct attention.
Augengläser	"goggles."
Augentränen bekommen	to lachrymate (*owing to gas*).
Augenverbindung	visual connection.
Ausarbeiten (der Ladekammer)	chambering (*mining*).
Ausbau	consolidation or completion (*of a position*); construction, improvement (*of defences*).
Ausbilden	to train.
Ausbildung	training.
Ausbildungslager	instructional camp.
Ausbreiten	to extend.
Ausbruch	a breaking out, outbreak.
Ausdauer	endurance, steadiness.
Ausdehnen	to extend, spread.
Ausdehnung	extent, extension.
Auseinanderziehen	to deploy.
Ausfall	sortie.
Ausfallstufe	sortie step.
Ausfragen	to interrogate.
Ausführung (kartographischer Arbeiten)	(map) reproduction.
Ausführungskommando	executive word of command.
Ausgabemagazin	refilling point.
Ausgabestelle	refilling point, ammunition distributing depôt.
Ausgang	exit, entrance.
Ausgangsfront	original front.
Ausgangsgraben	"down" trench.
Ausgangsstellung	"departure" *or* "jumping off" trench (*of an attack*).
Ausgebeplatz	refilling point.

Ausgediente Leute	time-expired men.
Ausgehobener	recruit.
Ausgesprochen	decided, obvious, clear.
Ausgleicher / Ausgleichfeder	balance spring (*of gun carriage*).
Ausheben	to recruit; to construct, dig (*trenches*).
Aushebung	levy, conscription.
Aushebungsbezirk	recruiting district.
Aushöhlung	hollowing out, burrowing.
Auskunftei	intelligence office.
Auslade-Kommissar	detraining inspector.
Ausladen	to unload, detrain.
Ausladepersonal	detraining personnel.
Ausladeort / Ausladestelle	unloading *or* detraining place.
Auslandsnachricht	information received from abroad (*on casualty lists*).
Ausläufer	spur (*of chain of hills*).
Ausmustern	to discharge, reject.
Auspuff	upshaft (*ventilation*).
Ausrauchen	to smoke out.
Ausräumen	to clear out.
Ausrücken	to march out, evacuate.
Ausrückstärke	marching out strength.
Ausrüsten	to equip.
Ausrüstung	equipment.
Ausrüstung, die gesamte (die volle)	full marching order.
Ausrüstung der grossen Bagage	train equipment.
Ausrüstungsgegenstände	articles of equipment.
Ausrüstungsstück	article of equipment.
Aussage (Gefangenen-)	(prisoner's) statement.
Ausschachtung	excavation.
Ausschalten	to switch off, disconnect (*electricity*).
Ausscheiden	to retire, withdraw from; to keep separate; to reserve, detail; to be excluded.
Ausscheiden (aus dem Kampfe)	to put out of action.
Ausschirren	to unharness.
Ausschlag	deflection (*magnetic compass*).
Ausschlaggebend	determining, deciding (*factor*).
Ausschliessen	to lock out; to exclude.
210 schliesst aus, 469 Meldung	"210 get off the line, 469 is sending a report."
Ausschlüpfen	to slip out, creep forth.

Ausschwärmen	to form a line of skirmishers.
Aussendung	transmission (*wireless, &c.*).
Aussenfort	detached fort.
Aussenposten	advanced post.
Aussenwache	outlying piquet.
Aussenwerk	outwork.
ausser Dienst (a.D.)	retired (*of officers*).
Aussetzen	to post (*e.g., an outpost detachment*); to expose.
Ausstatten	to equip, provide with.
Ausstattung	equipment, furnishing.
Aussteifen	to strut (*engineering*).
Aussteigeplatz	arrival platform.
Ausstellen	to post (*a sentry*).
Austausch	exchange, relief.
Auswechseln	to exchange (*prisoners, &c.*).
Ausweichgraben	support trench.
Ausweichstelle	passing place (*in trench, light railway, &c.*).
Ausweichstellung	alternative position (*for gun*).
Ausweis	authority, permit; notice, instructions; consignment note.
dieser Fernspruch gilt als Ausweis	this telephone conversation serves as authority.
Ausweisen, Einwohner	to expel inhabitants.
Ausweiskarte	pass, permit.
Auswerfer	ejector.
Auswerten	to exploit, utilize, compile results.
Auswertungs-Stelle	plotting office, headquarters of survey section.
Auszieher	extractor.
Auszimmerung	timbering of galleries (*mining*).
Auszug	extract (*e.g., from orders*); departure.
in einen Auszug bringen	to epitomize.
Automobilkorps	Automobile Corps.
Autoverkehr	motor traffic.
Avancieren	to promote.
Avantgarde	advanced guard, vanguard.
Aviatik	"Aviatik" (*a particular make of aeroplane*); aviation.
Awumba (Artillerie Waffen-und Munition-Beschaffungsamt)	Artillery Munitions Department of the War Ministry.
A-Zeit	period in front line.

B.

Backtrog	trough (*sometimes formed into a raft*).
Bäckerei	bakery.
Bagage (Gefechts, Grosse)	transport (1st line, train).
Bagageführer	regimental transport officer.
Bahnanlagen	railway buildings, &c.
Bahnarztbezirk	railway medical zone.
Bahnbauten	railway constructional works.
Bahn-Beauftragter (Bba.)	Railway Representative (at Army H.Q.).
Bahn brechen, sich	to push one's way.
Bahndamm	railway embankment.
Bahngestänge	railway fences.
Bahnhof	railway station.
Bahnhofskommandantur	office of railway station commandant.
Bahnlänge	pitch (*bombing practice*).
Bahnnetz	railway net, system.
Bahnsteig	platform (*railway*).
Bahnübergang	level crossing.
Bahnwärter	plate-layer; signalman.
Bajonett	bayonet; dog leg in a gallery (*mining*).
aufgepflanztes Bajonett	fixed bayonet.
mit dem Bajonett beginnen	to commence the dog-legging (*of galleries*).
mit gefälltem Bajonett	with bayonet at the charge.
Bajonettgriff	bayonet hilt.
Bajonetthaft	bayonet stud.
Bajonetthals	} bayonet socket.
Bajonetthülse	
Bajonettring	bayonet clasp.
Bajonettstoss	pointing with the bayonet; bayonet thrust.
Balken	baulk, log.
Ballon-Abwehr-Kanonen-Zug (B.A.K.Z.)	anti-aircraft gun section (*obsolete—see Flak*).
Ballon-Abwehr-Maschinen-Kanone	anti-aircraft automatic gun.
Ballonbrandgeschoss	incendiary bullet for use against balloons.
Ballon-Gruppen-Kommandeur	balloon group commander.
Ballonhülle	envelope of balloon.

Ballonkampfgruppe	balloon battle group.
Ballon-Zentrale A.O.K. (4)	(Fourth) Army Balloon Report Centre.
Ballonzug	balloon section.
Band	driving band (*of a projectile*).
Band, weisses	surveyor's tape.
Bandenkrieg	guerilla warfare.
Bandolier	bandolier.
Bank	parapet, bank.
Bannwaren	contraband goods.
Baracke	hut.
Barackenbau	hutting.
Barackenlager	hut camp.
Basis	base.
Bataillon	battalion.
Bereitschafts-Bataillon	battalion in support.
Ruhe-Bataillon	battalion at rest.
Stellungs-Bataillon	battalion in line.
Bataillonsbagage	battalion transport.
Bataillons-Bureau (-Geschäftszimmer)	battalion orderly room.
Bataillonskommandeur	battalion commander.
Bataillonsschreiber	orderly room clerk.
Bataillonstambour	battalion serjeant-drummer.
Batterie	battery.
besetzte Batterie	a battery which is occupied.
bespannte Batterie	horsed battery.
eingeschnittene Batterie.	dug-in battery; battery located by intersection on the flashes.
fahrende Batterie	field (artillery) battery.
fühlbare Batterie	effective battery.
gedeckte Batterie	concealed battery.
in geöffneter Zugkolonne	battery column.
reitende Batterie	horse (artillery) battery.
schwimmende Batterie	floating battery.
Batterie-Baupark	battery construction park.
Batteriechef	battery commander.
Batterieplan	battery board.
Batterierichtkreis	battery director.
Batterietrupp	reconnaissance personnel of field battery (*with telescope, flags, directors, telephone*).
Bauabteilung	entrenching detachment.
Baudirektion	Works Department.
Baugrube	shaft.
Baukommando	working party.
Baukompagnie	entrenching company, construction company.

Baulichkeiten	buildings.
Baumaterial	engineer material, building material.
Baumbeobachtung	tree observation post.
Baumverhau	abatis of trees.
Bautrupp	construction squad.
Bauweise	method of building.
Bauwesen (Militär)	(Military) Works Department.
Bayerisch	Bavarian.
B-Bataillon	battalion in support.
Beagid	*an inflammable product composed of carbide and other substances, used in acetylene safety lamp.*
Beamter	official.
Bedienung	gun detachment (*artillery*); gun team (*machine gun*).
Bedienungsmannschaften (einer Batterie)	personnel, (gun) detachment.
Befehl	order.
Befehligen	to command a regiment; to be in command of.
Befehlsausgabe	issue of orders.
Befehlsempfänger	representatives of formations for receiving orders.
Befehlshaber	General Officer Commanding.
Befehlsstand	} command post.
Befehlsstelle	
Befehlsübermittlung	transmission of orders.
Befestigung	fortification.
Befestigungsanlagen	defences.
Befestigungsarbeit	defence work.
Befestigungsbauten	defensive works.
Befördern	to promote; to dispatch.
Beförderung	promotion; transport.
Beförderung ausser der Reihe	promotion by selection.
Beförderung dem Dienstalter nach	promotion by seniority.
Beförderungsliste	promotion roll.
Beförderungsmittel	means of transport.
Befreiung	exemption.
Befürworten	to recommend.
Begegnungsgefecht	encounter battle.
Begleitflugzeug	escorting aeroplane.
Begleitkommando	escort.
Begleitmannschaft	escort; men detailed to assist.
Begleitung	escort.
Begraben	to bury.
Behandlung	treatment, handling.

Behelf	expedient, makeshift; subterfuge.
Behelfsbrücke	temporary bridge.
Behelfskonstruktion	makeshift type (*e.g.*, *of hand grenade*).
Behelfsmässig	improvised.
Behelfsschlitten	improvised sledge (*machine gun*).
Beherrschen	to rule over, command, overpower, control.
Behörde	authority.
Feldverwaltungs-Behörden	Field Administrative Authorities.
Beigetriebenes Material ...	requisitioned material.
Beilage	annexe; enclosure; appendix.
Beilpicke	pickaxe.
Beinwickel	puttee.
Beitreibung	requisitioning.
Beiwacht	bivouac.
Bekämpfen	to engage.
Bekleidung	clothing; revetting (*of a trench*).
Bekleidungsabteilung... ...	Clothing Section of the Intendance.
Bekleidungsamt (B.A.) ...	clothing office *or* depôt.
Bekleidungsordnung... ...	Clothing Regulations.
Bekleidungsstärke	clothing strength.
Bekleidungsstück	article of clothing.
Bekleidungsvorschrift ...	Clothing Regulations.
Beköstigung	messing.
Belag	roadway *or* planking (*of a bridge*).
Belagern	to besiege.
Belagerung	siege.
Belagerungsarmee	besieging army.
Belagerungsartillerie	siege artillery.
Belagerungskrieg	siege warfare.
Belagerungs-Park	siege park.
Belagerungs-Telegraphen-Abteilung	siege telegraph detachment.
Belagerungs-Train	siege train.
Belagerungszustand verhängen	to proclaim a state of siege.
Belebungsmittel	restoratives.
Beleg	document, proof, voucher.
Belegen	to cover; to occupy; to shell.
Belegen mit Schnellfeuer ...	to open rapid fire on.
Belegung	occupation; imposition, levy.
Belegungsfähigkeit	maximum levy which a town can sustain; billeting capacity.
Belegungsraum	billeting area.
Beleuchtung	illumination; light (*in shooting, &c.*).
Beleuchtungsmittel	illuminating material.
Beleuchtungswagen	searchlight wagon.

Benachrichtigung	informing, transmission of information.
Benzinbehälter	petrol tank.
Benzinvorrat	petrol supply.
Beobachter	observer.
Beobachtung	observation.
Beobachtungslatte	observation pole.
Beobachtungsmittel	means of observation.
Beobachtungsposten	look-out man.
Beobachtungsspiegel	periscope.
Beobachtungsstelle Beobachtungsstand	} observation post.
Beobachtungswagen	observation wagon (*field and foot artillery*).
Beobachtungswarte	observation post.
Bereich	zone, area.
ausser Bereich	out of range.
im Schussbereich	within range.
Bereifung	tyre (*of a wheel*).
Bereiten	to prepare; to break in (*a horse*).
Bereitlegen	to make ready for use.
Bereitschaft (in)	in readiness, in support.
Bereitschaften	supports.
Bereitschaftsbataillon-Kommandeur	commander of the support battalion.
Bereitschaftsbüchse Bereitschaftskapsel	} " alert " box (*gas*).
Bereitschaftskompagnie	support company.
Bereitschaftsstellung	support line.
Bereitstellen	to assemble (troops); to place in readiness.
Batterie, aufgeprotzt bereitgestellt	battery in " position in readiness."
Bereitstellungsraum	point of assembly.
Bergehalle (eines Luftschiffes)	airship shed.
Bergelohn	reward (*for collecting or bringing in captured material*).
Bergeholz	rubbing strake (*pontoon*).
Berghang	hill side.
Bergkompagnie	tunnelling company; mining company.
Bergmann-Maschinengewehr	Bergmann light machine gun.
Bergmännisch	relating to miners, mining.
Bergstrich	hachuring, hatching (*topog.*).
Bergung	salvage.
Bericht erstatten	to make a report, report.
Berichten	to report.

Berittener Feldjäger	mounted courier.
Berme	berm.
Berufungsrecht	right of appeal.
Berührung	contact.
Besatz	braid (*on cap, pantaloons, &c.*).
Besatzstreifen	cap band.
Besatzung	garrison.
Sicherheits-Besatzung	emergency garrison.
Beschaffenheit	nature, character.
Beschaffungsstelle	supply depôt.
Beschiessen	to shell, bombard, fire on.
der Länge nach beschiessen	to enfilade.
Beschotterung	road metal.
Beschlag	metal fittings (*of helmet, rifle, &c.*); shoeing (*of horses*).
Beschlagnahme	requisition, seizure.
Beschlagschmied	shoeing smith (*below the "Fahnenschmied" in rank*).
Beschlagzeug	farrier's tools.
Beschwerde führen	to lodge complaints.
Beseitigen	to neutralize (*artillery*); to remove (*obstacles, &c.*).
Besichtigung	inspection.
Besiegen	to defeat, conquer.
Besoldungs-Vorschrift	Pay Regulations.
Bespannungsabteilung	draught horse detachment (*foot artillery*).
Bespannung einer Batterie	battery team.
Bespannt	horsed; with teams hooked in.
Besprechung	conference (*e.g., of officers*).
Bestand	supply; strength (*of a regiment*).
Bestand (eiserner)	iron ration.
Beständigkeit	stability.
Bestandsaufnahme	inventory.
Bestandteil	constituent part.
Bestätigen	to confirm.
Bestätigung	confirmation, sanction.
Besteck	case of instruments (*e.g., surgical*); knife and fork, &c.
Bestrafen	to punish.
Bestreichen	to sweep (*e.g., with artillery fire*).
Bestreichung (toter Winkel)	sweeping (dead ground).
Beteiligen (sich, an)	to participate in.
Beton	concrete.
Betonarbeit	concrete work.
Betonbau	concrete structure.
Betonbaukompagnie	concrete construction company.

Betoniert	made of concrete.
Betonschicht	apron of concrete.
Betonstärke	thickness in concrete.
Betontrupp	concrete construction section.
Betonunterstand	concrete dug-out.
Betreffend (betr.) Betreffs (betr.)	} concerning, with reference to.
Betriebsabteilung	operating traffic department (*railway, &c.*).
Betriebsamt	operating traffic office (*railway*).
Betriebseinheit	traffic unit.
Betriebsgebiet	traffic district.
Betriebsinspektion	traffic inspectorate.
Betriebskompagnie	operating traffic company (*railway*).
Betriebsmaterial	rolling-stock.
Betriebsplan	time table (*railway traffic*).
Betriebswerkmeisterei	local traffic maintenance repair shop (*railway*).
Betriebswerkstätte	rolling stock repair shop (*railway*).
Bettung	platform, bedplate.
Bettungsstaffel	platform échelon (*in mortar battery*).
Beunruhigungsfeuer	harassing *or* disturbing fire.
Beurlauben	to give leave.
Beurlaubtenstand	officers and men on furloughed lists in peace time, *i.e., officers and men liable to military service who are not actually with the colours.*
Beurlaubter	man absent on leave.
Beute	booty.
Beutegeschütz	captured gun.
Beutepark Beutesammelstelle	} salvage dump for captured material.
Beutezug	raid.
Bevorstehend	imminent, impending.
Bewachung	guard, guarding.
Bewaffnung	arms, arming, armament.
Bewähren, sich	to prove of value, justify itself.
Bewaldet	wooded.
dicht bewaldet	closely wooded.
Bewässern	to irrigate.
Beweglichkeit	mobility.
Bewegungskrieg	open *or* field warfare.
in der Bewegung	on the move.
eine Bewegung ausführen lassen	to manœuvre.

Bewilligung	approval, concession, grant.
Bewurf	plastering, mortar.
Bezeichnung	designation (*of units*).
Beziehen	to take possession of; to draw (*rations*).
die Wache beziehen	to mount guard.
ein Lager beziehen	to pitch camp.
einen Posten beziehen	to occupy a post.
Quartier beziehen	to go into billets.
Bezirk	district.
Bezirkskommando	District Command.
Bezirksoffizier	district officer.
B.-Gelände	zone of the battalion in support.
Bildoffizier	photographic officer.
Binde	bandage; belt, sash.
Bindeleine	lashing.
Bindestränge	traces.
Birne	electric light bulb.
Biwak	bivouac.
Offizier vom Biwaksdienst	officer on bivouac duty.
Ortsbiwak	close billets.
Biwaksbedürfnisse	bivouac requisites.
Biwakskommandant	bivouac commander.
Biwaksplatz	bivouac ground.
Blanke Waffen	cold steel.
Blasebalg	bellows.
Blasen	to blow, to sound (*bugle calls*).
Blasgas	cloud gas.
Blasverfahren	emission of gas clouds.
Blatt	leaf, sheet; record.
Blaue Bohnen	bullets (*colloquial*).
Blaukreuzmunition	" blue cross " gas shell.
Blaupause	blue print.
Blaupunkt	reference point on map.
Blausäure	prussic acid.
Blech	sheet iron.
Blechbüchse	tin box; container (*for gas mask*).
Blechflasche	tin water-bottle.
Blechtafel	corrugated iron sheet.
Blechtornister	water-can (*slung like a pack*).
Bleikabel	lead-covered cable.
Bleikern	lead core (*of bullet*).
Blende	loophole; screen.
Blendlaterne	dark lantern.
Blick	glimpse, view.
Blind	blind.
Blind feuern	to fire with blank.
Blindgänger	a " blind."

Blind laden	to load with blank.
Blindschuss	a round of blank.
Blinken	to signal (*with lamps*; *replaces the word " signalisieren "*).
Blinker	lamp signaller.
Blinkertrupp	lamp signalling detachment (*replaces " Lichtsignaltrupp "*).
Blinkerzug	lamp signalling section.
Blinkfeuer	occulting lights (*used at airship sheds*).
Blinkgerät	lamp signalling apparatus (*replaces " Signalgerät "*).
Blinklampe	signal lamp.
Blinklicht	lamp signalling.
Blinkmeldung	lamp signal message.
Blinkstation	lamp signalling station.
Blinkverfahren	lamp signalling.
Blinkverkehr	lamp signal communication.
Blinkzeichen	lamp signal.
Block	machine gun emplacement.
Blockhaus	block house (*also used to describe a machine gun emplacement*).
Blockstation	signal box (*railway*).
Blosslegen	to expose.
Bluse	jacket, field service jacket (*latest pattern without buttons*).
Bock	box of a vehicle; trestle (*bridging*).
vom Bock fahren	to drive from the box.
Bockbein	trestle leg.
Bockbrücke	trestle-bridge.
Bockgerät	trestle gear.
Bockholm	transom.
Bockkeil	wedge.
Bockwagen	trestle wagon.
Bockwinde	block and tackle.
Boden	ground, earth.
Bodenbedeckung	features (*of landscape*).
Bodenfläche	surface of the ground.
Bodenkammer	base (*of a shell*).
Bodenständig	permanent (*of officers or units who remain permanently in a sector*).
Bodenstück	ground sill of a frame (*mining*).
Bodenzünder	base fuze.
Bogenbahn	trajectory.
Bogenschuss	high angle fire.
Bogohl (Bomben - Geschwader der Obersten Heeres - Leitung)	Bombing Squadron under General Headquarters.

Bohle	thick plank, board, "duck board."
Bohrer	drill.
Bohrloch	bore hole, auger hole.
Bohrmaschine	boring machine.
Bohrmine	bored mine (*mining*).
Bohrpatrone	*small cylindrical blasting cartridge, used in auger holes, &c.*
Bohrriefe	groove (*of rifling*).
Bohrschuss	shot *blasting*).
Bohrzange	bore pincers (*mining*).
Böig	squally, gusty.
Böller	small mortar.
Bolzen	bolt.
Bolzen zum Abzugsstück	trigger bolt (*field gun*).
Bolzen zum Spannstück	cocking bolt (*field gun*).
Bombe	bomb (*used by aeroplanes*).
Bombenflug	bombing raid (*aeroplane, &c.*).
Bombengeschwader	bombing squadron (*aviation unit*).
Bombensicher (*see also* "Schusssicher")	shell-proof (*against continuous bombardment by 8-in. guns and heavy "Minenwerfer," or single hits by heavier natures*).
Bombenwurf	bombing (*aeroplane, &c.*).
Böschung	slope (*of a parapet*); gradient (*of a road*).
Bote	messenger.
Brandbombe	incendiary bomb.
Brandgeschoss	} incendiary shell.
Brandgranate	
Brandloch	gas escape hole.
Brandlochverschlussplatte	escape-hole disc.
Brandmine	*Minenwerfer* incendiary shell.
Brandrakete	incendiary rocket.
Brandrohr	incendiary flare.
Brandsatz	powder train.
Brandschatzenabteilung	requisitioning detachment.
Brandwirkung	incendiary effect.
Brecheisen	crowbar.
Brechreizend	acting as an emetic (*gas shell*).
Brechstange	crowbar.
Breite (geographische)	latitude.
Breitenstreuung	dispersion, lateral error in shooting.
Bremse	brake.
Bremsflüssigkeit	liquid for filling recoil buffer.
Bremshebel	brake lever.
Bremsschuh	brake-shoe.

Bremswelle	spindle of brake (*field gun carriage*).
Bremszylinder	recoil buffer.
Brenndauer	time of burning (*of fuze*).
Brennlänge	time of burning, *or* setting of fuze.
Brennpunkt	focus; point of burst; centre (*of an attack*).
Brennzeit	time of burning (*of fuze*).
Brennzünder (Bz.)	time fuze.
Bresche	breach.
Bresche schiessen	to make a breach.
Brett	plank; chess (*bridging*).
Brettern, bekleidet mit	revetted with planks.
Bretterroste	"duck boards."
Bretterschuppe	wooden shed.
Brettstapelbrücke	wooden bridge on piles.
Bretttafel	tail board (*of vehicle*).
Brieftaube	carrier pigeon.
Brieftauben-Abteilung	carrier pigeon detachment.
Brieftaubenschirrmeister	carrier pigeon service, staff-serjeant of.
Brieftaubenschlag	carrier pigeon loft.
Brieftaubenstation	pigeon station.
Brigade	(1) "Brigade" of field artillery = 2 regiments = 12 batteries (*obsolete*). (2) Brigade of infantry = 2 or 3 regiments. (3) Brigade of cavalry = 2 regiments.
Brigade-Befehl Brigade-Kommando-Ordnung	} Brigade order.
Brigadier	Lieutenant-colonel of military police (Prussia): military policeman (Saxony).
Brillen	spectacles, goggles (*gas mask*).
Brillen mit Cellongläsern	goggles with Cellone eyepieces.
Brisante Eigenschaft	shattering effect.
Brisanzpulver	high explosive (H.E.).
Brisanzwirkung	high explosive (H.E.) effect.
Bronze-Mörser	(21 cm.) bronze mortar.
Brotbeutel	haversack.
Brotbeutelband	haversack strap.
Bruchpunkt	re-entrant (*of a trench*).
Bruchteile	fragments; disconnected portions (*of trench, &c.*).
Brücke	bridge.
fliegende Brücke	flying bridge.

Brückengerät	bridging material.
Brückenleitung	laddered circuit (*electrical*).
Brückenpfeiler	bridge pier.
Brückensteg	footbridge.
Brückentrain	bridging train.
Brückenwage	weighing machine, weigh-bridge.
Brückenwagen	bridge wagon.
Brunnenbaukommando	company for sinking and constructing wells.
Brustklappe	plastron (*of lancer's tunic*), breastplate.
Brustpanzer	} breastplate.
Brustschild	
Brustwehr	parapet, breastwork.
Buchhalter	bookkeeper.
Büchse	shot-gun (*slang for rifle*).
Büchsenmacher (*now* = Waffenmeister)	armourer.
Bügel	stirrup; ring, hoop; trigger guard.
Bundesrat	Federal Council.
Bunker (Betonunterstand)	concrete dug-out.
Bürgerlicher Beruf	occupation in civil life.
Bursche	officer's servant.
Burschenzimmer	orderlies' room.
Bussole	magnetic compass.
Buntmunition	gas shell.
B-Zeit	period in support.

C.

Cadre	cadre.
C-Bataillon	battalion in reserve.
Cellon	"Cellone" (*a material like celluloid*).
Cellongläser	Cellone eyepieces (*in goggles of gas mask*).
Central	(*see* Zentral).
Cernieren	to invest, besiege, blockade.
Cernierungsheer	investing army, besieging forces.
C-Gelände	zone of the battalion in reserve.
C-Geschoss	stream-line shell.
Charakterisiert	brevet (*rank*).
Chargen	officers and non-commissioned officers.
Chargenpferd	officer's charger.
Chargierten	officers and non-commissioned officers.
Chaussee	main road, high road.
Chefarzt	Senior Medical Officer.
Chef des Feldeisenbahnwesens	Director of Railways.
Chef des Feldkraftfahrwesens	Director of Mechanical Transport in the Field.
Chef des Feldsanitätswesens	Director-General of Medical Services of the Field Army.
Chef des Generalstabes (des Feldheeres)	Chief of the General Staff (of the Field Army).
Chef des Nachrichtenwesens	Director of Signals.
Chevaulegers	(*not translated; German term retained*) Bavarian light cavalry.
Chiffre	cipher.
Chiffreschrift	cipher writing.
Chiffrieren	to encipher.
Chlorgas	chlorine (*gas*).
Chlorkalk	bleaching powder, chloride of lime.
Chlorkohlenoxyd	phosgene (*gas*).
Cirka	about (*circa*).
Civil (in)	in plain clothes.
Civilversorgung	guarantee of civil employment for soldiers.
C-Zeit	period of rest.

D.

Dachpappe	roofing felt.
Dachsbau	dug-out (*colloquial*).
Dampfablassschlauch	condenser tube (*machine gun*).
Dampfstrassenzugmaschine	steam tractor.
Darstellung	representation.
Dauer	durability, duration.
Dauerbefehle	standing orders.
Dauerbrandfackel	long-burning torch.
Dauerfeuer	continuous bombardment.
Dauerfleisch	preserved meat.
Dauerlauf	running exercise.
Dauerlicht	continuous *or* steady beam of light (*signalling*).
Dauermarsch	forced march, long march.
Dauernd untauglich	permanently unfit.
Dauerschlacht	continuous battle.
Dechiffrieren	decipher.
Deckabstand	gap (*distance between top and bottom planes of an aeroplane*).
Deckband	cap band cover.
Deckbezeichnung	code designation, code name.
Deckblatt	corrigendum, amendment; wrapper.
Decke	cover, blanket; tarpaulin; roof of a gallery (*mining*); roof of a dug-out.
Deckenstärke	thickness of cover, strength of cover.
Deckenstück	top sill of a frame (*mining*).
Deckname	code name.
Decknamenverzeichnis	list of code names.
Deckoffizier	warrant officer (*Navy*).
Deckpause	code.
Deckplan	wagon cover tarpaulin.
Deckplatte	cover plate (*of breech action of light field howitzer*).
Deckring	middle guide ring (*of gun*).
Deckung	cover.
künstliche Deckung	artificial cover (*e.g., trenches*).
Deckung gegen Sicht	cover from view.
Deckungsgraben	support trench, cover trench.
Deckungslager	camp protected from view, but not from fire; concealed camp.
Deckungslinie	line of defence.
Deckungsmannschaft	escort; covering party.

Deckungsmaterial	roofing.
Deckungstruppen	covering party.
Deckwort	code word.
Degen	sword (*infantry and engineers*).
Degengefäss	} sword grip.
Degengriff	
Degenklinge	sword blade.
Degenknauf	} sword pommel.
Degenknopf	
Degenkoppel	sword belt.
Degenscheide	scabbard.
Degenschneide	sword edge.
Degenspitze	sword point.
Degenstoss	sword thrust.
Deichsel	pole (*of a vehicle*).
Demobilmachung	demobilization.
Demontieren (ein Geschütz)	to disable, cripple (a gun).
Depesche	despatch, telegram.
Depot	depôt, dump.
Detonation	detonation.
Detonieren	to detonate.
Dewumba (Waffen- und Munitions - Beschaffungsamt Depôt)	Depôt of the Munitions Department of the War Ministry.
Diebel	pin (*metal work*).
Dienen	to serve, to be in the army.
von der Pike auf dienen	to rise from the ranks.
Dienst	duty, service.
innerer Dienst	routine duty.
vom Dienst	on duty.
Dienstabzeichen	distinguishing mark *or* badge.
Dienstalter	seniority.
Dienstanweisung	training manual.
Dienstanzug	drill order.
Dienstbeschädigung	wounds or injuries contracted on service.
Diensteintritt	entry into the service.
Dienstfähig entlassen	discharged as fit.
Dienstgrad	rank.
Dienstleistung	duty.
zur Dienstleistung kommandiert	temporarily attached for duty.
Dienstlicher Schriftverkehr	official correspondence.
Dienstpferd	troop horse.
Dienstpflicht	liability for service.
Dienstraum	office.
Dienstsiegel	official seal.

Dienststelle	authority, office, headquarters, unit, formation.
Dienststempel	official stamp.
Diensttauglich...	fit for service.
Diensttuend	doing duty.
Dienstunfähig ⎫ Dienstuntauglich ⎭	disabled, non-effective, unfit *or* incapacitated for service.
Dienstunterricht	instruction, drill.
Dienstvorschrift(en)	regulations.
Dienstweg	official channel.
Dienstzeit	period of service.
Dienstzweig	branch of service.
Diesig	overcast, cloudy.
Difua (Divisions-Funker-Abteilung)	divisional wireless detachment (*permanently allotted to a divisional sector : formerly " Fukla," frequently " Divfua."*).
Dina	divisional signalling detachment.
Direktion	Directorate.
Diskushandgranate	disc hand grenade.
Disposition, zur (z.D.) ...	on half pay (*of officers*).
Distriktsoffizier...	district officer of military police.
Disziplinarstrafordnung ...	Disciplinary Regulations.
Divferna (Divisions - Fernsprech-Abteilung)	divisional telephone detachment.
Divfua *or* Divfunka (Divisions-Funker-Abteilung)	divisional wireless detachment (*permanently allotted to a divisional sector: formerly " Fukla"*).
Division	division.
Divisionsadjutant	divisional administrative staff officer.
Divisionsarzt	Assistant Director of Medical Services of a Division.
Divisionsauditeur	Divisional Judge-Advocate.
Divisionsbefehl	divisional order.
Divisionsbeobachtungsstelle	divisional observation post.
Divisionsbrückentrain ...	divisional bridging train.
Divisionsfunkerabteilung ...	divisional wireless detachment (*permanently allotted to a divisional sector; formerly " Fukla,"* see above—Difua).
Divisions-Gas-Offizier... ...	Divisional Gas Officer.
Divisionsgefechtsstand ...	divisional battle headquarters.
Divisions-Generalstab ...	General Staff of the Division.
Divisionsintendant	Divisional Intendant.
Divisionskraftwagenkolonne...	divisional M.T. column.

Divisionsnachrichtenmittel-Abteilung (Dina)	divisional signalling detachment.
Divisionspfarrer	Divisional Chaplain.
Divisionsstabsquartier	Divisional Headquarters.
Divisions-Verfügung	} divisional order.
Divisions-Verordnung	
Dolch	dagger.
Dolchmesser	clasp knife.
Doll	thole pin (*boat*).
Dolmetscher	interpreter.
Doppeldecker	biplane.
Doppelferngläser	binoculars.
Doppelfernrohr	binocular telescope.
Doppelgeleise	double track (*railway*).
Doppelkolonne	column of subsections (*artillery and machine guns*).
Doppelläufig	double-barrelled.
Doppelleitung	double circuit; metallic circuit.
Doppelposten	double sentry post.
Doppelsterne	lights showing a double star.
Doppelzünder (Dz.)	time and percussion fuze.
Dornbalken	"pin" baulks (*bridging*).
Drachenballon	kite balloon (*sausage-shaped*).
Drachenwarte	kite balloon meteorological station.
Dragoner	dragoon.
Dragoner-Regiment	dragoon regiment.
Dragoner-Schützenregiment	regiment of dismounted dragoons.
Draht	wire.
blanker Draht	bare wire (*electrical*).
Drahteinzäunung	wire fence.
Drahtgeflecht	wire netting.
Drahtgeschütz	wire gun.
Drahtgitter	wire netting.
Drahthindernis	"wire," wire entanglement.
Drahtleitung	wire, lead (*electrical*).
Drahtlose Telegraphie	wireless telegraphy.
Drahtnagel	wire nail.
Drahtnetz	wire entanglement.
Drahtrolle	wire cylinder (*of entanglements*).
Drahtschere	wire-cutter, wire shears.
Drahtscherertrupp	wire-cutting squad.
Drahtschlinge	wire loop.
Drahtseil	wire rope.
Drahtverhau	"wire," wire entanglement; soup made of dried vegetables (*colloquial*).
Drahtwalzenhindernis	cylinder of wire (*for entanglements*.

Drahtzange	wire nippers, pliers.
Drahtzaun	wire fence.
Drall	twist of rifling (*gun or rifle*).
gleichbleibender Drall	uniform twist.
zunehmender Drall	increasing twist.
Draufgehen	to advance, rush forward.
Drawa (Drachenwarte)	kite balloon meteorological station.
Drehgestell	pivot mounting (*e.g., for a machine gun*).
Drehbank	lathe.
Drehbolzen	pivot bolt.
Drehbrücke	swing bridge.
Drehen	to turn, to wheel.
Drehscheibe	turn table (*on railway*); traversing plate (*of trench mortar*).
Drehung	rotation, turn, twist.
Dreieckpunkt	triangulation station.
Dreifuss	tripod.
Dreifusslafette	tripod mounting.
Dreischichteneinsatz	3-layer drum (*for gas mask*).
Dressieren	to train, break in.
Drilchanzug	canvas clothing.
Drillich *or* Drilch	canvas, drill.
Drohen	to threaten, be imminent.
Dröhnen	to boom.
Druckarbeiten	printing work.
Drückeberger	malingerer; shirker.
Drücker	trigger.
Druckpumpe	force pump.
Druckpunkt	pull-off (*of a rifle*).
Druckschraube	pusher (*aeroplane*).
Druckvorschriften-Etat (D.V.E.)	Numbered Index of Official Publications.
Durcharbeiten	to elaborate, work through.
sich durcharbeiten	to force one's way through.
Durchbrechen	to break through, penetrate, pierce.
eine Blockade durchbrechen	to run a blockade.
Durchbruch	breaking through, penetration.
strategischer Durchbruch	strategical penetration.
Durchdringen	to penetrate, force one's way through.
Durchführen	to accomplish, carry out.
einen Angriff durchführen	to drive home an attack.
Durchführung (einer Belagerung)	prosecution (of a siege).
Durchgang	gangway; passage, thoroughfare.
Durchgangsschein	permit.

Durchgebildet	well trained.
Durchlassposten	examination post.
Durchlaufender Erdaufwurf	continuous parapet.
Durchlaufendes Drahthindernis	continuous wire entanglement.
Durchlöchern	to riddle with bullets.
Durchmesser	diameter.
Durchrufen	to pass the word down.
Durchschiessen	to cut by fire.
Durchschlag	carbon copy. breaking into the enemy's gallery (*mining*).
Durchschlagen	to penetrate.
Durchschlagskraft	penetration (*of a projectile*).
Durchschneiden	to cut through, intersect.
Durchschnitt	average.
Durchschnittszeichnung	sectional sketch.
Durchstoss	breaking through, inroad.
Durchstossung	bayonet wound, wound caused by a stab or thrust.
Durchwaten	to ford, wade through.
Düsig	overcast, cloudy.
Dynamit	**dynamite.**

E.

Eben	even, level (*adjectives*).
Ebene	plain (*subst.*).
Ebnen	to make level, flatten (*artillery bombardment*).
Eckbalken	corner post.
Eckbrett	bracket.
Eckhölzer	squared timber.
Ecksäule	corner pillar.
Egge	harrow; also a plank with nails driven and projecting through it, used as an obstacle.
Ehrenbezeugungen	military compliments (*e.g., saluting*).
Ehrengericht	court of honour.
Eichenspreize	oak stay.
Eid	oath.
Fahneneid	oath on the colours (*when recruits are sworn in*).
Eierhandgranate	"Egg" hand grenade.
Eigenmächtig	unauthorized.
Eile	hurry.
Eilig	urgent.
Eilmarsch	forced march.
Einarbeiten	to acquaint oneself thoroughly with.
Einarbeiten, gegenseitiges	mutual acquaintance with each other's methods.
Einbau	digging in, mounting.
Einbauen (der Batterien)	digging in (of batteries).
Einbauten	structures in field fortification (*e.g., shelters, observation posts, &c.*).
Einbautrupp	working party for constructing emplacements.
Einberufen	called out (*e.g., Landwehr*).
Einbeziehen	to make use of, to take advantage of.
Einbrechen	to invade.
Einbruch	raid, breaking in, penetration, invasion.
Einbruchstelle	point of entry (*of a raid*).
Eindecker	monoplane.
Eindeckung	overhead cover, recess.
Eindeckungen (fortlaufende)	continuous recesses (*under parapet*).
Eindringen	to break into, penetrate, enter.
Einerden	to earth (*telegraph, &c.*).

Einfachleitung	earth return circuit (*telegraph, &c.*).
Einfall	collapse; invasion; idea.
Einfallen	to fall in; to invade; to occur (*of an idea*).
Einfallswinkel	angle of descent.
Einfordern	to call in; to demand.
Eingedeckt (schusssicher)	in shell-proof emplacement.
Eingedeckt werden	to be covered in, *or* completely "blinded" (*trench, or other works*).
Eingeschnitten	dug-in (*e.g., battery*).
Eingleisige Bahn	single-line railway.
Eingraben (sich)	to dig oneself in.
Eingreif-Division	counter-attack division (*as opposed to "Kampf-Division" or front line division*).
Eingreifen	to come into action.
Einheit	unit; unity.
Einheits-Geschoss	universal or combined (H. E. and shrapnel) shell.
Einheitsscheibe	standard target.
Einheitsmütze	universal pattern cap.
Einimpfen	to inoculate.
Einjährig-Freiwilliger	one-year volunteer.
Einkehlen	to groove; to provide with a gutter.
Einleben	to become thoroughly acquainted with (*e.g., a new position*).
Einleiten einen Angriff	to prepare an attack; to begin an attack.
Einmessen	to fix (*e.g., battery aiming points*).
Einmündung	entrance (*e.g., where a communication trench enters a fire trench*).
Einnehmen	to occupy, conquer.
Einquartieren	to billet, quarter troops.
Einrichten	to erect, organize, arrange, settle, prepare.
Einrichtung	arrangement, order.
nach Einrichtung der neuen Stellen	after the installation of the new stations.
Einrücken	moving in (*e.g., of troops into billets*); to be called up (*of recruits*).
Einsatz	engagement, employment, bringing into action; breathing drum of gas mask (*in which case it is a contraction for "Atemeinsatz"*).
Munitionseinsatz	expenditure of ammunition.
Einschalten	to switch on (*electrical*); to insert (*a unit between other units in line*).
Einschärfen	to inculcate.

Einschichteneinsatz	single layer drum (*for gas mask*).
Einschienenbahn	monorail.
Einschiessen, sich	to register, begin registration, find the range.
Einschiessensverfahren	registration.
Einschiffen	to embark.
Einschlagen	to strike (*of projectiles*).
Einschlagsknall	report of a shell burst.
Einschliessen	to comprise, include; envelop.
Einschliessung	investment (*fortress*); envelopment.
Einschneiden	to dig in.
Einschnitt	emplacement, embrasure, railway cutting.
Einschneidetrupp	flash spotting detachment.
Einschraubzünder	fuze (*which is screwed in*).
Einsetzen	to introduce, insert; to put in (*e.g., troops into the line, into the fight, &c.*), engage.
am Apparat eingesetzt	engaged at the telephone (*colloquial*).
Artilleriefeuer einsetzen	open fire with artillery.
Einsitzer	single-seater (*aeroplane*).
Einspannen	to hook in (*horses*).
Einspielen	co-operation, co-ordination.
Einspringender (Winkel)	re-entrant (angle).
Einspritzen	to inject.
Einsteigbrücke	gangway (*for entraining purposes*), ramp.
Einstellen	to put in; to suspend.
einen Stollen einstellen	to stop a gallery (*mining*).
ein Pferd einstellen	to stable a horse.
Feuer einstellen	to cease fire.
in einen Truppenteil eingestellt werden	to be posted to a unit.
Rekruten einstellen	to allot recruits to a unit.
sich wieder einstellen	to return.
Einstellung	recruiting, enlistment; suspension.
zeitweilige Einstellung	temporary suspension; intermission.
Einsturz	collapse, fall, downfall.
Einsturz eines Schachtes	caving in of a shaft.
Einteilen	to divide into, detail.
Einteilung	division, graduation, disposition; "order of battle."
Eintragen	to enter in a note book.
Eintrefftag	date of arrival (*e.g., on a movement order*).

Eintreten	to enter, to join the army.
Eintrittskante	leading edge (*plane of aeroplane*).
Einverleibt	absorbed.
Einvernehmen	understanding.
Einweiser	guide (*into the trenches*).
Einzelaufzählung	detailed enumeration.
Einzelfeuer	independent fire.
Einzelheiten	details.
Einzelscharte	ordinary loophole.
Einzelschuss	single round.
Einzeltreffer	single direct hit.
Einziehen	to withdraw, confiscate.
Einzug	entry (*of troops into a town, &c.*)
Eisenbahnarbeiterkompagnie	railway labour company.
Eisenbahnbaukompagnie	railway construction company.
Eisenbahnbetriebsamt	railway traffic office.
Eisenbahnbetriebskompagnie	railway traffic company.
Eisenbahndamm	railway embankment.
Eisenbahndurchschnitt	railway cutting.
Eisenbahnnetz	network of railways, railway system.
Eisenbahnschiene	rail.
Eisenbahnschwelle	sleeper.
Eisenbahntruppen	railway troops.
Eisenbereifung	iron tyre.
Eisenbeton	reinforced concrete.
Eisenbetonkuppel	reinforced concrete cupola.
Eisenbewehrung	reinforcement (*ferro-concrete*).
Eisenblechrahmen	sheet-iron frame.
Eisendraht	iron wire.
Eisenflechtung	reinforcement (*ferro-concrete*).
Eisenklammer	dog (*in timber work*).
Eisenklingeln	metallic noise.
Eisenmeissel	iron chisel.
Eisenpfahl	iron stake, post.
Eisenpfosten	iron post.
Eisenplatte	iron plate.
Eisenstange	iron rod.
Eisenteile	iron *or* metal parts.
Eisenträger	iron girder.
Eiserner Bestand	iron ration (*also used in connection with artillery ammunition*).
Eiserne Portion	iron ration.
Eisernes Kreuz (E.K.)	Iron Cross.
Eisnägel	frost nails.
Eissporn	ice spade (*on trail of gun*).
Elektrikertrupp	electrician detachment.

Elemente (unklare)	suspects.
Elevationswinkel	elevation of a gun.
Ellbogenfühlung	close touch.
Empfangsabteilung	reception section (*of main dressing station*).
Empfangsbescheinigung	receipt voucher.
Empfangsstation	receiving station (*wireless, &c.*).
Empfangsstelle	receiving station.
Endstation	terminus.
Engländerwache	guard for British prisoners of war.
Engpass	pass, defile.
Engquartier	close billets.
Ente	" dud " shell (*colloquial*).
Entblössen	to lay bare ; to expose (*a wing*).
Entfalten	to deploy.
Entfaltung	deployment.
Entfernung	distance, range.
Entfernung aus der Armee	expulsion from the army.
Entfernungsmesser	telemeter, range finder.
Entfernungsschätzer	range taker.
Entgegengehen	to go to meet, encounter.
Entgehen, einem	to escape one's notice ; to lose ; to miss.
Entkeimen	sterilize.
Entkommen	to escape.
Entladen	to unload, discharge.
Entlastungsangriff	attack to relieve pressure elsewhere.
Entlausen	to disinfest, rid of vermin.
Entlausungsstube	disinfestation room.
Entlüfter	suction pump for extracting bad air from a mine.
Entsatz	relief.
Entsatzarmee	relieving army.
Entsatzmannschaft	relief-column.
Entscheidung	decision.
Entscheidungskampf Entscheidungsschlacht	} decisive battle.
Entschlammen	to free from mud.
Entsetzen (eine Festung)	to relieve, succour (a fortress).
Entseuchen	to disinfect.
Entsprechend	suitable, corresponding.
Entstänkerungspatrone	deodorizing cartridge (*for getting rid of gas*).
Entwaffnen	to disarm.
Entwässerungsanlagen	drainage arrangements.
Entwässerungsgraben	draining trench.
Entweichen	to escape.
Entwicklung	deployment, extension ; development.

Entwurf	draft (*of document*), rough sketch, project, provisional edition (*text-books, regulations, &c.*).
Entziehen	to withdraw, screen (*from view, fire, &c.*).
Entziffern	to decipher.
Entzünden	to inflame, light.
Epauletten	epaulettes.
Equitations-Anstalt	School of Equitation (Bavaria).
Erbeuten	to secure, capture (*booty*).
Erdarbeit	digging.
Erdaufwurf	heap of earth, mound.
Erdaufwurf (durchlaufender)	continuous parapet.
Erdbeobachtung	ground observation.
Erden	earths (*telephone, &c.*).
Erdfunkerdienst	ground wireless service.
Erdkabel	buried cable.
Erdklemme	earth terminal (*electrical*).
Erdleitung	earth, earth line (*electricity*).
Erdmine	"earth mortar" projectile (*a large canister bomb*).
Erdmörser	earth mortar, buried trench mortar.
Erdoberfläche	surface of the ground.
Erdpolster	cushion of earth.
Erdsappe, flüchtige	flying sap.
Erdstation	ground station.
Erdtelegraph	power buzzer (*telegraphy*).
Erdtelegraphie	earth current telegraphy, power buzzer.
Erdtelegraphenstand / Erdtelegraphenstation	power buzzer station.
Erdung	earth (*electrical*).
Erdvorlage	layer of earth (*in front of concrete wall, &c.*).
Erfahrungsgemäss	as a result of experience.
Erfordern	to demand, request, ask for.
Erforderlich	requisite.
Erfordernis	requirement.
Erfüllen	to observe, fulfil.
Ergänzend	supplementary, completing.
Ergänzung	complement; recruiting.
Ergänzungsbedarf	deficiency.
Ergänzungsmannschaften	drafts.
Ergänzungsplanquadrat	supplementary squaring of a map.
Ergänzungszug	supplementary section (*applied to extra machine gun units formed in 1916. The term is now obsolete*).
Ergeben (sich)	to surrender.

Ergebnis	occurrence; result, consequence, sequel.
Ergreifen	to seize, take up (*arms*).
Erhebung	elevation, rising ground.
Erhebungen und Falten des Geländes	undulations in the ground.
Erhöhen	to increase.
Erhöhung	elevation, height, hill, commanding point.
Erhöhungswinkel	angle of elevation.
Erkennen	to recognise; to detect (*a target*).
Erkennungsmarke	identity disc.
Erkennungswort	watchword, countersign.
Erkennungszeichen	distinguishing mark.
Erklärung	declaration.
Erkunden	to examine, reconnoitre.
Erkundung	reconnaissance.
Erkundung, gewaltsame	reconnaissance in force.
Erkundungsabteilung	reconnoitring party.
Erkundungsergebnisse	results of reconnaissance
Erkundungspatrouille	reconnoitring patrol.
Erkundigen, sich nach	to inquire after.
Erkundigung	inquiry.
Erkundigungsabteilung	reconnoitring detachment.
Erkundigungskommando	} reconnoitring patrol.
Erkundigungspatrouille	
Erlass	order.
kriegsministerieller Erlass	War Ministry order.
einen Befehl erlassen	to issue, publish an order.
Erlaubnisschein	permit.
Erläuterung	explanation.
Erledigen	to settle, finish; to stop, repulse.
Erledigungsschein	receipt.
Erleiden	to suffer.
Ermächtigung	authorization.
Ermitteln	to ascertain, determine.
Ernennen	to nominate, appoint.
Ernte	harvest.
Erntekompagnie	harvesting company.
Eröffnen (Feuer)	to open (fire).
Eröffnung	opening, beginning.
Ersatz	"Ersatz," supplement, reinforcement, draft, depôt; substitute.

The word "Ersatz," when used alone means "draft" or "reinforcement." When prefixed to the title of a unit, e.g., "Ersatz Bataillon," it either means "depôt" or "supplementary unit formed by a depôt."
(See also "Ersatz Reserve.").

Ersatzbehörden	recruiting authorities.
Ersatzgestellung	substitute, replacement.
Ersatzglas	spare mirror (*for periscope*).
Ersatzkompagnie	depôt company, "Ersatz" company.
Ersatzmagazin	reserve depôt.
Ersatzmannschaften	drafts.
Ersatzmittel	spare parts (*telephone, &c.*).
Ersatzreserve	"Ersatz Reserve" (*category of men surplus to the annual contingent required for the Army in peace*).
Ersatzreservist	"Ersatz" reservist.
Ersatzstollen	substitute (alternative) gallery (*mining*).
Ersatzstück	spare part.
Ersatztruppen	depôt troops.
Ersatztruppenteil	depôt unit.
Ersaufen	to be swamped, drowned.
Erschiessen	to shoot dead, execute.
Erschütterungshalbmesser	radius of rupture (*mining*).
Erstatten (Bericht)	to make a report.
Ersticken (im Keime)	to nip (in the bud).
Erstickendes Gas	suffocating *or* asphyxiating gas.
Erstrecken, sich	to extend (*e.g.*, "*das Feuer erstreckte sich bis zum rechten Kompagnieabschnitt*"=*the fire extended as far as, &c.*).
Erstürmen	to take by assault.
Erstürmung	taking by assault.
Ersuchung	request, demand.
Erweis	proof, demonstration.
Erwerbungsfähig	capable of earning one's living.
Erwiderungsfeuer	retaliation fire.
Erzwingen	to force, gain by force.
Eskadron	squadron.
Eskadronskolonne	squadron column.
Etappen	Lines of Communication (L. of C.).
Etappenanfangsort	Home base.
Etappenarzt	Deputy Director of Medical Services (L. of C.).
Etappendelegierter	Delegate for the L. of C.
Etappendepotmagazin	depôt on L. of C.
Etappen-Eisenbahn-Direktion	L. of C. railway directorate.
Etappen-Fernsprech-Depôt	L. of C. telephone depôt.
Etappen-Flug-Park	L. of C. aviation park.
Etappenfuhrparkkolonne	L. of C. supplypark.
Etappengebiet	L. of C. area.
Etappen-Haupfort	L. of C. main depôt.

Etappenhilfsbäckereiabteilung	L. of C. auxiliary bakery detachment.
Etappenhilfskompagnie ...	L. of C. auxiliary company.
Etappen-Inspektion	L. of C. Inspectorate.
Etappen-Kommandantur ...	L. of C. Commandant's office.
Etappen-Kraftwagenkolonne	L. of C. M.T. column.
Etappen-Lazarett	L. of C. stationary hospital.
Etappenmagazin	depôt on L. of C.
Etappen-Ort	post on L. of C.
Etappen-Sammelkompagnie...	L. of C. collecting company.
Etappen-Sanitätskraftwagen-Abteilung	L. of C. motor ambulance detachment.
Etappen-Sanitäts-Depot ...	advanced depôt of medical stores.
Etappen-Telegraphen-Direktion	L. of C. telegraph directorate.
Etappenverwendungsfähig ...	fit for service on the L. of C.
Etat (niederer, höherer) ...	establishment (higher, lower); budget.
Etatsmässig	on the establishment.
Exerzieren	to drill.
Exerziermarsch	drill step.
Exerziermässig	as if it were a drill.
Exerzierreglement	drill book.
Exerzierpatrone	dummy cartridge.
Exerzierplatz	drill ground.
Explosionsmotor	internal combustion engine.
Exzellenz	Excellency (*title given to Lieut.-Generals and senior ranks in the German Army*).

F.

Fabrik	factory.
Fabrikleitung	factory management.
Fach	compartment (*in a box*); branch, department; trade, profession.
Facharbeiter	technical worker.
Fachleute	specialists.
Fachwerkbrücke	truss bridge.
Fadenkreuz	cross hairs (*of telescope, &c.*).
Fahndung	search for a deserter.
Fahndungsersuch	request to search for a man who has left his unit without leave.
Fahne	flag, colours, standard.
Fahne, auf Dienst bei der	on service with the colours.
Fahneneid	oath on the colours (when recruits are sworn in).
Fahnenflucht	desertion.
Fahnenflüchtiger	deserter.
Fahnenjunker	aspirant officer (first stage).
Fahnenschmied	farrier.
Fähnrich	aspirant officer (second stage), ensign.
Fähnrichsprüfung	ensigns' examination (*of cadets before posting as ensign, &c.*).
Fahrbar	practicable for wheeled traffic; mobile.
Fahrbare Station (Funken-)	mobile (wireless) station.
Fahrbündel	float (*for improvised floating bridge*).
Fahrplan	time table (*railway*).
Fähre	ferry, raft.
Fahrende Batterie	field artillery battery.
Fahrer	driver.
Fahrgestell	undercarriage (*of aeroplane*).
Fahrrad	bicycle.
Fahrtanweis Fahrtliste	} time table *or* itinerary (*railway*).
Fahrtnummer	number given to draft of reinforcements.
Fahr- und Marsch-Tafeln	tables of railway movements and marches.
Fahrzeug	vehicle.
Fällen	to fell.
das Bajonett fällen	to bring the bayonet to the charge.
Fallbrücke	drawbridge.
Fallschirm	parachute.
Fallschirmrakete	parachute light.
Fallwinkel	angle of descent.
Faltboot	collapsible boat.

Faltbootbrücke	bridge of collapsible boats.
Falte	fold, hollow.
Falten (Erhebungen und) des Geländes	undulations in the ground.
Falzartiger Halter	grooved charger *or* strip (*magazine rifle*).
Fangschnur	cap lines, busby lines.
Faschine	fascine.
Faschinenbekleidung	fascine revetment.
Fassen	to hold, to seize (*slang for* "beziehen," *to draw rations*).
Fassung	loading space, holding capacity (*railway*).
Fassungsvermögen	holding capacity (*dug-outs, &c.*).
Fausthandschuh	mitten.
Faustriemen	sword-knot.
Fechten	to fight, fence.
Federgehäuse	casing of brake spring (*gun carriage*).
Federspannung	tension of spring (*in machine gun, &c.*).
Fedrawa (Feld-Drachenwarte)	field kite balloon meteorological station.
Fehlanzeige	nil report.
Fehlen	to miss, err; to lack.
Fehler	fault, mistake, miss.
Fehlerhaft	faulty.
Fehlgehen	to miss one's way.
Fehlschlagen	to miscarry.
Fehltritt	false step.
Fehlwurf	misfire (*especially applicable to* "Lanz-" *or* "Wurf-Mine").
Feile	file (*tool*).
Feind	enemy.
Feindlich	hostile, the enemy's.
Feka (Fern-Kampf-Artillerie)	long-range artillery.
Feld	field; land (*of rifling*).
das Feld behaupten	to hold the field.
das Feld räumen	to quit the field.
ins Feld rücken	to take the field.
Feld-Apotheker	Senior Pharmacist Officer of the Army.
Feld-Artillerie	field (and horse) artillery.
Feld-Artillerie-Schiess-Schule	Field Artillery School of Gunnery.
Feldbäckerei	field bakery.
Feldbackofen	field oven.
Feldbahn	field railway (*metre gauge*).
Feldbahnbetriebsabteilung,	field railway traffic section.
Feldbahnbetriebsamt	field railway traffic office.

Feldbahndepot	field railway depôt.
Feldbahnlore	field tramway truck
Feldbefestigungskunst ...	art of field fortification.
Feldbinde	waist belt (*officers*).
Feldbrief	letter (*written in the field*).
Felddienst	field service.
Felddienst-Ordnung	Field Service Regulations.
Feldeisenbahnchef	Director of Railways.
Feldeisenbahnwesen	Field Railway Service.
Feldflasche	water bottle.
Feldflieger-Abteilung ...	reconnaissance flight (*aviation unit; obsolete term, now known as "Fliegerabteilung."*)
Feldflieger-Abteilung (A) ...	artillery flight (*aviation unit; obsolete term, see "Fliegerabteilung (A)".*)
Feldflugwesen	Field Aviation Service (*obsolete*).
Feldgeistlicher...	chaplain to the forces.
Feldgendarmerie	field police.
Feldgerät	stores.
Feldgericht	court-martial.
Feldgeschrei	password.
Feldgeschütz	field gun.
Feldgranate	field gun high explosive (H.E.) shell.
Feld-Haubitze	field howitzer.
Feldheer	Field Army.
Feldhilfsarzt	Surgeon Probationer.
Feldhose	field service trousers or pantaloons.
Feldjäger	King's Messenger.
Feldjäger (berittener) ...	mounted courier.
Feldkabelleitung	cable line.
Feldkanone	field gun.
Feldkessel	dixie, camp kettle.
Feldkochgerät	field cooking utensils.
Feldkompagnie	field company (*active company of a pioneer battalion*).
Feldkoppel	field service belt.
Feldkraftfahrchef	Director of Mechanical Transport.
Feld-Krieg	field warfare.
Feld-Kriegs-Kassen-Verwaltung	field treasury officials.
Feldküche	travelling kitchen.
Feldlazarett	field hospital, casualty clearing station.
Feldluftschiffer-Abteilung	balloon detachment.
Feldmagazin	field depôt.
Feldmarschall	Field-Marshal.

Feldmarschmässig	for active service.
Feld-Maschinen-Gewehr-Zug	machine gun section (*obsolete*).
Feldmineurwagen	mining store wagon.
Feldmütze	field service cap.
Feldoberpostinspektion ...	Chief Inspector of Field Post Offices.
Feldoberpostsekretär ...	Chief Field Post Office Secretary.
Feldpatrone	field gun cartridge (*fixed ammunition*).
Feldpionier-Dienst	Manual of Field Engineering.
Feldpionier-Kompagnie ...	pioneer field company.
Feldpolizei, geheime	secret police.
Feldpostamt	field post office (Corps H.Q.).
Feldpostexpedition	field post office (Divisional H.Q.).
Feldpostmeister	field postmaster.
Feldpoststation	field post office.
Feldpostwesen...	Field Postal Service.
Feldprobst	Chaplain-General.
Feldproviantamt	field supply depôt.
Feldrekrutenbataillon ...	recruit battalion in the field.
Feldrekrutendepot	field recruit depôt.
Feldsanitätswesen	Medical Service of the Field Army.
Feldschanze	field work.
Feldschmiede	field forge.
Feldschrapnelpatrone ...	field gun shrapnel cartridge (*fixed ammunition*).
Feldsignalabteilung	field signalling detachment (*cavalry*).
Feldsignaltrupp	field signal section (*obsolete*).
Feldstecher	field glass.
Feldstiefel	field service boots.
Feldtrain-Eskadron	field train squadron.
Feldverwaltungs-Behörden ...	field administrative authorities.
Feldverwaltungs-Schreiber ...	superintending clerk.
Feldwache	piquet.
Feldwebel	serjeant-major (*company serjeant-major of infantry, pioneers, or foot artillery*).
Feldwebel-Leutnant	serjeant-major-lieutenant (*only appointed in war*).
Feldwetterstation	meteorological station.
Feldwetterwarte	field meteorological station.
Feldzahlmeister	field paymaster.
Feldzeugmeister	Master of the Ordnance.
Feldzeugmeisterei	Ordnance Department.
Feldzug	campaign.
Feldzugsplan	plan of campaign.
Felge	felloe (*of wheel*).

Ferngespräch	telephone conversation.
Fernglas	telescope.
Fernhörer	telephone receiver.
Fernkampfgruppe	long-range group (*artillery*).
Fernmündlich	by telephone (*conversation " in clear," as opposed to " durch Fernspruch," i.e., telephoned in code*).
Fernpatrouille	distant patrol.
Fernrohr	telescope.
Fernrohraufsatz	telescopic sight.
Fernrohrbüchse	rifle with telescopic sight.
Fernsprecher	telephone.
Fernsprech-Abteilung (Trupp)	telephone detachment (squad).
Fernsprechapparat	telephone instrument.
Fernsprech-Doppelzug	divisional telephone detachment.
Fernsprechgerät	telephone stores.
Fernsprechleitung	telephonic communication, telephone line.
Fernsprechnetz	telephone system.
Fernsprech-Offizier	telephone officer.
Fernsprechschlüssel	telephone code book.
Fernsprechstelle	telephone station.
Fernsprechverbindung / Fernsprechverkehr	telephonic communication.
Fernsprechzentrale	telephone exchange.
Fernspruch	telephone message (*in code*).
Fernstecher	field glasses.
Fesselballon	captive balloon.
Fester Sitz!	Screw firmly home!
Feste Station	fixed station (*wireless*).
Festlegen (im Plan)	to plot.
Festlegepunkt	reference point.
Festlegung	definition, location, fixing, determination.
Festnehmen	to arrest.
Feststellen	to identify, establish, fix.
Feststellung	identification.
Festung	fortress.
Festungen, Kampf um	fortress warfare.
Festungsanlagen	fortifications.
Festungsartillerie	fortress artillery.
Festungsbaubeleuchtungstrupp	fortress searchlight section.
Festungsbaufeldwebel	fortress construction serjeant-major.
Festungsbauleutnant	2nd lieutenant in the fortress construction service.

Festungsbauoffiziere	Corps of Fortress Constructors.
Festungsbauwärter	superintendent of fortifications.
Festungsdienstordnung	Fortress Service Regulations.
Festungsfliegerabteilung	fortress flight.
Festungsfunkerabteilung	fortress wireless detachment.
Festungsluftschiffertrupp	fortress balloon detachment.
Festungsmaschinengewehrkompagnie	fortress machine gun company.
Festungsscheinwerferzug	fortress searchlight section.
Festungsstab	fortress staff.
Festungsstation	fortress (wireless) station.
Festungswerk	fortification.
Fettdose	box of grease.
Feuer	fire ; bombardment.
bei Feuer stehen	to be under fire.
bestreichendes Feuer	grazing fire, enfilade fire.
ein heftiges Feuer unterhalten	to maintain a heavy fire.
Feuer einschalten, eröffnen	to open fire.
Feuer feindwärts verlegen !	Lift your fire !
flankierendes Feuer	flanking, enfilading fire.
lebhaftes Feuer	rapid firing.
ruhiges Feuer	deliberate fire (*artillery*).
Sperrfeuer	barrage, barrage fire.
Störungsfeuer	harassing fire.
Vernichtungsfeuer	annihilating fire.
wirksames Feuer	effective fire.
Wirkungsfeuer	fire for effect.
Zerstörungsfeuer	destructive fire.
Feuerabriegelung	barrage.
Feuerarme Zone	area lightly shelled.
Feuerart	nature of fire (*e.g., rapid or deliberate fire*).
Feuerbereit	in readiness to open fire.
Feuerbereich	zone of fire, danger zone.
Feuerbündel	faggot.
Feuererscheinung	flame effect.
Feuergarbe	cone of fire.
Feuergeschwindigkeit	rate of fire.
Feuerkraft	fire power, intensity of fire.
Feuerlärm	fire alarm.
Feuerleerer Raum	an area not swept by fire.
Feuerleitung	fire control; telephone line used for directing fire.
Feuerleitungsplan	large scale map for fire control.
Feuerleitungsübungen	fire control (command) exercises.
Feuerleitungsstelle	fire control post.
Feuerlinie	firing line.

Feuerordnung	method of fire (*e.g.*, *rapid or deliberate fire*).
Feuerpause	pause *or* interval during firing.
Feuerrichtung	direction of fire.
Feuersäule	column of flame.
Feuerschein	reflection (*of gun flash*).
Feuerstärke	volume of fire.
Feuerstellung...	fire position, battery position.
Feuerstellung der Batterie	battery position.
Auswahl der Feuerstellung	selection of battery position.
Feuerstrahl	gun flash.
Feuertiefe	depth of fire.
Feuerüberfall	burst of fire.
Feuerüberlegenheit ...	superiority of fire.
Feuervereinigung ...	concentration of fire.
Feuerverteilung	distribution of fire.
Feuerverteilungsheft ...	fire distribution book.
Feuerwerker	serjeant-artificer.
Feuerwerks-Offizier ...	artificer-officer.
Feuerwirkung...	fire effect.
Fewewa (Feldwetterwarte) ...	field meteorological station.
Filialdepot	branch depôt.
Filtermasse	drum-contents (*i.e.*, *contents of a gas drum*).
Filzschuh	felt boot.
First	roof of gallery (*mining*).
Flachbahn	flat trajectory.
Flachbahngeschütz ...	flat trajectory gun.
Flächenrückbiegung ...	sweep-back (*of aeroplane*).
Flachfeuer	flat trajectory fire.
Flachfeuerbatterie ...	flat trajectory battery.
Flachswerg	waste, tow waste.
Fladdermine	*sometimes used for* camouflet (*mining*).
Flagge	flag, standard (*naval*).
Flaggenzeichen	flag signals.
Flak (Flug - Abwehr - Kanone)	anti-aircraft gun.
Flakbatterie	anti-aircraft battery.
Flak-Ersatz-Abteilung ...	anti-aircraft depôt.
Flakfernsprechnetz	anti-aircraft telephone system.
Flakgruko (Flug - Abwehr- Kanonen - Gruppen - Kommandeur)	A. A. Group Commander.
Flakgruppe	anti-aircraft gun group.
Flakschule	anti-aircraft gun school.
Flakschutz	**anti-aircraft protection.**

Flakzug	anti-aircraft section.
Flamga	(*see* "Flug-Abwehr-Maschinengeehr-Abteilung").
Flammenstoss	} jet of flame.
Flammenstrahl	
Flammenwerfer	*Flammenwerfer or* flame projector.
Flammenwerfertrupp	*Flammenwerfer* squad.
Flanke	flank.
Flankenangriff	flank attack.
Flanken aufdecken	to expose the flanks.
Flankenbewegung	flank march.
Flankenfeuer	enfilade fire, flanking fire.
Flankenstollen	branch gallery (*mining*).
Flankieren	to enfilade.
Flankierende Stellung	position from which enfilade fire can be brought to bear.
Flankierendes Artilleriefeuer	enfilade artillery fire.
Flankierung	flanking fire, flanking position.
Flankierungsanlagen	flanking defences.
Flankierungsgeschütz	gun for flanking fire.
Flasche	flask, bottle (*has been known to be used for trench mortar bombs*).
Flaschengas	gas from cylinders, cylinder gas.
Flaschensauerstoff	oxygen in cylinders.
Flaschenzug	pulley.
Flechtwerk	hurdle-work.
Flickmaterial	material for repair of clothing.
Fliegende Brücke	flying bridge.
Fliegende Division	independent division.
Fliegende Kolonne	flying column.
Fliegenschrank	meat-safe.
Flieger	aviator; airman.
Gruppenführer der Flieger (Grufl)	Group Aviation Commander.
Fliegerabteilung	reconnaissance flight (*aviation unit*)
Fliegerabteilung (A)	artillery flight (*aviation unit*).
Fliegerabwehr	anti-aircraft measures.
Fliegeralarm	aircraft alarm.
Fliegerangriff	aerial attack, air raid.
Fliegerantenne	aeroplane wireless receiving station.
Fliegeraufnahme	aeroplane photograph.
Fliegerbeobachtung	aeroplane observation.
Fliegerbeschuss	anti-aircraft firing.
Fliegerdeckung !	"Put on the screens !"; keeping under cover from aeroplanes.
Fliegerdeckung aufgehoben !	"Remove screens."
Flieger-Ersatz-Abteilung (Fea)	training squadron (*aviation depôt*).

Fliegergefechtsstation	...	aviation wireless fighting station (*ground station*).
Fliegergefechtsstation (E)	...	aviation wireless fighting station, receiving only (*ground station*).
Fliegergruppenführer	...	Commander of Group of Aviation Troops, Wing Commander.
Fliegerkampf	...	aerial combat.
Fliegerkompagnie	...	flying company (Bavaria) (*now obsolete*).
Fliegerkorn	...	foresight (*on rifle : for use against aerial objectives*).
Fliegernotsignal	...	aerial distress signal.
Fliegerpfahl	...	A.A. pivot mounting (*for machine gun*).
Fliegerphotographie ...	...	aeroplane photograph.
Fliegerschiessen	...	anti-aircraft fire.
Fliegersicht	...	view from aircraft.
Fliegerstörer ...	...	aeroplane jamming station.
Fliegertauglichkeit	...	fitness for flying.
Fliegertruppen... ...	...	Flying Troops (*equivalent to aeroplane units of Royal Air Force*).
Fliegertuch	...	cloth sheet (*for signalling to aeroplanes*).
Fliegerverfolgungsstelle des A.O.K.		Army Centre for enemy aircraft activity.
Fliegerwache	...	aeroplane observation post.
Fliegerwarnungsdienst	...	arrangements for giving warning of the approach of aircraft.
Fliegerwarte	...	aeroplane observation post.
Fliehbolzen	...	centrifugal bolt (*in fuze, &c.*).
Floss	...	(*a*) float, raft ; (*b*) fin, steadying fin in a dirigible.
Flossbrücke	...	floating bridge.
Flottenatmer	...	*a rescue apparatus similar to the " Dräger Selbstretter" or oxygen breathing apparatus.*
Flüchtige Befestigung	...	hasty entrenchment.
Flug	...	flight (*the act of flying*).
Flug-Abwehr-Kanone (Flak)		anti-aircraft gun.
Flug-Abwehr-Kanonen-Gruppen-Kommandeur		A.A. Group Commander.
Flug-Abwehr-Kanonen-Schule		anti-aircraft gun school.
Flug-Abwehr-Kanonen-Zug ...		anti-aircraft section.
Flug-Abwehr - Maschinengewehr-Abteilung		machine gun anti-aircraft detachment.
Flugbahn	...	trajectory.
Flügel	...	wing, flank ; aileron (*aeroplane*).
Flügel-Adjutant	...	Aide-de-camp to the Emperor.

Flügelfeder	wing tip.
Flügelkompagnie	wing company.
Flügelmine	trench mortar bomb with fins.
Flügelminenwerfer	*not translated.*
Flügelmutter	wing nut.
Flügelrippe	wing rib (*aeroplane*).
Flügelweise	side by side.
Flügelzug	flank platoon.
linker Flügelzug	platoon on left wing of sector
Flughafen	aerodrome, hydroplane base.
Flughafenstation	aerodrome (wireless) station.
Flughalle	hangar.
Flugmaschine	aeroplane.
Flugmeldeabteilung	aircraft report detachment.
Flugmeldedienst	aircraft reporting service.
Flugmeldestelle	aircraft reporting station.
Flugplatz	aerodrome.
Flugposten	aircraft sentries.
Flugschule	flying school.
Flugwache	aircraft look-out station.
Flugweite	range (*of a projectile*).
Flugwesen	aviation.
Flugzeug	aeroplane.
Ft.-Flugzeug	aeroplane fitted with wireless.
Flugzeugbordstation	aeroplane wireless set.
Flugzeugführer	pilot (*of aeroplane*).
Flugzeugführerabzeichen	pilot's badge.
Flugzeuggeschwader	squadron of aeroplanes.
Flugzeugschuppen	aeroplane shed, hangar.
Fluma (Flugmeldeabteilung)	aircraft report detachment.
Flurschäden	damage to property on manœuvres.
Flüstertute	megaphone.
Förderbahn	field tramway (60 *cm. gauge*).
Formation	formation *or* unit.
Fortifikations-Beamter	engineer official.
Fortlaufende Eindeckungen	continuous recesses (*under parapet*).
Fouragieren	to forage.
Franzosenwache	guard for French prisoners of war.
Freiliegen	to be unencumbered.
Freimachen (des Schussfeldes)	clearing (the field of fire).
Freisprechen	to acquit.
Freiwillige Krankenpflege	voluntary aid.
Freiwilliger	volunteer.
Freiwilliges Automobil-Korps	Volunteer Automobile Corps.
Freiwilliges Motorboot-Korps	Volunteer Motorboat Corps.
Fressbeutel	nose bag.
Frieden	peace.
ein fauler Frieden	a hollow truce.

Friedens-Besoldungsvorschrift	Pay Regulations (Peace).
Friedensfahrplan	peace time-table (*railway*).
Friedensfuss	peace footing.
Friedensmässig	obtaining in peace time.
Friedenspräsenzstärke ...	peace strength law.
Friedens-Sanitätsordnung ...	Medical Regulations (Peace).
Friedensstand	peace conditions.
Friedens-Verpflegungsvorschrift	Supply Regulations (Peace).
Frontausdehnung	extent of front held.
Frontbeobachtungsstelle ...	forward observing station.
Frontlänge	frontage, front.
Front machen	to front.
Front-Offizier	regimental officer.
Frontstärke	strength of the fighting troops.
Frühsprenger	premature burst.
Fuchsloch	small shelter, "funkhole."
Fühlung	touch.
in engster Fühlung bleiben	to remain in closest touch.
Führen	to lead, guide, convey.
Führer	commander, leader, guide.
Führer der grossen Bagage ...	commander of the train.
Fuhre	transport.
eine Fuhre Heu	a load of hay.
Fuhrkosten	cost of transport.
Fuhrpark	transport park.
Fuhrparkkolonne	supply park.
Fuhrparkwagen	supply park vehicle.
Führung	Higher Command; conduct; guiding.
Führungsbolzen	guide bolt.
Führungsklaue	guide (*of gun carriage*).
Führungsleiste	guide rib.
Führungsnut	guiding groove.
Führungsring	driving band (*of a projectile*).
mit vorderem Führungsring	with forward driving band (*shell*).
Fuhrwesen	horsed transport services.
Fufa (Funker-Feld-Abteilung)	field wireless detachment.
Fukla (Funker-Klein-Abteilung)	trench wireless detachment (obsolete: see *Difua*).
Füllpulver 02 (Fp. 02) ...	1902 pattern explosive (T.N.T.).
Füllstoff	liquid (*used to fill gas shell*).
Füllung	the bursting charge of a shell.
Funkeins (Funker-Ersatz-Abteilung 1)	No. 1 Wireless Depôt Detachment.
Funken...	to spark; to send a wireless message, transmit by wireless.
Funkenapparat	wireless apparatus.

Funkenempfangsstation	wireless intercepting station *or* receiving station.
Funkengrossstation	large (high-power) wireless field station.
Funkenstation	wireless station.
Leichte Funkenstation	light wireless station.
Schwere Funkenstation	heavy wireless station.
Funken-Telegraphen-Abteilung	wireless telegraph detachment.
Funkentelegraphie (Ft.)	wireless telegraphy (W/T.).
Ft. Dienst	wireless telegraphy.
Ft. Einrichtung	wireless installation.
Ft. Flugzeug	aeroplane fitted with wireless.
Versagen der F.T.	breakdown of wireless apparatus.
Funker	wireless operator.
Funkerabteilung	wireless detachment.
Funker-Ersatz-Abteilung	wireless depôt detachment.
Funkerfeldabteilung	field wireless detachment.
Funkerkleinabteilung	trench wireless detachment (*obsolete: see Difua*).
Funkerkommando	wireless headquarters.
Funkerkompagnie	wireless telegraph company (*peace*).
Funkerstand	wireless station.
Funkerverbindung	wireless communication.
Funkerverkehr	wireless communication.
Funkspruch	wireless message.
Funktionieren	to work (*mechanical term*).
Furagierleine	forage cord.
Furier	quartermaster-serjeant (*for supply*).
Füsilier	private of fusilier battalion *or* regiment.
Fuss-Artillerie	foot artillery.
Fuss-Artillerie-Munitions-Kraftwagenkolonne	foot artillery M.T. ammunition column.
Fussbekleidung	foot gear.
Fusskranke	men with sore feet.
Fuss-Artillerie-Schiess-Schule	Foot Artillery School of Gunnery.
Fusslappen	foot bandages.
Fussscheibe	disc for foot of trestle (*bridging*).
Futter	fodder, forage; lining of clothes; bush (*metal work*).
Futtersack	corn sack.
Futterwagen	forage wagon.

G.

Gabel	fork; bracket (*in ranging*).
Gabeln (einen Schacht)	to run out a branch gallery (*mining*).
Gabeln, sich	to branch off (*mining*).
Galerie	cross gallery (*mining*).
Galopp	gallop.
Gamaschen	gaiters, leggings.
Gang	gait, pace, step; carriage, bearing; alley (*trench*); course or progress (*of events, fight, &c.*).
ausser Gang sein	to be out of gear (*machinery*).
Ganzboot	cavalry pontoon composed of two half-pontoons ("*Halbbooten*").
Ganzponton	whole pontoon of the Corps equipment (*as opposed to "Halbponton," bipartite pontoon*).
Garbe (eines Maschinen-Gewehrs)	cone of bullets of a machine gun.
Garde	Guard.
Garde-Regiment zu Fuss (G.R. z.F.)	Foot Guards Regiment.
Gardes du Corps	(*not translated; the "Gardes du Corps" Regiment is one of the Guard Cavalry Regiments.*).
Gardist	private of Foot Guards and Body Guard regiments (*e.g.*, 115th).
Garnison-Bauwesen	Barrack Construction Department.
Garnisondienst	garrison duty.
Garnisondienstfähig	} fit for garrison duty.
Garnisondiensttauglich	
Garnisonsauditeur	Garrison Judge-Advocate.
Garnisonsbataillon	garrison battalion.
Garnisonslazarett	station hospital.
Garnisonsverwendungsfähig	fit for garrison duty.
Garnison-Verwaltung	garrison administrative officials.
Garnison-Verwaltungs-Direktor	Director of Garrison Administration.
Garnison-Verwaltungs-Inspektor	Inspector of Garrison Administration.
Garnison-Verwaltungs-Ober-Inspektor	Chief Inspector of Garrison Administration.
Garnitur	articles of uniform.
Gasalarm	gas alarm.
Gasabwehrmittel	means of defence against gas.
Gasangriff	gas attack.
Gasbereitschaft	gas readiness, precautions against gas, "gas alert."
Gasbereitschaft (erhöhte)	"special gas alert."

Gasflasche	gas cylinder.
Gasgranate	gas shell.
Gaskampf	gas warfare.
Gaskolonne	gas column (*balloon troops*).
Gaskrank	"gassed."
Gasmaske	gas mask.
Gasmaskpatrone	gas mask drum.
Gasmine	*Minenwerfer* gas shell.
Halbe schwere Gasmine	half-sized heavy *Minenwerfer* gas shell.
Mittlere Gasmine	medium *Minenwerfer* gas shell.
Leichte Gasmine	light *Minenwerfer* gas shell.
Gaspipette	gas sampling tube.
Gasregiment	pioneer regiment employed on gas duties.
Gasschutzlager	gas defence supply depôt.
Gasschutzpäckchen	anti-gas respirator.
Gasschutzbrillen	gas goggles.
Gasschutzmaske	gas mask, helmet.
Gasschutz-Offizier (G.S.O.)	anti-gas officer.
Gasstellung	*alternative battery position from which gas shelling is carried out.*
Gassumpf	gas pocket.
Gasvergiftet	"gassed."
Gaswolke	gas cloud.
Gattung	arm of the service.
Gaze	gauze.
Gebiet	area, district.
Gebirgsfunkenstation	mountain wireless station.
Gebirgs-Funkerabteilung	mountain wireless detachment.
Gebirgshaubitze	mountain howitzer.
Gebirgskanone	mountain gun.
Gebirgskrieg	mountain warfare.
Gebirgs-Maschinen-Gewehr-Abteilung	mountain machine gun detachment.
Gebirgs-Minenwerfer Kompagnie	mountain *Minenwerfer* company.
Gebiss	set of teeth; bit for horses.
Stangengebiss	curb.
Trensengebiss	snaffle.
Gebrauchsladung	normal charge (*gun ammunition*)
Gebührnisse	allowances.
Gedrücktes Pferd	horse with saddle galls.
Geerdet werden	to be earthed (*electrical*).
Gefahr	danger, risk, peril.
Gefährden	to endanger, risk, imperil.
Gefahrlosigkeit	safety.
Gefahrsmoment	critical moment.

Gefälle	slope (*of a road*); fall (*of a river*).
Gefangenenaussage	prisoner's statement.
Gefangenentransport ...	convoy of prisoners.
Gefangener	prisoner.
einen Gefangenen verhören	to interrogate a prisoner.
Gefangenschaft	captivity.
Gefecht...	fight, fighting, engagement, action, combat, battle.
ausser Gefecht gesetzt werden	to be put out of action.
ein hinhaltendes Gefecht ...	a containing action.
örtliches Gefecht	local engagement.
Gefechtsabschnitt	battle sector.
Gefechtsaufklärung	close reconnaissance (*during an action*).
Gefechtsauftrag	objective.
Gefechtsbagage	first line transport.
Gefechtsbataillon	battalion in line.
Gefechtsbatterie	firing battery.
Gefechtsbefehl...	operation order.
Gefechtsbefehlstelle	battle headquarters.
Gefechtsbereitschaft	readiness for action.
Gefechtsbereitschaft (erhöhte)	increased readiness for action; "stand to."
Gefechtsbereitschaft (höchste)	instant readiness for action; "stand to."
Gefechtsbericht	tactical report.
Gefechtsbreite	frontage.
Gefechtsfall, im	in case of an engagement.
Gefechtsfeld	battlefield, scene of action.
Gefechts-Ft-Station	wireless station near the firing line.
Gefechtshandlung	conduct of operations.
Gefechtslage	tactical situation *or* conditions.
Gefechtslandeplatz	advanced landing ground (*aviation*).
Gefechtsordonnanz	orderly, runner.
Gefechtsstaffel...	wagon line (*of a field battery in action*).
Gefechtsstand	battle headquarters.
Gefechtsstärke	fighting strength.
Gefechtsstelle	battle headquarters, command post.
Gefechtsstellung	battle station.
Gefechtsstreifen	battle zone, battle sector, zone of combat.
Gefechtstätigkeit	action during an operation.
Gefechtszweck...	objective, tactical consideration.
Geflecht	plaiting, hurdle-work, wicker-work.
Gefreitenknopf	*button (small) worn on collar as badge of rank for lance-corporal.*

Gefreiter	lance-corporal, acting bombardier.
Gegenangriff	counter-attack; *sometimes* methodical counter-attack *as compared with* "*Gegenstoss*" or *immediate counter-attack*.
Gegenbefehl	counter-order.
Gegenmassregel	counter-measure.
Gegenmine	countermine (*mining*).
Gegenstand	article, object, affair.
Gegenstoss	counter-attack (*sometimes* an immediate counter-attack, *as compared with* "*Gegenangriff*," *a methodical counter-attack*).
Gegenstoss - Division (Regiment)	counter-attack division (regiment).
Gegenzeichnen	to countersign.
Gegner	enemy, opponent, foe.
Gegnerisch	hostile.
Gehalt	pay (*of officers*).
Geheim (geh.)	secret.
streng geheim	strictly secret.
Geheimschrift	cipher, code.
Gehöft	farm.
Gehölz	copse.
Gehorsamsverweigerung	refusal to obey orders.
Geisel	hostage.
Geistlicher	chaplain.
Gekofern (General-Kommando-Fernsprech-Kommando *or* Kommandeur)	Corps Telephone H.Q. (*or* Commander).
Gekofunk (General-Kommando-Funker-Kommando *or* Kommandeur)	Corps Wireless H.Q. (Commander).
Gekofusta (Gruppen- (General Kommando) Funkenstation)	Group (Corps) wireless station.
Geladen (gel.)	loaded.
Gelände	ground, country, terrain.
A-Gelände	zone of the battalion in line.
B-Gelände	zone of the battalion in support.
C-Gelände	zone of the battalion in reserve.
abfallendes Gelände	a falling slope.
aufsteigendes Gelände	a rising slope.
bedecktes Gelände	close country.
durchschnittenes Gelände	intersected country, close country.
freies Gelände	open country.
welliges Gelände	undulating country.

Geländeabschnitt	area.
Geländefalte	fold in the ground.
Geländegestalt	nature of the ground.
Geländekunde	topography.
Geländepunkt	topographical feature.
Geländerholz	upright for handrail (*bridging*).
Geländerleine	railrope (*bridging*).
Geländespiegel	panoramic mirror, periscope.
Geländeteil	area.
Geländeverhältnisse	nature of the ground.
Geländewinkel	angle of sight.
Gelbkreuzmunition	" yellow cross " gas shell.
Gelegenheitsziel	fleeting target.
Geleise (Gleis)	line of rails *or* track (*railway*).
Geleit	} escort.
Geleitmannschaft	
Gelenkstab	jointed stick.
Gelingen	to succeed, be successful.
Gemeinde	commune.
Gemeiner	private soldier.
Gemüsebaukommando	market gardening detachment.
Gendarme	gendarme.
Gendarmerie	military police.
Gendarmerie-Wachtmeister	serjeant-major of the gendarmerie.
Genehmigt	approved.
General	General.
General-Adjutant	Aide-de-Camp to the Emperor.
Generalarzt	Colonel (*medical*).
General-Auditeur	Judge-Advocate-General.
Generaldelegierter	Delegate-General (*at Army H.Q. in connection with " voluntary aid "*).
General der Artillerie	General of Artillery (*commands a Corps*).
General der Infanterie	General of Infantry (*commands a Corps*).
General der Kavallerie	General of Cavalry (*commands a Corps*).
General der Telegraphentruppen	Director of Signals.
General-Feldmarschall	Field-Marshal (*usually commands a Group of Armies*).
General-Inspekteur des Etappen- und Eisenbahnwesens	Inspector-General of Lines of Communication and Railways.
General-Inspektion	General Inspectorate.
General-Intendant	Intendant-General.

Generalität	General Officers.
General-Kommando	Staff of an Army Corps, Corps Headquarters.
Generalleutnant	Lieutenant-General (*commands a Division*).
Generalmajor	Major-General (*commands a Brigade*).
General-Oberst	" General-Oberst " (*usually commands an Army*).
Generaloberarzt	Lieutenant-Colonel (*medical*).
Generalprofoss	Provost-Marshal.
General-Quartiermeister ...	Quartermaster-General at G.H.Q. (*a General Staff officer*).
Generalstab	General Staff.
Generalstabsarzt	Lieutenant-General (Director-General of Medical Services).
Obergeneralarzt und Sanitäts-Inspekteur	Major-General (*medical*).
Generalarzt	Colonel (*medical*).
Generaloberarzt	Lieutenant-Colonel (*medical*).
Oberarzt	Lieutenant (*medical*).
Oberstabsarzt	Major (*medical*).
Stabsarzt	Captain (*medical*).
Assistenzarzt	Second-Lieutenant (*medical*).
Generalstäbler...	General Staff Officer (*unofficially used instead of* " Generalstabs-Offizier ").
Generalstabschef	Chief of the General Staff.
Generalstabskarte	staff map.
Generalstabs-Offizier ...	General Staff officer.
Generalveterinär	Colonel (*veterinary*).
Genesungsabteilung ...	convalescent depôt.
Genesungskompagnie Genesendekompagnie	} convalescent company.
Genesungsheim	sanatorium, convalescent home.
Genfer Abkommen ...	Geneva Convention.
Geniekorps	Corps of Engineers.
Geniewesen	engineering.
Gent Minenwerfer	(*not translated*).
Geöffnet	at full interval.
Geöffneter Linie (Batterie in)	battery in line at full interval.
Gepäck	pack, kit, baggage.
Gepäck ablegen	to take off packs.
Gepäckbrett	kit-board (*railway transport*).
Gepäckhalter	luggage carrier (*bicycle*).
Gepäcklatte	kit-stanchion (*railway transport*).
Geplänkel	skirmish among outposts.

(B 11413)   C

Gerade ...	straight; even.
gerade Rotten	even files.
ungerade Rotten	odd files.
Geradlinig	rectilinear.
Gerät (e)	stores; implements.
Artilleriegeräte	artillery equipment.
Gerät fordern	to indent for stores.
Gerätedepot	store depôt.
Gerätewagen	pioneer store wagon.
Gerichtsdienst	court martial duty.
Gerippe	framework.
Geröllboden	rubble, loose ground (*e.g., at the bottom of a mine crater*).
Gesamtstärke	total strength.
Geschäfts-Anweisung für die Bahnbevollmächtigten	Regulations for Railway Traffic Officers.
Geschäftszimmer	orderly room, office.
Geschickt	skilful, clever, wise.
Geschirr	harness; gear, utensils (*e.g.*, cooking).
Geschirrtau	trace-rope.
Geschlossen	closed, in close order, at close interval.
geschlossene Schützengräben	closed works.
Geschoss	projectile, bullet, shell.
Brand-Geschoss	incendiary shell.
C-Geschoss	stream line shell.
Geschosse (zu kurz gehende)	"shorts."
Granate-Geschoss	H.E. shell.
Geschossart	nature, type, kind *or* pattern of projectile.
Geschossaufschlag	fall of the shell.
Geschossbahn	trajectory.
Geschossgarbe	cone of fire (*of bullets, &c.*).
Geschosskopf	head (*of shell*).
Geschosskorb	shell basket.
Geschossraum	chamber (*of a gun*).
Geschosssicher	*shell*-proof (*not* bomb-proof); (*also* "bullet-proof," *but this depends on context*).
Geschossspitze	point (*of shell*).
Geschosssplitter	splinter (*of shell*).
Geschosstrichter	shell crater, shell hole.
Geschosswand	wall of shell.
Geschütz	gun.
Geschützbedienung	gun detachment (*artillery*); gun team (*machine gun*)

Geschützbettung	gun platform.
Geschützeinschnitt	gun pit.
Geschützdepot	gun depôt.
Geschützführer	No. 1, gun captain.
Geschützinstandsetzungswerkstatt	gun repair shop.
Geschützkampf	artillery duel.
Geschützpark	gun park.
Geschützrohr	barrel of a gun.
Geschützstand	gun emplacement.
Geschützzwischenraum	interval between guns.
Geschwader	squadron (*naval or air service*).
Geschwindigkeit	speed, rapidity, velocity; rate of fire.
Geschwindschritt (im)	at the double.
Gesicht	face; sight, vision.
Gesichtsfeld } Gesichtskreis }	field of vision *or* view.
Gesichtspunkt	aspect, point of view.
Gestaffelt	staggered (*aeroplane*); écheloned.
tief gestaffelt	distributed in depth (*not* "écheloned").
Gestellung	summons, calling up (*of recruits, &c.*); appointment (*of a man*); provision (*of carts, &c.*).
Gestellungsaufschub	postponement of summons, "putting back."
Gesuch	request.
Getreidefeld	cornfield.
Getrennt	separated, isolated.
Getriebe	driving-gear.
Getriebholz	frames and sheeting (*as opposed to* "Schurzholz," *or continuous casing in mining*).
Gewähr	guarantee.
Gewähr leisten	ensure, guarantee, enable.
Gewalt	power, force.
Gewaltmarsch	forced march.
Gewaltsam	vigorous, powerful, heavy (*attack*).
Gewandt	intelligent, smart, skilful.
Gewehr	rifle.
An die Gewehre!	Stand to!
Gewehr ab!	Order arms!
Gewehr auf!	Shoulder arms!
Gewehr über!	Slope arms!
mit Gewehr bei Fuss stehen	to be at the order.
Gewehrbatterie	rifle battery.

Gewehrfeuer	rifle fire.
Gewehrführer	gun captain (*machine gun*).
Gewehrgestell	rifle rack.
Gewehrgranate (14)	(1914 pattern) rifle grenade.
Gewehrgranatengestell	rifle grenade stand.
Gewehrhaken	rifle clip.
Gewehrkolben	butt of rifle.
Gewehrpanzergeschoss	armour-piercing bullet.
Gewehrpyramide	piled arms.
Gewehrriemen	rifle sling.
Gewehrschaft	stock of rifle.
Gewehrschloss	breech mechanism of rifle.
Gewehrschusslänge	range of a rifle.
Gewehrstärke	combatant *or* rifle strength.
Gewehrstütze	arm rack.
Gewehrträger	apparatus for carrying a machine gun.
Gewehrtragende	men who carry rifles.
Gewehrweise	in order of guns (*machine guns*).
Gewindegang	thread (*of a screw*).
Gezeichnet (gez.)	signed (*in copies of documents*).
Gezogen	rifled.
Giftgas	asphyxiating gas, lethal gas.
Gitterbrücke	lattice girder bridge.
Gitterleitung	laddered circuit (*telephone*).
Gitternetze	grid, squaring (*on map*).
Gitter-Schwanzträger	open booms (*of aeroplane*).
Gitterwerk	truss (*engineering*).
Gkofunk (see "Gekofunk")	Corps Wireless H.Q.
Glatt	smooth, smooth bore.
Gleichförmigkeit	uniformity.
Gleichschritt	march in step.
Gleichstrom	continuous current (*electrical*).
Gleis (Geleise)	line of rails *or* track (*railway*).
Gleisbreite	wheel track; gauge of railway.
Gleitbahn	slipway.
Gleitflug	volplane.
Gleitkufe	skid (*aeroplane*).
Gleitriegel	sliding pin (*actuating breech block of gun*).
Gleitrolle	snatch block (*balloon*).
Glied	rank.
Gliedern	to organize.
Gliedern nach der Tiefe	to organize in depth.
Gliederung	distribution, organization, formation.
Kriegsgliederung	order of battle.

Glockenzeichen	... ...	signals given by bells or gongs.
Glühlampe	... ...	glow lamp; incandescent lamp (*electric*).
Glühzündapparat	... ...	dynamo-exploder.
Glühzünder	... ...	electric fuze.
Gondel ...	... ...	nacelle (*of aeroplane*).
Graben	... ...	trench.
erster Graben	... ...	front trench.
zweiter Graben	... ...	support trench.
dritter Graben	... ...	reserve trench.
Annäherungsgraben	...	communication *or* approach trench.
Laufgraben ...	... ...	} communication trench.
Verbindungsgraben	...	
Verkehrsgraben	... ...	supervision *or* lateral communication trench.
Grabenbekleidung	... ...	revetment.
Grabenbesatzung	... ...	men in the trenches, trench garrison.
Grabenkanone	... ...	trench gun.
Grabenposten ...	... ...	sentries in the fire trenches.
Grabenroste	... ...	" duck boards."
Grabensohle	... ...	sole *or* bottom of trench.
Grabenspiegel ...	... ...	trench mirror.
Grabenstärke ...	... ...	trench strength.
Grabenstück	... ...	length *or* section of trench.
Grabentiefe	... ...	depth of trench.
Grabenwand ...	... ...	side of trench.
Grabenwehr ...	... ...	rifle pit, *sometimes* trench garrison.
Grad ...	... ...	degree.
Gradabzeichen	... ...	badge of rank.
Gradbogen	... ...	graduated arc; sextant.
Granate	... ...	grenade.
Granate	... ...	} high explosive (H.E.) shell (*also* common shell).
Granate (Spreng.-)	... ...	
Granate-Geschoss	... ...	
Granateinschlag	... ...	shell burst.
Granatenhülse	... ...	shell case.
Granatenwerfer	... ...	" stick " bomb-thrower (*usually not translated; the modern term is* " Granatwerfer.")
Granatfüllung ...	... ...	explosive used for filling shell; bursting charge of shell.
Granatloch	... ...	shell hole.
Granatmine	... ...	Lanz *Minenwerfer* bomb.
Granatring	... ...	driving band on shell.
Granatsignal ...	... ...	flare signal fired from " *Signalwerfer* " or " *Granatwerfer*."

Granattrichter...	shell crater, shell hole.
Granatwerfer ...	see "Granatenwerfer" (*for which it is a recent contraction*).
Granatwurfmine Lanz (Gr. W.M.L.)	9·1-cm. Lanz *Minenwerfer* H.E. shell.
Granat-Zünder (Gr. Z.)	percussion fuze for H.E. shell.
Grasschollen ...	sods.
Grate ...	scorings (*e.g., in the bore of a gun*).
Grauguss ...	cast iron.
Greifzange ...	grip strap (*bridging*).
Grenadier ...	grenadier.
Grenadier-Regiment ...	grenadier regiment.
Grenze ...	limit, boundary, frontier.
Grenzgruppen ...	flank groups (*of a unit in the trenches*).
Grenzwächter Grenzwache	frontier guard.
Griffhebel ...	actuating lever (*breech action of light field howitzer*).
Groftrupp (Grosser-Flammenwerfer-Trupp)	large *Flammenwerfer* squad.
Gros ...	main body.
Grosse Bagage ...	baggage section of the train.
Grosser Generalstab ...	Great General Staff.
Grosses Hauptquartier ...	General Headquarters.
Grossstation ...	large (high-power) wireless station.
Grufl (Gruppenführer der Flieger)	Group Aviation Commander; wing commander.
Grukonach (Gruppen-Nachrichten-Kommandeur)	Group Signal Commander.
Grundlinie ...	base line, datum line.
Grundrichtung (einer Batterie)	zero line (of a battery).
Grundriss ...	design, sketch, plan.
Grundsatz ...	principle.
Grundsohle ...	mine level.
Grundwasser ...	surface water.
Grundzahlen ...	theoretical figures, not allowing for error (*artillery*).
Grünkreuzmunition ...	"green cross" gas shell.
Gruppe ...	Group (*equivalent to a Corps*) or group (8 *men under a N.C.O.*).
Gruppen-Fernsprech-Kommando (Kommandeur)	Group Telephone H.Q. (Commander).
Gruppenfeuer ...	volley firing.
Gruppenführer ...	group commander (lance-corporal).
Gruppen-Funkenstation (Grufusta)	Group (Corps) wireless station.
Gruppen-Funkerabteilung ...	Group (Corps) wireless detachment.

Gruppen-Funker-Kommando (Kommandeur)	Group Wireless H.Q. (Commander).
Gulaschkanone	travelling kitchen (*colloquial*).
Gummi	rubber, india-rubber.
Gummilösung	rubber solution.
Gurt	girth ; belt (*machine gun*).
Tragegurt	belt (*e.g., for carrying an infantry shield, &c.*).
Gürtel	belt.
S.M. in Gürteln	S.A.A. in belts (*machine gun*).
Gürtelbahn	circular railway.
Gürtelwagen	"wheel belt" waggon (21 *cm. mortar battery*).
Gürten	to fill a machine gun belt.
Gurtstelle	belt store (*machine gun*).
Gutachten	opinion.
Güterbahnhof	goods yard.
Güterschuppen	goods shed.
Guttaperchazündschnur	gutta-percha safety fuze.

H.

Haarbusch	plume.
Hacke	pick; heel.
Häcksel	chaff.
Hafendirektion	Dock Directorate.
Haft	arrest, imprisonment; clasp, holder.
Haftpfahl	hook-picket.
Haftpflock	steel picket (*bridging*).
Hahn	cock, tap.
den Hahn am Gewehr spannen	to cock a rifle.
Hahnspitze	striker (*of a pistol*).
Haken und Ösen	hooks and eyes.
Hakennagel	spike.
Halbmesser	diameter.
Halbponton	half-pontoon (*of the bipartite divisional equipment*).
Halbscherenfernrohr	director with single telescopic sight (*see* "Scherenfernrohr").
Halfter	halter, headcollar; holster.
Halfterriemen	head rope.
Halde	slag heap.
Halle	hangar (*aeroplane*).
Halsbinde	scarf.
Halt	Halt; support.
Halt geben	to support.
Halt! Wer da?	Halt! Who goes there?
Signal auf Halt	signal at danger (*railway*).
Hälter, falzartiger	grooved charger *or* strip (*magazine rifle*).
Haltetau	guy.
Haltung	carriage, bearing, behaviour.
Handbetriebbahn	trench tramway (50 *cm. gauge*).
Handbombe	hand grenade.
B-stoffhandbombe	asphyxiating hand grenade.
Handfeuerwaffen	small arms.
Handgemenge	hand to hand fight.
Handgranate	hand grenade.
Behelfshandgranate	extemporised hand grenade.
Brandhandgranate	incendiary hand grenade.
entschärfte Handgranate	hand grenade without detonator.
scharfe Handgranate	live hand grenade.
scharf machen	to insert a detonator in.
Stielhandgranate	cylindrical grenade with handle.
Übungshandgranate	dummy hand grenade.
Handgranatenkapsel	detonator for hand grenade.

Handgranatennische ...	grenade recess.
Handgranatenoffizier	bombing officer.
Handgranatenstand ...	ground set aside for hand grenade training.
Handgranatentrupp ...	bombing party.
Handgranatenwerfer ...	"thrower," bomber.
Handgriff	handle.
Handhabung	handling, use, management.
Handlüfter	rotary blower (*mining*).
Handpferd	led horse.
Handschuh	glove.
Handschutz	hand guard (*rifle*).
Handseite	off side ("*Sattelseite*," *near side*).
Handstreich	coup-de-main, surprise attack.
Handwaffen	small arms.
Handwerker	workman, tradesman, artisan, artificer.
Handwerkerabteilung	artificer's detachment.
Handwerkerabteilung des Trains	tradesmen of the Train.
Handwerksmeister ...	master mechanic.
Handwerkszeug	tools.
Handwerkskiste	tool box.
Hang	slope; deep level (*in mining*).
Hängematte	hammock.
Hartfutter	corn (*ration*).
Hartschier (Hatschier)	halbardier, archer, soldier of the Bavarian Body Guard of Halbardiers.
Hartspiritus	solidified alcohol, solidified methylated spirits.
Haube	false cap (*on shell*).
Haubengranate	H.E. shell with false cap.
Haubengeschoss	projectile with false cap.
Haubitze	howitzer.
Küsten-Haubitze	coast defence howitzer.
Turm-Haubitze	howitzer in turret.
Leichte (Schwere) Feld-Haubitze	light (heavy) field howitzer.
Haubitz-Batterie	howitzer battery.
Haubitz-Granate	howitzer (H.E.) shell.
Haubitz-Zünder	howitzer fuze.
empfindlicher Haubitz-Zünder	sensitive, *i.e.*, instantaneous howitzer fuse.
Haufen	dump (*mining*).
Hauptarm	main gallery (*mining*).
Hauptgestell	head stall.

Hauptinhalt	synopsis.
Hauptkadettenanstalt	Central Cadet Institution (Gross Lichterfelde).
Hauptkampflinie	main fighting line.
Hauptkrankenbuch	hospital register.
Hauptleute und Rittmeister	Captains (*of dismounted and mounted arms*).
Hauptlinie	axis.
Hauptmacht	main body.
Hauptmann	Captain (*of infantry, artillery or engineers*).
Hauptmessstelle	central survey office.
Hauptquartier	headquarters.
Grosses Hauptquartier	General Headquarters.
Hauptrichtung	main direction; zero line.
Hauptstellung	main position, main emplacement.
Hauptstollen	main gallery (*mining*).
Haupttrupp	main body of advanced or rear guard.
Hauptverbandplatz	main dressing station.
Hauwewa (Haupt-Wetterwarte [der Heimat])	chief meteorological observatory (in Germany).
Hebebaum	lever, handspike.
Heer	Army.
das stehende Heer	Standing Army.
Heeresartillerie	artillery reserve under orders of G.H.Q.
Heeresbericht	official communiqué.
Heeresgasschule	Army Gas School (Berlin).
Heeresgruppe	Group of Armies.
Heeresgruppen-Kommando	H.Q. of a Group of Armies.
Heeres-Kavallerie	Independent Cavalry.
Heeresleitung, Oberste	Commander-in-Chief, General Headquarters, Higher Command.
Heeresreserve	G.H.Q. reserve.
Heeres-Sauerstoff-Schutzgerät	military oxygen protective apparatus.
Heereszeitung	Army Gazette.
Heimat	home (*usually translated as Germany, &c.*).
Heimatluftschutz	aerial defence in Germany.
Heimatschlag	homing loft (*carrier pigeon*).
Heimatsgebiet	The Home Territory.
Heimatsheer	The Home Army (*as opposed to "Feldheer"*).
Helm	helmet.

Helmbeschlag	helmet furnishings
Helmüberzug	helmet cover.
Hemmkette	drag-chain.
Hemmklotz	brake-shoe; block placed behind a wheel to prevent a cart moving backwards down a slope.
Hemmschuh	drag-shoe.
Hemmung	jam, stoppage (*e.g., in rifle or machine gun*).
Henkel	handle (*of a camp kettle*).
Heran	up.
Heranführung	supply; bringing up.
Heranmarschieren	to march up, come up, approach.
Heranschaffen	to bring up (*e.g., ammunition*).
Heranschleichen	to creep forward (up).
Heranziehen	to detail; to bring up.
Heranziehung	requisitioning (*e.g., of horses*).
Herausziehen	to withdraw; to comb out.
Herbstmanöver	autumn manœuvres.
Hereinmarsch	march into the trenches.
Hergestellte	recovered wounded.
Herrschen	to rule, reign, prevail.
Herstellung	fitting, fixing up, construction, production, recovery.
Hervorlocken	to entice out, to draw (*e.g., fire*).
Hilfeleistung	rescue work, first aid.
Hilfsbahn	auxiliary railway.
Hilfsbeobachter	auxiliary observer.
Hilfsdienstpflicht	auxiliary service.
Hilfsgerätewagen	breakdown train (*railway*).
Hilfskorn	auxiliary foresight (*rifle*).
Hilfskräfte	auxiliary personnel.
Hilfskrankenträger	auxiliary stretcher bearer.
Hilfslafette	auxiliary mounting (*machine gun*).
Hilfslazarett	auxiliary hospital.
Hilfslazarettzug	temporary *or* improvised ambulance train.
Hilfstruppen	auxiliary troops.
Hilfsziel	aiming point.
Himmel, am	"in the air."
Hinausragend	projecting.
Hindernis	obstacle, wire entanglement, "wire."
elektrisches Hindernis	electrified wire entanglement.
versenktes Hindernis	sunken obstacle.
Hinhalten (den Feind)	to delay, detain (the enemy).
Hinten (nach)	in rear.

Hinterhalt	ambush.
Hintergelände	ground behind the line, back area.
Hintergestell eines Wagens	back part of a wagon.
Hinterkaffe	stern (*of a pontoon*).
Hinterkante	trailing edge (*plane of aeroplane*).
Hinterlader	breech-loader.
Hinterwagen	wagon body.
Hin- und Rückleitung	complete metallic circuit.
Hinweis	indication, direction, reference.
Hirschfänger	short hunting knife ; side arm of *Jäger*.
Hoboist	bandsman.
Hochbahn	elevated railway.
Hochdruck	high pressure (*mining*).
Hochempfindlich	highly sensitive (*of a telephone, &c.*).
Hochleitung	aerial line (*telephone*).
Hochofen	blast furnace.
Hochspannungsabteilung	detachment for running a high tension installation.
Hochspannungsleitung	high tension wire.
Hochstand	raised, commanding *or* elevated position.
Höchstzahl	maximum.
Hocken	to crouch.
hockende Schützen im Graben	troops sitting in trenches.
Höhe	height, hill.
Höhenmesser	altimeter (*aviation*).
Höhenrauch	haze.
Höhenrichtmaschine	elevating gear.
Höhenrichtwelle	shaft of elevating gear (*gun*).
Höhenrücken	ridge, crest.
Höhensteuer	diving rudder, elevating plane (*aviation*).
Holm	transom ; beam ; wing spar (*aeroplane*).
Hohltraverse	hollow traverse.
Hohlweg	sunken road.
Holz	wood.
Holzattrappe	wooden dummy (*e.g., bomb for instructional purposes*).
Holzbauten	wooden buildings.
Holzbohrer	auger, gimlet.
Holzdeckel	wooden lid *or* plug.
Holzfäller-Abteilung	tree-felling detachment.
Holzhammer	mallet.
Holzkasten zum Sümpfen	wooden sump box.

Holzkohle	charcoal.
Holzmeissel	wood chisel.
Holzrahmen	wooden frame.
Holzscheibe	wooden target.
Holzwolle	wood shavings.
Horchapparat	listening apparatus (*mining*).
Horchdienst	listening service.
Horchen	to listen.
es wird gehorcht	a " listen " will be made.
Horchergebnis	results of listening.
Horchgang	listening gallery.
Horchmeldung	listening report.
Horchminengang	listening gallery.
Horchpatrouille	listening patrol.
Horchpause	listening period (*mining, &c.*).
Horchposten	listening post, listening sentry.
Horchpostengraben	listening post sap.
Horchpostenloch	listening post.
Horchsappe	listening sap.
Horchstollen	listening gallery.
Horchzeit	listening time.
Hörer	receiver (*telephone*).
Hornist	bugler.
Horn	bugle, horn (*musical instrument and horn of cattle, &c.*).
Hubvermögen	lifting capacity (*aeroplane, &c.*).
Huf	hoof.
Hufeisen	horse-shoe.
Hufeisentasche	shoe-case.
Hufkratzer	hoof-pick.
Hülle	cover (*e.g., for breech of rifle*).
Ladungshülle	} canister bomb.
Minenhülle	
Hüllen	casing (*mining*).
Hülse (Patronen-)	cartridge case.
Hülsenliederung	obturation by means of the cartridge case.
Hundetrupp	dog section.
Hupen	to hoot (*aeroplane doing contact work*).
Hupsignal	hooting signal (*aeroplane*).
Husar	hussar.
Husaren-Regiment	hussar regiment.
Hüttenlager	hutments.
Hygieniker	hygienic adviser, sanitary officer.

I.

Note.—The initial letter " I " is frequently written and printed as " J " in German; *e.g.*, " Jnfanterie."

Ifl (Infanterie-Flieger)	infantry aeroplane, contact patrol.
Iflen	to act as contact patrol.
Ika (Infanterie-Kampf-Artillerie)	artillery detailed for the engagement of the enemy's infantry.
Immobil	on home service; stationary.
Impfen	to vaccinate, inoculate.
Impfliste	vaccination list.
Ina (Nachrichtenmittel-Abteilung eines Infanterie-Regiments)	infantry regimental signalling detachment.
Infanterie	infantry.
Infanterieausbildung	infantry training.
Infanterie-Flieger ...	infantry aeroplane, contact patrol.
Infanteriefliegerstation	infantry aeroplane station (*wireless*).
Infanterie-Funkerzug	infantry wireless section (*of divisional wireless detachment*).
Infanteriegeschütz	"infantry gun."
Infanteriegeschützbatterie ...	battery of "infantry guns."
Infanterie-Kampf-Artillerie...	artillery detailed for the engagement of the enemy's infantry.
Infanterie-Konstruktions-Bureau	Infantry Technical Section (of Technical Institute).
Infanterie-Munitions-Kolonne	infantry ammunition column (heavy).
Infanterie-Panzer	infantry armour, body armour.
Infanteriepionierkompagnie ...	infantry pioneer company.
Infanterie - Regiments - Nachrichtenzug	infantry regimental signalling section.
Infanteriereglement	"Infantry Training" (*abbreviation of "Exerzier-Reglement für die Infanterie"*).
Infanterie-Schiess-Schule ...	School of Musketry.
Infanterie-Schiess-Vorschrift	Infantry Musketry Regulations.
Infanterieschild	infantry shield.
Infanterie-Sturm-Batterie ...	infantry assault battery.
Infanterist	infantry soldier.
Ingenieur-Komitee ...	Engineer Committee.
Ingenieur-Korps	the Corps of Engineers (*as distinct from the Corps of Pioneers*).
Inhaltsangabe	statement of contents.
Inhaltsverzeichnis	list of contents.

Innenwache	inlying piquet.
Innen-Zünder	internal fuze.
Inselwache-Bataillon	coast defence battalion.
Inspekteur	Inspector-General.
Inspektion	Inspectorate (*or district, &c., under inspector*).
Instandhaltung	maintenance.
Instandsetzung	repair.
Instandsetzungswerkstatt	repair shop.
Instanzenweg, auf dem	through the officially recognised channel.
Instellunggehen (das)	going into the line.
Intendant	"Intendant" (*not translated; an Intendant is an administrative official*).
Intendantur	Intendance (*i.e., the service dealing with pay, finance, barracks, supply, and clothing*).
Intendantur-Assessor	Intendance assessor.
Intendantur-Beamter	Intendance official.
Intendantur-Rat	Intendance councillor.
Intendantur-Registrator	Intendance registrar.
Intendantur-Sekretär	Intendance clerk.
Interimsbahn	temporary railway.
Intervalle (Zwischenraum)	interval.
Irrläufer	runner who has lost his way.
Irrung	error.
Isolator	insulator (*electrical*).
Isolierband	insulating tape.
Isoliert	isolated; insulated.
Iststand } Iststärke }	actual strength (*as opposed to "Etatsstärke" or establishment*).
Iststärkenachweisung	statement (*or* list) showing actual strength.
I-Träger	steel joist *or* girder.
Iwumba (Infanterie-Waffen- und Munitions-Beschaffungsamt)	Infantry Section of the Munitions Department of the War Ministry.

J.

Note.—The initial letter "I" is frequently written and printed as "J" in German; *e.g.*, "Jnfanterie."

Jacke	jacket.
Jagdgeschwader	pursuit squadron (*aviation unit*).
Jagdstaffel	pursuit flight (*aviation unit*).
Jagdstaffelgruppe	pursuit flight group (*aviation unit*).
Jäger	"Jäger" (*not translated; corresponds to our "Rifles" or "rifleman"*).
Jäger-Kraftwagenkolonne	Jäger M.T. column (*obsolete*).
Jäger zu Pferde	"Jäger zu Pferde" (*not translated; the title of certain cavalry regiments*).
Jahresklasse	yearly class of recruits, annual recruit contingent.
Jahrgang	the year of birth of a recruit contingent or class.
Jasta (Jagdstaffel)	pursuit flight (*aviation unit*).
Jeweilig	for the time being.
Joch	bay (*of bridge*).
Jochbrücke	pile bridge.
Jod	iodine.
Jodtinktur	tincture of iodine.
Jugend-Kompagnie	a military training company for boys.
Jugend-Wehr	organization for giving boys a semi-military training.

K.

K-Munition	armour-piercing ammunition (*rifle or machine gun*); K-shell (*asphyxiating gas shell*).
Kabel ... Kabeldraht ...	} cable.
Kabelleitung ...	cable line.
Kabelstrecke ...	length of cable.
Kabelkiste ...	test box.
Kabelwerfer ...	cable-thrower.
Kader ...	cadre.
Kadettenhaus ... Kadettenschule ...	} cadet school.
Kafunka (Kavallerie-Funker-abteilung)	cavalry wireless detachment.
Kagohl (Kampf-Geschwader, Oberste Heeresleitung)	Bombing Squadron under G.H.Q.
Kahnfähre ...	ferry by rowing boat.
Kaiserlicher Kommissar u. Militär-Inspekteur	Imperial Commissioner (*of voluntary aid units*).
Kaliber...	calibre (*gun, rifle &c.*).
schweres Kaliber (15 u. 21 cm.)	heavy artillery (15 and 21 cm.).
kleinkalibrig	small bore.
Kalipatrone ...	potash cartridge.
Kamm ...	comb; crest of a hill, ridge.
Kammer ...	chamber, bolt (*of rifle*).
Kammerhülse ...	central tube (*of shrapnel*).
Kammerknopf...	knob (*of rifle bolt*).
Kammerunteroffizier ...	N.C.O. *or* quartermaster in charge of clothing.
Kampf ...	battle, fight, combat, engagement, action.
Kampf-Bataillon	battalion in line.
Kampf-Division	front line division (*as opposed to "Eingreif-Division" or counter-attack division*).
Kampf-Einsitzer-Staffel (Kest)	single-seater fighting flight.
Kampferfahrung ...	experience of fighting.
Kampf-Geschwader ...	bombing squadron (= 6 bombing flights).
Kampffront ...	front line, fighting front.
Kampfgas ...	battle gas.
Kampfgraben ...	fire trench.

Kampfhandlung	method of fighting.
Kampflage	tactical situation.
Kampfmittel	means of warfare.
Kampfstaffel	bombing flight.
Kampftagesrate	daily allotment of gun ammunition for active operations.
Kampfunfähig zu machen	to put out of action.
Kampfverhältnisse	tactical situation.
Kampfzweck	objective.
Kanal-Direktion	Inland Water Transport Directorate.
Kandare	curb (of *bridle*).
Kaninchenloch	" funk hole " (*recess under parapet*).
Kanne	can (*of a food carrier*).
Kanone	gun.
Küstenkanone	coast defence gun.
Mantelkanone	jacketed gun.
Marinekanone	naval gun.
Revolverkanone	revolver gun.
Ringkanone	gun with chase rings.
Turmkanone	gun in turret.
Schützengrabenkanone	trench gun.
Kanonen-Granate	gun (H.E.) shell.
Kanonen-Zünder	gun fuze.
Kanonier	gunner.
Kantholz	squared timber.
Kantine	canteen.
Kappe	cap (*e.g., of fuze, shell, &c.*).
Kapelle	chapel ; band.
Kapellmeister	bandmaster.
Kapitulant	re-engaged man.
Kapitulieren (um weiter zu dienen)	to re-engage.
Kapitulieren (einer Festung)	to surrender, capitulate.
Kapsel	detonator.
Kapuze	cape.
Karabiner	carbine.
Karabinerfutteral	carbine bucket.
Karabinier-Regiment	Carbineers (*cavalry regiment*).
Karbidlampe	acetylene lamp.
Karbol, Karbolsäure	carbolic acid.
Karbonsäure	carbonic acid.
Kardätsche	body-brush.
Karo	army bread (*colloquial*).
Karriere	career ; gallop.
Kartätsche	case shot.
Karte	map.

Karten aufziehen	to mount maps.
Kartenausschnitt	section of map.
Kartenlager	map depôt.
Kartenstelle	map office, topographical section.
Kartenvervollständigung	incorporation into maps.
Kartenzeichen	conventional signs (*maps*).
Kartenzeichnen	map drawing.
Kartographische Abteilung	cartographical department (*of Survey*).
Kartonzünder	cardboard (*electric*) fuze.
Kartuschdeckel	lid of cartridge case (*gun ammunition*).
Kartusche	cartridge (*of gun, not rifle*).
Kartuschenbeutel	cartridge bag.
Kartuschhülse	cartridge case (*gun : in the case of " separate " ammunition*).
Kartuschkorb	cartridge basket (*gun ammunition*).
Kartuschvorlage	flash reducer (*gun ammunition*).
Kasematte	casemate.
Kasemattenlafette	casemate mounting.
Kaserne	barracks.
Kasernenarrest	confined to barracks.
Kasernenhof	barrack square.
Kasernenkrankenstube	regimental sick and inspection room.
Kasino	mess.
Kasinovorstand	mess president.
Kassation	cashiering, military degradation.
Kassieren	to cashier, dismiss.
Kasse	safe, money chest; cashier's office.
Kassenabteilung	Finance section of the Intendance.
Kassendienst	pay department.
Kassenverwaltung	cashier's or paymaster's office; financial administration.
Kassierer	cashier.
Kastenwagen	instrument wagon (fortress searchlight section).
Kavallerie	cavalry.
Kavallerieattacke	cavalry charge.
Kavallerie-Division	cavalry division.
Kavallerie-Funkerabteilung	cavalry wireless detachment.
Kavallerie-Kraftwagenkolonne	cavalry M.T. column.
Kavalleriemassen	cavalry forces.
Kavallerieschleier	cavalry screen.
Kavallerie-Schützen	cavalry rifles (dismounted cavalry).
Kavallerie-Telegraphenschule	Cavalry Telegraph School.
Kavallerie-Telegraphenpatrouille	cavalry telegraph patrol.

Kavallerie-Unteroffizier-Reitschule	Cavalry Non-commissioned Officers' Riding School.
Kavallerist	cavalry soldier.
Kegelwinkel	angle of cone of dispersion (*of a bursting shell*).
Kehle	throat; gorge (*of a fort*).
Kehren	to turn about.
Kehrt!	About turn!
Keil	wedge, scotch; wedge breech block.
Keilfläche, vordere	front face of wedge (*field gun breech block*).
Keilverschluss	wedge breech action (*of Krupp gun*).
Keim	bud, embryo, germ.
im Keime ersticken	to nip in the bud.
Keimfrei	sterilized.
Kennbuchstabe	identification letter.
Kenntlich	conspicuous, clear, distinct.
Kenntnisnahme (zur)	"to note" (*at foot of orders*).
Kennwort	password.
Kennzeichen	distinguishing mark.
Kentern	to turn turtle.
Kern	kernel, core (*e.g., lead core of a bullet*).
Kerngeschoss	armour-piercing bullet.
Kernpunkt	strong point consisting of a fortified building or buildings.
Kerntruppen	picked troops.
Kernschussweite	point blank range.
Kessel	kettle, boiler.
Kest	see "Kampf-Einsitzer-Staffel."
Kette	chain.
Kettenbrücke	suspension bridge.
Keule	club, knobkerry.
Kielflosse	fin (*aeroplane*).
Kies	gravel.
Kiesbettung	road ballast.
Kiesel	pebble.
Kieselguhr	"Kieselguhr" (*not translated; a fossil earth used as an absorbent for nitroglycerine in the manufacture of dynamite*).
Kieselstein	flint.
Kiesgrube	gravel pit.
Kimme	backsight.
Kinnriemen	chin strap.
Kitt	cement.

Klammer	dog (*timber work*); bracket (*in printing, &c.*).
Klappbett	folding bed.
Klappe	jack (*telephone*); aileron (*of aeroplane*).
Klappenschrank	indicator board (*telephone*).
Klappensicherung	centrifugal safety device (*fuze*).
Klappkragen	stand and fall collar (*tunic*).
Klebestreifen	adhesive tape (*of gas mask*).
Kleiftrupp (Kleiner-Flammenwerfer-Trupp)	small *Flammenwerfer* squad.
Klemme	terminal (*electrical*), binding screw.
Klemmen	to squeeze, jam.
Klemmer	riveter.
Klinge	blade (*of sword*).
Klingelausschalter	bell-push.
Klingelzeichen...	bell signal.
Klopfeinrichtung	mechanical dummy pick (*mining*).
Klopfschacht	inclined gallery in which a dummy pick is worked (*mining*).
Knagge	chock (*nailed on a baulk to prevent lashing from slipping*).
Knaggenbalken	chock baulk (*bridging*).
Knall	report.
Knallquecksilber	fulminate of mercury.
Knallsatz	detonating composition.
Knebel	toggles.
Kneifzange	pliers.
Kneifzange, schraubensichere	round-nosed pliers.
Knie	knee; salient; elbow *or* bend (*of a pipe*).
Kniestellung	salient.
Knopf	button.
Knotenpunkt	junction (*railways, &c.*).
Knüppel	club; winch.
Knüppel, Knüppelrost ...	baulk, round timber.
Knüppeldamm	corduroy road.
Knüppelgitter...	"duck boards."
Kochgerät	cooking utensil.
Kochgeschirr	cooking utensil, mess tin.
Kochkessel	camp kettle.
Kochnische Kochstelle }	cooking place.
Kodofea (Kommandeur der Flieger-Ersatz-Abteilungen)	Commander of aviation depôts.
Kofl *or* Koflieg (Kommandeur der Fliegertruppen)	Army Aviation Commander.

Koflak (Kommandeur der Flug-Abwehr-Kanonen)	Commander of the Anti-aircraft Guns.
Kofu (Kommandeur der Funkertruppen) Kofunk	Commander of Wireless Troops (*at Army H.Q.*)
Kogen-Luft (Kommandierender General der Luftstreitkräfte)	Commander of the Air Forces.
Kohldampf	hunger (*colloquial*).
Kohlenmonoxyd (Papier) ...	carbon monoxide (test-paper).
Kohlenoxyd	carbon monoxide.
Kohlensäure	carbonic acid.
Kokarde	cockade (*a circular metal badge, two of which are worn on the field service cap; they show the Imperial* (*upper cockade*) *and State* (*lower cockade*) *colours in concentric rings*).
Kolben	butt (*rifle*).
Kolbenhals	small of the butt.
Kolbenbeschlag Kolbenkappe ...	butt plate.
Koller	cuirassier's tunic.
Kolonne	column.
Kolonnenbrücke	bridge for all arms.
schwere Kolonnenbrücke ...	heavy *or* reinforced bridge for all arms.
Kolonnengebiet	back billeting area.
Kolonnenweg	track.
Koluft (Kommandeur der Luftschiffer)	Balloon Commander.
Kommandantur	Commandant's office.
Kommandeur	Commander.
Kommandeur der Kraftfahrtruppen (K.d.K.)	Commander of the Army Mechanical Transport Troops.
Kommandieren	to detail, detach.
Kommandierender General ...	General Officer Commanding an Army Corps.
Kommandiert	man on detachment, attached (*e.g., to General Staff*).
Kommando	H.Q. staff; party, detachment, command; word of command. (*See also* " Armee-Oberkommando.")
das Kommando führen ...	to be in command.
ein Kommando haben ...	to be on duty.
Höhere Kommandostelle ...	the Higher Command.
Kommandowort	word of command.

Kommiss	(*a prefix meaning army, e.g.,* "*Kommissbrot,*" *army bread*).
Kommiss-Stiefel	ammunition boot.
Kommissar (Auslade-)	detraining inspector.
Kompagnie	company.
Kompagnieführer	company commander.
Kompass	magnetic compass.
Königliche Dienstsache	On His Majesty's Service.
Konserven	preserved food.
Konservenbüchse	preserved food tin.
Konserven-Verpflegung	tinned rations.
Konstatieren	to state as a fact ; to observe, find out ; to conclude.
Kontrolle	supervision, control.
Kontroll-Liste	muster roll.
Kontrollschiessen	checking registration.
Kontroll-Station	policing set (*earth current telegraphy*).
Kontroll-Versammlung	muster of reserves.
Kopfbedeckung	head-dress.
Kopfdeckung	protection for the head.
Kopffernhörer	head-receiver (*telephone*).
Kopframpe	end-loading ramp.
Kopfringscheibe	head target with rings (*musketry*).
Kopfscheibe	head target (*musketry*).
Kopfschützer	Balaclava helmet.
Kopfstation	railhead.
Kopfstück	top sill of a frame (*mining*).
Kopf-Zünder	nose fuze.
Kopie	copy (*e.g., carbon copy*).
Koppel	belt.
Koppelschloss	belt buckle.
Koppelzeug	belt.
Korb	basket (*of kite balloon*).
Korbtrupp	balloon party.
Korn	foresight of a rifle.
feines Korn	fine sight.
gestrichenes Korn	medium sight.
volles Korn	full sight.
Körperbeschaffenheit	physique.
Körperlage	physical condition.
Körperpflege	hygiene, personal cleanliness.
Körperstrafe	corporal punishment.
Korporalschaft	section ($\frac{1}{2}$ *of a* "*Zug*" *; consists of* 2 "*Gruppen,*" *i.e.,* 18 *men under an under-officer*).

Korps	Corps.
Korps-Apotheker	Corps Pharmacist.
Korpsarzt	Director of Medical Services (*with Corps*).
Korpsbrückentrain	Corps bridging train (*obsolete*).
Korps-Intendant	Corps Intendant.
Korps-Intendantur	Intendance of the Corps.
Korps (-Ober) -Auditeur	Corps (Chief) Judge-Advocate.
Korps-Stabsveterinär	Major (*veterinary*).
Korpstagesbefehl	Corps Order of the Day.
Korpstruppen	Corps troops.
Korrektur	correction.
Korridorgraben	gangway trench.
Korridorunterstand	gallery dug-out.
Kost	food.
Kosten	expenses.
Kot	mud, mire ; excreta.
Kräfte	forces, effectives.
Kräfteverteilung	distribution of forces, order of battle.
Kraftfahrbataillon	mechanical transport battalion.
Kraftfahrrad	motor bicycle.
Kraftfahrtruppen	mechanical transport troops.
Kraftfahrwesen	mechanical transport service.
Kraftlastwagen	mechanical transport lorry.
Kraftradfahrer	motor cyclist.
Kraftradfahrer-Abteilung	motor cyclist detachment.
Kraftwagen	motor lorry.
Kraftwagenflak	A.A. gun on motor lorry.
Kraftwagengeschütz	
Kraftwagenkolonne	mechanical transport column.
Kraftwagenpark	mechanical transport park.
Kraftwagenpark des Gr. H.Q. (des Oberbefehlshabers Ost)	G.H.Q. (East) M.T. park.
Kraftwagenstaffel	lorry train.
Kraftzugpark	tractor park.
Kragen	collar.
Klappkragen	stand and fall collar.
Stehkragen	stand up collar.
Kragenpatten	collar patches.
Kran	crane (*engineering*).
Krankenabschub	transport, evacuation of sick.
Krankenlager	field dressing station.
Krankenliste	sick list.
Krankenkraftwagen	motor ambulance.
Krankenlöhnung	sick pay, pay while in hospital.
Krankenpflege (freiwillige)	voluntary aid.

Krankensammelpunkt	⎫ collecting station (*for wounded*).
Krankensammelstelle	⎭
Krankenstube...	Medical Inspection Room.
Krankentrage ...	stretcher.
Krankenträger	stretcher-bearer
Krankentransport-Abteilung	sick and wounded transport detachment, ambulance section.
Krankenwärter	hospital orderly, sick attendant.
Krankenwagen	ambulance wagon.
Krankenzug ...	passenger train for sick and wounded.
Kratzhacke ...	long scraper.
Kreis (*Kr. in a postmark*)	district.
Kreisbeamte ...	district official.
Kreisen	to move in a circle, circle (*of aeroplanes*).
Kreiskorn	circular foresight (*anti-aircraft sight for machine guns*).
Kreisleitung ...	omnibus circuit (*electrical*).
Kreisschlagen	to signal with the arms.
Krepieren	to explode (*of shells*); to die (*of animals*).
Kreuz ...	cross gallery (*mining*).
Kreuz (Eisernes)	Iron Cross.
Kreuzfeuer	cross fire.
Kreuzhacke	pickaxe.
Kreuzmuffe	3-way joint (*electrical*).
Kreuzstelle	junction (*of roads, &c.*).
Kreuzung	crossing.
Kriegerverein	Military Veterans' Society.
Kriegs-Akademie	Staff College.
Kriegs-Akademiker	Staff College graduate.
Kriegsamt	War Bureau (Department of War Ministry).
Kriegsanruf	⎫ call to arms.
Kriegsaufgebot	⎭
Kriegsausrüstung	war equipment.
Kriegsbedarf ...	munitions of war, military stores.
Kriegsbehörde	military authorities.
Kriegsbekleidungsamt	War Clothing Depôt; clothing centre of Army Corps.
Kriegsbereitschaft	readiness for war.
Kriegsbericht	war record, communiqué.
Kriegsberichterstatter	war correspondent.
Kriegsbücherei, fahrbare	mobile library.
Kriegsdienst ...	active military service.
Kriegsdienstpflichtiger	conscript.

Kriegsdrangsal	horrors of war.
Kriegsentschädigung	war indemnity.
Kriegsetat	war footing.
Kriegsfähig	fit for field service.
Kriegsfreiwilliger	war-volunteer.
Kriegsführung	conduct of war.
Kriegsfuss, auf, setzen	to mobilize.
Kriegsgebrauch	customs of war.
Kriegsgefangenen - Arbeiter Bataillon	prisoners of war labour battalion.
Kriegsgefangener	prisoner of war.
Kriegsgerät	war stores, war equipment.
Kriegsgericht	district court martial.
Kriegsgerichtsrat	Judge-Advocate-General.
Kriegsgesetz	martial law.
Kriegsgliederung	order of battle.
Kriegshilfsdienst	auxiliary service in war-time.
Kriegshund	war dog.
Kriegskunde	the art of war.
Kriegskunst	strategy, art of war.
Kriegslazarett (Abteilung)	clearing hospital (detachment).
Kriegslist	stratagem.
Kriegsmarsch	tactical march.
Kriegsministerium	War Ministry.
Kriegsministeriumserlass	War Ministry order.
Kriegsnot	stress of war.
Kriegsportion	field service ration.
Kriegsrangliste	nominal roll of officers in a unit.
Kriegsrat	council of war.
Kriegsrecht	martial law.
Kriegsschauplatz	theatre of operations *or* front.
Kriegsschule	War School (*somewhat similar to the R.M.C. Sandhurst and R.M.A. Woolwich*).
Kriegsstammrolle	nominal roll.
Kriegsstand	war strength, establishment.
Kriegstagebuch	war diary.
Kriegsstark	at war establishment.
Kriegsunbrauchbar	unfit for service.
zeitig kriegsunbrauchbar	temporarily unfit.
Kriegsvermessungswesen	Military Survey Service.
Kriegsverpflegungsamt	commissariat.
Kriegsverwaltung	war administration.
Kriegsverwendungsfähig	fit for active service.
Kriegsvollbahn	standard gauge military railway.
Kriegswesen	military affairs, war department.
Kriegszahlamt	army pay office.

Kriegszahlmeister	army paymaster.
Kriegszufälle	contingencies of war.
Krimstecher	field-glass.
Kroki	sketch map.
Krümper	cast horse kept on for fatigues.
Kruppe	crupper.
Kübel	bucket, pail.
Kuckuck	travelling kitchen (*colloquial*).
Kugel	bullet, ball.
Kugelfest	bullet-proof.
Kugelhandgranate	ball hand grenade.
Kugellager	bearing block, ball bearing.
Kugelmine	spherical trench mortar shell.
Kugel, schwebende	parachute flare.
Kugelsicher	bullet-proof.
Kühler	water-jacket, radiator.
Kumt	collar (*harness*).
Kunde	news, note, intelligence.
Kundschaft	scouting, espionage.
Kundschafter	scout.
Kunstbauten	bridges, tunnels, &c.
Künsteleien	artificial methods.
Kupferleitungsdraht	copper line wire.
Kuppe	round hill-top, knoll.
Kuppel	cupola.
Kuppeln	to couple.
Kürassier	cuirassier.
Kürassier-Regiment	cuirassier regiment.
Kurbel	crank.
Kurbelwelle	crank shaft.
Kursbuch	railway time table.
Kursus	course of instruction.
Kurve	curve (*railway*).
Kurzschluss	short circuit (*electrical*).
Kurzschuss	a " short " (*artillery*).
Küste	coast.
Küsten-Haubitze	coast defence howitzer.
Küsten-Kanone	coast defence gun.
Küstenlafette	coast defence mounting.
Küsten-Mörser	coast defence mortar.
Küstenverteidigung	coast defence.
Küster	sacristan.

L.

Labeflasche	bottle of cordial (*medical*).
Labung	refreshment, treatment (*medical*).
Ladefähig	in serviceable condition (*of ammunition*).
Ladehemmung	jam (*e.g., in rifle or machine gun*).
Ladekammer	chamber (*mining*).
Ausarbeiten der Ladekammer	chambering.
Ladekommando	battery charging detachment (*wireless*).
Ladeloch	loading aperture (*field gun*).
Lademaschine	battery charging machine.
Laderampe	ramp.
Ladestelle	entraining station, loading platform; accumulator charging station (*wireless, &c.*).
Ladestock	ram rod.
Ladestörung	jam (*e.g., in rifle or machine gun*).
Ladestreifen	charger *or* strip (*for loading magazine rifle*).
Ladung	charge (*gun, mine, &c.*).
geballte Ladung	concentrated charge.
eine kleine Ladung sprengen	to blow a camouflet.
Ladungsabstand	L.L.R. *or* line of least resistance (*mining*).
Ladungshülle	canister bomb (*used with light* "*Ladungswerfer*").
Ladungsmine (Wurfladung)	canister bomb (*used with heavy* "*Ladungswerfer*").
Ladungsraum	chamber (*of gun*).
Ladungswerfer	"*Ladungswerfer*" (*not translated; a form of trench mortar*).
Lafette	gun carriage.
Kasemattenlafette	casemate mounting.
Küstenlafette	coast defence mounting.
Oberlafette	top carriage.
Panzerlafette	shielded mounting.
Schirmlafette	carriage with overhead shield.
Unterlafette	lower carriage.
Lafettenkasten	trail box (*gun carriage*).
Lafettenplatte	trail plate.
Lafettenrücklauf	recoil.
Lafettenschwanz	trail (*of gun*).
Lafettensitz	seat on gun carriage.

Lafettensporn	spade of gun carriage, trail spade.
Lafettenwand	trail bracket of gun carriage.
Lage	situation, state of affairs, condition, state, position; fall (*of shell, &c.*).
Lagekarte	situation map.
Lager	camp, depôt; bed; bearing.
Lager aufheben	to strike camp.
Lager aufschlagen	to pitch camp.
Lager, äusseres	external pivot of cradle (*field gun carriage*).
Lager für den Verschlussbolzen	recess for locking bolt (*of field gun breech action*).
Lagerpfahl	picket post.
Lagerplatte	platform.
Lagerplatz	depôt, dump.
Lagerstroh	straw for bedding.
Lagerung	storage.
Lagewinkel	angle of sight (*gunnery*).
Lähmen	to disable, paralyze, neutralize.
Lahmlegung	silencing or neutralizing (*of artillery, &c.*).
Landbrücke	abutment.
Landesaufnahme	Survey Department (*of War Ministry*).
Landesfahrzeug	country cart.
Landesfarben	national colours.
Landeskokarde	State cockade (Bavarian, etc.)
Landespferdekolonne ...	cart-horse column.
Landeswappen	national arms.
Landgendarmerie	territorial police (Prussia).
Landjägerkorps	territorial police (Württemberg).
Landkarte	map.
Landmacht	land forces.
Landmine	land mine.
Landsturm	"Landsturm" (*not translated*).
Landsturmmann (gedienter)...	(trained) Landsturm man.
Landsturmmann (ungedienter)	(untrained) Landsturm man.
Landung	landing.
Landungsgestell	landing gear (*aeroplane*).
Landwehr	"Landwehr" (*not translated*).
Landwehrmann	Landwehr man.
Länge von Greenwich ...	longitude of Greenwich.
Längenabweichung	error in range.
Längenrampe	long ramp, platform.
Längenstreuung	errors in range due to the gun.
Langgranate...	long shell.
Längsbestreichung }... Längsfeuer ...	enfilade fire.

Längsstabilität	longitudinal stability (*aeroplane*).
Langtau	drag rope (*gun carriage, &c.*).
Lanz	"Lanz" (*the name of a certain kind of trench mortar*).
Lanzenriemen	thong of lance.
Lanzenschuh	bucket of lance.
Lanze	lance.
Stahlrohrlanze	steel lance.
Lanzen zur Attacke gefällt	lances at the ready.
Lappen	rag.
Fusslappen	foot bandage.
Lärmsignal	sound signal.
Lasche	fish plate (*railway*).
Lastkraftwagen	motor lorry.
Lastmaschine	battery charging machine.
Lasttier	pack animal.
Lastzug	mechanical transport train.
Laterne	lantern.
Latte	lath.
Lattenroste	gratings, "duck boards."
Lattensteg	ladder bridge (*for crossing obstacles*).
Lauerstellung	position in observation (*artillery*).
Lauerstellung, Batterie in	battery in position in observation.
Lauf	course, run; barrel (*of rifle*).
Laufbretter	"duck boards."
Laufbrücke	light bridge.
Laufbrücke (verstärkte)	light bridge, suitable for field artillery.
Laufen	to run.
Laufend	current (*e.g., month, &c.*).
auf dem Laufenden halten	to keep up-to-date (*e.g., a list*).
Läufer	runner (*messenger*).
Läuferposten	runner post.
Läuferrelais	chain of runners.
Läuferstation	runner station.
Lauffeuer	running fire.
Laufgraben	communication trench.
Laufgrabendepot	trench depôt.
Laufgraben-Offizier	orderly officer in the trenches.
Laufgraben-Spiegel	trench periscope.
Laufmantel	barrel casing (*machine gun, &c.*).
Laufschiene	guide-rail (*bridging*).
Laufschritt	double time.
Lauschposten	listening post.
Läusefrei	free of vermin.
Lautverstärker	amplifier valve (*telegraphy*).
Lazarett	hospital.
Lazarettabteilung	hospital section of the Intendance.

Lazarettgehilfe	hospital assistant.
Lazarett-Inspektor	Inspector of Hospitals.
Lazarett-Ökonomie-Verwaltung	hospital administration officials.
Lazarettschiff	hospital ship.
Lazarettwagen	ambulance wagon.
Lazarettzug	ambulance train.
L.E.-Munition	L.E. ammunition (*explosive rifle bullets for anti-aircraft purposes*).
Lea (Luftschiffer-Ersatz-Abteilung)	training depôt for balloon troops.
Lebensbedingungen	conditions of living.
Lebensmittel	food.
Lebensmitteldepot	ration dump.
Lebensmittelempfänger	supply orderly.
Lebensmittelkiste	ration box.
Lebensmittelwagen	supply wagon.
Lebensretter	life-saving apparatus; oxygen breathing apparatus.
Lebhaft	vigorous, rapid (*of firing*).
Lederring / Lederscheibe	leather washer.
Leeren	to empty, *sometimes* to deflate.
Lehm	clay.
Lehmboden	clay soil.
Lehmgrube	clay pit.
Lehr-Batterie	instructional battery.
Lehrgang / Lehrkursus	course of instruction.
Lehr-Regiment	Instructional Regiment (*now one of the Guard Regiments*).
Lehrschmiede	instructional forge.
Leibbinde	body-belt.
Leibgarde der Hartschiere	Bavarian Bodyguard of Halbardiers.
Leibgendarmerie	Body Guard Police.
Leibgrenadier-Regiment	Body Grenadier Regiment.
Leib-Regiment	Body Regiment.
Leibriemen	belt.
Leibwache	life guard.
Leichtatmer	low resistance breathing drum (*gas*).
Leichte Funkenstation	light wireless field station (*mobile*).
Leichte Munitions-Kolonne	light ammunition column.
Leichte Nebelmine	light smoke-bomb.
Leichter Maschinen-Gewehr-Trupp	light machine gun section.
Leichtkranken-Abteilung	section for mild cases.
Leichtverwundeten-Sammelplatz	collecting station for slightly wounded.

Leistung	performance, work, achievement.
Leistungsfähigkeit	efficiency; capacity for work.
... ...	control battery (*for barrage, &c.*).
Leiten	to direct.
einheitlich leiten	to co-ordinate.
Leiterbrücke	ladder bridge.
Leitersystem	ladder circuit (*telephone*).
Leiterwagen	waggon with open sides.
Leitfeuer	slow match, safety fuze (*mining, &c.*).
Leitung	line, circuit (*e.g., of telephone*); command, direction, control.
Hin- und Rückleitung ...	complete metallic circuit.
Leitungsdraht	line wire, wire.
Leitungsgraben	telephone line trench.
Leitungskontrollieren	line testing.
Leitungsnetz	telephone system.
Leitungspatrouille (Mann) ...	lineman.
Leitungsprobe	line test.
Leitungsprüfer	testing apparatus (*electrical*).
Leitungsschnur	lead (*electricity*).
Leitungszeicher	galvanometer.
Leitwelle	cam actuating screw (*breech action of light field howitzer*).
Lenkballon	dirigible airship.
Lenken	to guide, direct (*fire*).
Lenkluftschiff	} dirigible airship.
Lenkschiff (*for* Lenkluftschiff)	
Leuchtapparat	illuminating apparatus.
Leuchtfackel	illuminating torch.
Leuchtgas	coal gas.
Leuchtgerät	illuminating apparatus.
Leuchtgeschoss	} star shell.
Leuchtgranate	
Leuchtkugel	light, light ball.
Leuchtmasse	phosphorescent compound.
Leuchtpatrone	light-pistol cartridge.
Leuchtpatronensignal ...	flare signal.
Leuchtpistole	light-pistol, illuminating pistol.
Leuchtrakete	light rocket.
Leuchtsatzfeuer	flare (*in cylindrical drum*).
Leuchtsignalgerät	flare signal stores.
Leuchtspurmunition	tracer ammunition.
Leuchtvisier	luminous sight.
Leuchtzeichen	flare signal.
Leuchtzeichen-Zwischenposten	intermediate flare-signal station.
Leukoplast	a make of adhesive tape.

Leutnant	Second-lieutenant.
Libelle	clinometer, level.
Libellenaufsatz	clinometer sight.
Libellenstück	level.
Libellenteil	clinometer graduation.
Lichtanlage	light installation.
elektrische Lichtanlage	electric light installation.
Lichtbildergerät	photographic apparatus.
Lichtfernsprecher	heliograph.
Lichtkegel	beam (*of searchlight or signal lamp*).
Licht-Mess-Trupp	observation group.
Lichtsignalapparat	lamp signalling apparatus.
Lichtsignal	luminous signal, lamp signal.
Lichtsignalstand	lamp signal station.
Lichtsignaltrupp	lamp signalling detachment.
Lichtspruch	lamp signal message.
Lichtung	clearing (*e.g., in a wood, the foreground, etc.*).
Lichtzeichentrupp	lamp signalling section.
Lichtzentrale	light and power station.
Liderung	obturation, gas check.
Liebesgaben	gifts to soldiers in the field, "comforts."
Lieferant	contractor.
Lieferung	supply, delivery.
Liegen	"fall" (*e.g., of shell*).
Liegen, richtig	to be accurate (*e.g., of artillery fire*).
Liegeraum	small shelter for cover, lying.
Liegestütz	lying *or* prone position.
Linie	line.
Linie, erste, zweite, &c.	1st, 2nd, &c., Line Position.
vorderste Linie	front *or* foremost line.
Linienführung (festlegen)	to mark out.
Linien-Kommandantur	Line Command; office of Line Commandant (*railway*).
Links um!	Left turn!
Links schwenkt!	Left wheel!
List	stratagem, trick, ruse.
Liste	list, roll.
Litewka	"Litewka" *or* loose blouse.
Litze	braiding.
Lochmannhindernis	Lochmann entanglement.
Lockern (sich)	to become loose.
Löhnung	pay (*of rank and file*).
Löhnungsappell	pay-parade.
Lore	lorry, truck.
Lose (Schützenlinie)	thin *or* extended (line of skirmishers).

Lösung...	solution (*cipher*); relief.
Losung... } Losungswort }	countersign.
Löten ...	to solder.
Löwenhöhle ...	small shelter, "funk hole."
Lowry ...	lorry.
Luchsen ...	to keep a sharp look out.
Lücke ...	gap.
Luft ...	air.
wir bekamen dicke Luft	we were heavily shelled (*colloquial*).
Luftangriff ...	aerial attack.
Luftaufklärung ...	air reconnaissance.
Luftbeobachtung ...	air observation.
Luftdruck ...	air pressure.
Luftdruckwirkung ...	effect of concussion.
Luftfahrzeug ...	aircraft.
Lufterkundung ...	air reconnaissance.
Luftmörser ...	pneumatic trench mortar.
Luftpumpe ...	air pump.
Luftröhrenentzündung ...	bronchitis.
Luftschiff ...	airship.
lenkbares Luftschiff	dirigible airship.
Luftschifffahrt...	aeronautics, airship voyage.
Luftschiffer ...	aeronaut, man of a balloon detachment *or* crew of airship.
Luftschiffer-Abteilung (Feld-)	balloon detachment.
Luftschiffer-Bataillon ...	air battalion.
Luftschiffer-Ersatz-Abteilung (Lea)	training depôt for balloon troops.
Luftschiffer-Trupp ...	airship section.
Luftschiffertruppen ...	airship and balloon troops.
Luftschiffführer ...	airship commander.
Luftschiffhalle ...	airship shed, hangar.
Luftschiffschraube ...	airship propeller.
Luftschiffschule ...	Airship School.
Luftschiff-Versuchsanstalt ...	Airship Experimental Establishment.
Luftschraube ...	aeroplane (airship) propeller.
Luftschutz! ...	Air protection! (*word passed down the telephone when hostile aircraft cross the line*); aerial defence.
Luftsperrabteilung ...	balloon barrage ("apron") detachment.
Luftsperre ...	defensive patrol (*aeroplane barrage*).
Luftstreitkräfte ...	air forces.
Lunte ...	match (*mining, &c.*).
Lupe ...	magnifying glass.
Lux-Offizier ...	observation officer.

M.

Magazin	magazine, store, depôt.
Magazinfuhrparkkolonne	depôt supply column.
Magazinportion	regulation ration.
Magazin-Verwaltung	magazine officials.
Magazin-Vorstand	quartermaster, magazine official.
Magnetnadel	magnetic needle.
Major	Major.
Mannschaft (arbeitende)	working party.
Mannschaften	rank and file, details.
Mannszucht	military discipline.
Manöver	manœuvre.
Mantel	greatcoat; jacket (*of gun*); barrel casing (*of m. g.*); envelope (*of bullet*).
Mantel-Kanone	jacketed gun.
Mantelriemen	greatcoat strap.
Marine	Navy.
Marine-Alarm-Signal	naval alarm signal (*probably some form of mechanical fog signal*).
Marine-Division (Brigade, &c.)	Naval Division (Brigade, &c.).
Marine-Infanterie-Regiment	marine infantry regiment.
Marine-Korps	Naval Corps.
Marine-Landflieger-Abteilung	naval land flight (*aviation unit*).
Marineluftschiff	naval airship.
Markant	marked, very visible.
Marketender	canteen personnel.
Marketenderei	canteen.
Marketenderwagen	canteen cart.
Markierter Feind	a "marked" enemy.
Markscheider	mine surveyor.
Marschbefehl	march orders.
Marschbereit	ready to move.
Marschdisziplin	march discipline.
Marschfähig	able to walk, fit for marching.
Marschgeschwindigkeit	rate of marching.
Marschieren	to march.
Marschkolonne	infantry in fours, column on the march, column of route.
Marschleistung	marching power.
Marsch! Marsch!	Double!
Marsch ohne Tritt	breaking step.
Marschordnung	order of march.
Marschpause	rest (*on the march*).
Marschtafel	march table.

Marschtag	"marching day" (*in a withdrawal e.g., to the Hindenburg Line*); date of departure (*on a movement order*).
Marschzucht	march discipline.
Maschenartig	like network.
Maschendraht	wire netting.
Maschensystem	network.
Maschinen-Amt	locomotive office.
Maschinen-Flug-Abwehr-Kanonen-Zug	anti-aircraft automatic gun section.
Maschinen-Gewehr	machine gun.
abgesetztes Maschinengewehr	detached machine gun.
abgespaltenes Maschinengewehr	isolated, detached machine gun.
Maschinen-Gewehr-Abteilung	machine gun detachment.
Maschinen-Gewehr-Ergänzungs-Zug	machine gun section (*obsolete*).
Maschinen-Gewehr-Kompagnie	machine gun company.
Maschinen-Gewehr-Scharfschützen-Kompagnie	machine gun marksman company.
Maschinen-Gewehr-Scharfschützen-Abteilung	machine gun marksman detachment.
Maschinengewehrschlitten	machine gun sledge.
Maschinen-Gewehr-Stand	machine gun emplacement.
Maschinengewehrstollen	machine gun shelter.
Maschinen-Gewehr-Trupp (Leichter)	light machine gun section.
Maschinen-Gewehr-Zug	machine gun section.
Maske	mask, gas mask.
Maskenstoff	fabric of a gas mask.
Maskieren	to mask, make invisible, screen.
Maskierung	camouflage.
Mass	measurement.
Massenfeuer	concentrated fire (*e.g., of artillery*).
Massenstreufeuer	intense distributed fire (*artillery*).
Massgebend	decisive, determining.
Massnahme	measure, disposition (*of troops*).
Massstab	scale, rule.
Mast	mast.
umlegbare Mast	telescopic mast.
Mastfernrohrtrupp	giant periscope section.
Material	equipment, material.
Materialanforderung	indent for stores.
Materialiendepot	supply dump.
Materialienwagen	material wagon (*telegraph equipment*).

Matrose	sailor.
Matrosen-Regiment	" Matrosen " regiment.
Mauerung	revetment.
Mauerwerk	masonry.
Maulesel } Maultier }	mule.
Meile	the German mile of 7.5 km. or 4.6 British miles.
Melasse	molasses.
Meldeblock	block of message forms.
Meldedienst	service of despatch riders, runners, &c.
Meldegänger	runner.
Meldeheft	message book, report book.
Meldehund (-Trupp) (-Staffel)	messenger dog (section) (depôt).
Meldekarte	message form.
Meldekette	chain of runners.
Meldekopf	signal communication head.
Meldeläufer	runner.
Meldeläuferkette	chain of runners.
Melden	to report.
Melder	runner, orderly.
Meldereiter	mounted orderly.
Meldesammeloffizier	intelligence officer (*at Corps or Divisional H.Q. for reconnaissance, observation, hostile activity, &c.*).
Meldesammelstelle	report centre.
Meldeverkehr	messenger traffic.
Meldeweg	the track followed by a chain of runners.
Meldewesen	Signals.
Meldewurfgranate	message bomb.
Meldung	report.
eine Meldung auffangen	to intercept a message.
Membrane	diaphragm.
Membransirene	diaphragm syren, Claxson.
Merkblatt	instructions, pamphlet.
Messbild	scale drawing.
Messe	mess (*naval*).
Messevorstand	mess president (*naval*).
Messingkartusche	brass cartridge case (*of gun, not rifle*).
Messingklemme	brass terminal.
Messkette	measuring chain.
Messplan	artillery plan, " plan directeur."
Messplan-Abteilung	survey section (*obsolete*).

Messstab	scale (*for stadia rod*).
Messstelle	survey post *or* station.
Haupt-Messstelle	central compiling and plotting station, central survey office.
Messtisch	plane table.
Messtrupp	survey section.
Messverfahren, akustisches	sound ranging.
Meuterei	mutiny.
Meutern	to mutiny.
Messzentrale	central survey office (*compiling and plotting station*).
Miete	shock, stook, rick, haystack.
Mikrophon	microphone.
Milchschmeisserei	light bombardment (*colloquial*).
Mildernde Umstände	extenuating circumstances.
Militär-Bäcker	military baker.
Militär-Bau-Verwaltung	Military Works Administration.
Militär-Bau-Wesen	Military Works Department.
Militär-Bevollmächtiger	military representative.
Militär-Eisenbahn-Direktion	Military Railway Directorate.
Militär-Eisenbahn-Werkstätten-Amt	Military Railway Workshop Office.
Militäreisenbahnwesen	Military Railway Service.
Militärfahrplan	military time table.
Militär-Fahrschein	railway warrant.
Militär-Flugwesen	Military Aviation Service.
Militär-Geistlicher	military chaplain.
Militär-General-Direktion der Eisenbahnen	General Directorate of Military Railways.
Militär-Gerichts-Aktuar	military actuary.
Militär-Krankenwärter	sick attendant.
Militär-Küster	military sacristan.
Militärmass	military standard.
Militär - Pharmaceutisches-Personal	personnel for Pharmacy Services.
Militär-Reit-Institut	School of Military Equitation.
Militärsanitätswesen	Army Medical Service.
Militär-Strafgesetzbuch	Military Criminal Code.
Militär-Strafgesetzordnung	Code of procedure for military tribunals.
Militär-Strafvollstreckungsvorschrift	Regulations for the carrying out of sentences of military tribunals.
Militär-Verkehrswesen	Military Communication Service.
Militärzensur	military censorship.
Militärischer Richter	member of a court martial.
Mine	mine *or Minenwerfer* shell.
Minenfeld	minefield.
Minenfeuer	*Minenwerfer or* trench mortar fire.

Minengalerie … … …	} gallery (*mining*).
Minengang … … …	
Minengarbe … … …	inverted cone in ground formed by firing a mine.
Minengraben … … …	mine trench (*in which entrances to mines are made*).
Minenhalle … … …	mine dug-out (*mining*).
Minenhülle … … …	canister bomb (*used with heavy "Ladungswerfer"*).
Minenhunde … … …	truck (*mining*).
Minenkammer … … …	mine chamber (*mining*)
Minenkratze … … …	clay adze (*mining*).
Minensperre … … …	minefield.
Minensplitter … … …	trench mortar bomb splinter.
Minensprengung … …	mine explosion, blowing of a mine.
Minenstollen … … …	mine gallery.
Minentrichter … … …	mine crater.
Minenwerfer … … …	*Minenwerfer* (*usually not translated*); trench mortar.
Minenwerfer-Abteilung …	*Minenwerfer* detachment.
Minenwerfer-Bataillon …	*Minenwerfer* battalion.
Minenwerfer-Kompagnie …	*Minenwerfer* company.
Minenwerfer-Trupp … …	*Minenwerfer* sub-section (*crew for 1 trench mortar*).
Minenwerfer-Zug … …	*Minenwerfer* section (*sub-division of a "Minenwerfer" company*).
Mineur … … … …	miner.
Mineurkompagnie … …	mining company.
Minieren … … …	to mine.
Misweisung der Magnetnadel	deviation of the compass.
Mithören … … …	to overhear, listen in.
Mitteilung … … …	message, report, information.
Mittelarrest … … …	light field punishment.
Mittelgang … … …	central passage (*of dug-out*).
Mittelpferd … … …	centre horse.
Mittelplatte … … …	centre plate.
Mittelschild … … …	main shield (*field gun*).
Mitwirkung … … …	co-operation.
Mobil … … … …	mobile, mobilized.
Mobilisieren … … …	to mobilize.
Mobilmachung … …	mobilization.
Mobilmachungsbefehl …	mobilization order.
Monteur … … …	mechanic (*aviation troops*).
Montieren … … …	to mount, to fit together.
Montierung … … …	clothing, equipment; mounting.
Montierungs-Depot-Verwaltung	clothing depôt officials.
Moritz … … … …	*name used to denote listening sets.*

Mörser	(21 cm.) mortar.
Bronze-Mörser	bronze mortar.
Erdmörser	buried trench mortar, "earth mortar."
Küsten-Mörser	coast defence mortar.
Mörserbatterie...	(21 cm.) mortar battery.
Morseschrift	Morse alphabet.
Motordefekt	motor breakdown.
Motorrad	motor cycle.
Motorwagen	motor car.
Mühle	mill.
Mulde	depression, hollow.
Mündlich	verbal.
Mundloch	fuze hole.
Mundlochbüchse	old pattern type of fuze.
Mundlochfutter	gaine (*of fuze*).
Mundscheibe	mouth opening (*of a gas mask*).
Mundschlauch	mouth tube.
Mundstück	muzzle (*of gun*).
Mündung	mouth, muzzle.
Mündungsblitz	gun flash.
Mündungsdeckel	muzzle cap.
Mündungsfeuer	gun flash.
Mündungsfeuer anschneiden	to obtain bearings on the flashes.
Mündungsfeuerdämpfer ...	flash reducer.
Mündungsfläche	face of muzzle (*of gun*).
Mündungsgeschwindigkeit ...	muzzle velocity.
Mündungskappe	muzzle cover (*gun*).
Mündungsschoner	muzzle protector.
Munition	ammunition.
Alder B-Munition	"Alder B" ammunition (*explosive bullet for anti-aircraft purposes*).
Blaukreuzmunition ...	"blue cross" gas shell.
gegürtete Munition... ...	filled belts (*machine gun*).
Gelbkreuzmunition ...	"yellow cross" gas shell.
getrennte Munition ...	separate ammunition (*as opposed to "fixed" ammunition*).
Grünkreuz-Munition ...	"green cross" gas shell.
K-Munition	armour-piercing ammunition (*rifle and machine gun*); K-shell (*asphyxiating gas shell*).
L.E.-Munition	"L.E." ammunition (*explosive rifle bullets for anti-aircraft purposes*).
Panzer-Munition	armour-piercing bullets.
S. m. K.-Munition	armour-piercing ammunition (*rifle and machine gun*).
S-Munition	"S" ammunition (*with the ordinary pointed rifle bullet*).

Spreng-Munition	the regulation explosive (*trinitrotoluol*).
T-Munition	T-shell (*lachrymatory gas shell*).
Munitionsausgabestelle	ammunition refilling point.
Munitionsbestand	stock of ammunition.
Munitionseinsatz	expenditure of ammunition.
Munitionsergänzung	ammunition supply.
Munitionsersatz	replenishment of ammunition.
Munitionskeller	deep dug-out for storing ammunition.
Munitionskolonne (n/A.)	new pattern ammunition column.
Munitionskolonne (leichte; leichte Feldhaubitze)	ammunition column (light; for light field howitzers).
Munitionslager	ammunition depôt.
Munitionsleute	ammunition party.
Munitionsnachschub	ammunition supply.
Munitionsniederlage	ammunition store.
Munitionsunterstand	ammunition dug-out.
Munitionstragetier	ammunition pack animal.
Munitionsverbrauch	expenditure of ammunition.
Munitionsvergeudung	waste of ammunition.
Munitionswagen	ammunition wagon.
Munitionswesen	supply of ammunition.
Munitionszug	ammunition train.
Musikmeister	bandmaster.
Muskete	automatic rifle.
Musketen-Bataillon	" Musketen " battalion (*armed with automatic rifles*).
Musketier	private (*of the Active category in a line infantry regiment*).
Muster	pattern.
Musterung	mustering (*of recruits*), examination (*of recruits*).
Mütze	cap.
Dienstmütze	peaked cap.
Einheitsmütze	universal pattern cap.
Feldmütze	field service cap.
Pelzmütze	fur cap, hussar busby.
Schirmmütze	peaked cap.

N.

Nachbardivision	division on the flank, neighbouring division.
Nachbrenner	hang fire (*mining*).
Nachen	barge, flat-bottomed boat.
Nachersatz	drafts.
Nachexerzieren	to do extra drill.
Nachfärben	to dye.
Nachforschung	investigation.
Nachfrage	inquiry, demand.
Nachhaltig	lasting, protracted.
Nachhut } Nachkommando }	rear guard.
Nachlieferung	supply.
Nachrichten-Abteilung	Intelligence Section; regimental signalling detachment.
Nachrichtendienst	Intelligence Service.
Officer vom Nachrichtendienst	information officer (*at Brigade H.Q.*).
Nachrichtengeschoss	message shell (*special projectile to contain a message*).
Nachrichten-Kommandeur	Signal Commander (*with Armies, &c.*).
Nachrichtenkopf	signal communication head.
Nachrichtenmine	message shell (*from light "Minenwerfer."*)
Nachrichtenmittel	means of communication.
Nachrichtenmittel-Abteilung	regimental signalling detachment.
Nachrichtenmittel-Offizier	regimental signalling officer.
Nachrichten-Offizier	intelligence officer; signalling officer.
Nachrichtensammelstelle	information centre.
Nachrichtensammlung	collection of intelligence.
Nachrichtentruppe	Signal Corps.
Nachrichtenwerfer	message projector.
Nachrichtenwesen	Signal Service.
Nachrichtenzug	signalling section.
Nachschub	supply (*of men and material, from rear to front*), drafts, reinforcements.
Nachsehen	to inspect.
Nachsetzen (jemandem)	to pursue.
Nachspitzenkompagnie	rearward point company.
Nachtdienst	night shift.
Nachtrab	rear, rear guard.
Nachtrag	addendum, supplement (*frequently met with in German orders*).

Nachträgliche Überbauung	addition (*i.e., which can be made to trenches*).
Nachtrupp	rear party.
Nachuntersuchung (ärztliche)	2nd medical examination.
Nachurlaub	extension of leave.
Nachwirkung	after effects (*e.g., of gas*).
Nachzügler	straggler.
Nahabwehrgeschütz	close defence gun.
Nahaufklärung	close reconnaissance.
Nähe	vicinity, nearness.
in erreichbarer Nähe	within striking distance.
Nahkampf	close combat.
Nahkampfbatterie	close-range battery.
Nahkampfgeschütz	close-range gun.
Nahkampfgruppe	close-range group (*artillery*).
Nahkampfmittel	close-range weapons.
Nahpatrouille	close patrol (*tactical reconnaissance*).
Nahrungsmittel	victuals, food supplies.
Nahtkommando	contact detachment (*see " Nahtkompagnie*).
Nahtkompagnie	contact company (*employed in trench warfare to ensure maintenance of touch between two formations when attacked*).
Namensanruf	roll call.
Namensverzeichnis	list of names.
Namenszug	regimental monogram.
Namo (Nachrichtenmittel-Offizier)	regimental signalling officer.
Nasenklemme	nose-clip (*gas*).
Nasensteg	nose-piece (*of goggles*).
Nationale	*details of birth, profession, &c.* (*found in pay books and other official documents*).
Nebel	mist, fog.
Nebelbereitschaft	readiness for action during fog, "fog alert."
Nebelbombe	smoke bomb.
Nebelhorn	foghorn.
Nebelkasten	smoke generator; smoke box.
Nebeltopf	smoke generator; smoke pot.
Nebeltrommel	smoke generator; smoke drum.
Nebelmine	smoke bomb.
Nebelwolke	smoke cloud.
Nebenabschnitt	neighbouring sector.
Nebenarm	minor branch of a branch gallery (*mining*).
Nebendepot	auxiliary depôt.

Nebenfluss	tributary.
Nebengeleise	siding
Nebenstrasse	} by-road, branch road.
Nebenweg	
Nebenwirkung	secondary effect.
Neigung	inclination, slope.
Nervenschock	shell shock.
Nest	nest, isolated post.
Netz	network, system.
Neuanlagen	new works.
Neuaufnahme	re-survey.
Neuer Art (n/A.)	new pattern.
Neueingestellte	newly arrived men.
Neugestalten	to re-organize.
Neuigkeit	news.
Neutralitätsabzeichen	badge for neutrals.
Nicht-Kombattant	non-combatant.
Nichttransportfähig	unfit for transport.
Niederhalten	to dominate, paralyze, neutralize.
Niederkämpfen	to silence (*a battery*).
Niederkämpfung	silencing, neutralizing (*e.g., of hostile artillery*); counter-battery work.
Niederlage	defeat.
Niedermetzeln	to massacre, slaughter.
Niederschiessen	to shoot down.
Niederspannungsleitung	low tension line (*electricity*).
Niet	rivet.
Nische	recess (*e.g., in parapet or trench*).
Nonius	vernier.
Normalspurbahn	standard gauge railway.
Notbehelf	expedient; emergency signal.
Notizbuch	note book.
Notbremse	emergency brake.
Notleitung	emergency line (*telephone, &c.*).
Notrampe	extemporised ramp (*for entraining purposes*).
Notsignal	S.O.S.
Nottrage	emergency stretcher.
Notverband anlegen	to give first aid.
Notzeichen	emergency signal, S.O.S. signal.
Nullpunkt	zero, freezing point.
Nullpunkt (Batterie)	battery aiming point.
Nullzeit	zero time (*time for the commencement of an operation*).
Nummer	number.
Nummerieren	to number off.
Nut	recess, groove, slot.
Nutzgewicht	useful load.

O.

Oberarzt	Lieutenant (*medical*).
Oberbäcker	chief baker.
Oberbefehlshaber	Commander-in-Chief.
Oberbefehlshaber Ost (Obost)	C. in C. on the Eastern Front.
Oberfahnenschmied	farrier-serjeant.
Oberfeldherr	Supreme Commander-in-Chief (*i.e.*, the Emperor).
Ober-Festungs-Bauwärter	Chief Superintendent of Fortifications.
Oberfeuerwerker	chief artificer.
Oberfeuerwerkerschule	School for Artificers.
Obergefreiter	bombardier of foot artillery.
Obergeneralarzt und Sanitäts-Inspekteur	Major-General (*medical*).
Obergurt	surcingle.
Oberhandwerker des Trains	chief tradesman of the Train.
Oberirdisches Kabel	overland cable.
Oberjäger	under-officer of rifles; King's Messenger.
Oberkommando	Headquarters Staff.
Oberkommando (**Armee-**)	Army Headquarters (Staff).
Oberkommando der Küstenverteidigung	Coast Defence Headquarters.
Ober (Korps)-Auditeur	Chief (Corps) Judge-Advocate.
Oberlazarettgehilfe	chief hospital assistant.
Oberleder	the uppers (*of boots*).
Oberleutnant	Lieutenant.
Obermeister	staff-serjeant of artillery technical establishments.
Oberquartiermeister	*not translated: Deputy Chief of the General Staff of an Army, or head of a section of the General Staff in the War Ministry.*
Erster-Oberquartiermeister	*not translated: Deputy Chief of the General Staff of the Field Army.*
Oberschild	upper shield (*of field gun*).
Oberst	Colonel.
Oberstabsapotheker	chief pharmacist.
Oberstabsarzt	Major (*medical*).
Oberstabsveterinär	brevet Major (*veterinary*).
Oberste Heeresleitung	Commander-in-Chief, General Headquarters, Higher Command.
Oberstleutnant	**Lieutenant-Colonel.**

Oberveterinär	Lieutenant (*veterinary*).
Oberwallmeister	staff-serjeant of fortifications.
Oberzündung (mit)	with overhead ignition (*pattern of 21 cm. mortar*).
Obost	abbreviation for "Oberbefehlshaber Ost."
Ofen	mine chamber (*mining*).
Offensive	offensive.
Offizier	officer.
Offizier der Ronde	Officer of the "Rounds," Visiting Rounds.
Offizier vom Tagesdienst	Officer of the Day.
Offizier-Aspirant	probationary *or* aspirant officer, cadet.
Offizierdiensttuer	acting officer.
Offizier-Reitschule	Officers' Riding School (*at Paderborn, Dresden, &c.*).
Offiziersprüfung	officers' examination (*examination for commission*).
Offizierstellvertreter	acting officer (*but usually not translated*).
Ökonomie-Handwerker	regimental tradesman.
Öllappen	oily rags.
Ölspritzflasche	oil can.
Operationsbasis	base of operations.
Operationsbefehl	operation order.
Operationsgebiet	zone of the field army.
Operativ	strategic.
O-Punkt	aiming point, reference point.
Ordnung (Tages-)	Order of the Day.
Ordnung (geschlossene)	close order.
Ordnung (offene)	open order.
Ordonnanz	orderly.
Ordonnanzdienst	orderly duty.
Ordonnanz-Offizier	orderly officer.
Organ	personnel; individual, subordinate member of section.
Orientierung	orientation, reconnaissance.
Orientierung	fire direction by means of prearranged light signals (*artillery*).
Orientierung im Gelände	knowledge of the ground.
Ort	place, village.
Ort	*in mining, used sometimes instead of "Spitze" for the face of a working.*
Ortsbefehl	local order.
Ortsbehörde	municipal *or* local authorities.
Ortsbiwak	close billets.

Ortschaft	locality, village, place.
Ortsdienst	orderly officer's duty in place where troops are billeted.
Ortsfeste-Flug-Abwehr-Kanonen-Zug	fixed anti-aircraft section.
Ortskommandant	Town Major, local commandant.
Ortskommandantur	Town Major's office.
Ortskrankenstube	medical inspection room.
Ortslazarett	local hospital.
Ortsquartier	billet.
Ortsunterkunft	billets (*ordinary*).
Ortsvorstand	local authorities, mayor.
Ortsverkehr	local correspondence; local traffic.
Öse	eye, shank, lug.
Otto	*a type of German aeroplane engine.*

P.

Packpferd	packhorse.
Packtasche	wallet.
Packwagen	baggage wagon.
Paletot	greatcoat (*officer's*).
Pallasch	straight sword (*of heavy cavalry*).
Panjepferd	Russian horse (*requisitioned*).
Panjewagen	Russian cart (*requisitioned*).
Panne ...	breakdown (*Fr. panne*).
in der Panne sein	} to have a breakdown.
eine Panne haben	
Panzerauto	armoured car, "tank."
Panzerbatterie	armoured battery.
Panzerbeobachtungsstand	armoured observation post.
Panzerbeobachtungsturm	armoured observation turret.
Panzergeschoss	} armour-piercing shell.
Panzergranate...	
Panzerkabel	armoured cable.
Panzerkopf	armour-piercing head (*of shell*).
Panzerkraftwagen	armoured car, "tank."
Panzerkuppel	armoured cupola.
Panzerlafette	shielded mounting.
Panzermunition	armour-piercing bullets.
Panzerplatte	armour plate.
Panzerschild	armoured shield.
Panzerstahlgranate	steel armour-piercing shell.
Panzersturmwagen	armoured car, "tank."
Panzerturm	armoured turret.
Panzerwagen	armoured car, "tank."
Panzerzug	armoured train.
Parabellum	*types of German automatic pistol and rifle.*
Parade...	review.
Paradeanzug	full dress.
Paradeschritt	"goose" step, drill step.
Parkieren	to park.
Park-Kompagnie	park company.
Parkplatz	park (*for ammunition, &c.*).
Parkstaffel	stores depôt (*of Army aircraft park*).
Parlamentär	bearer of a flag of truce.
Parole ...	countersign, parole.
Parolebuch	order book.
Parolelosung	countersign.
Pass	pass, permit, passport.
Patent	officer's commission.
Patentiert	commissioned.

Patrone	cartridge (*in the case of a gun, only when it is fixed ammunition*).
gegürtete Patronen	cartridges in the belt (*machine gun*).
ungegürtete Patronen	loose rounds (*machine gun*).
Patronenhülse	cartridge case.
Patronenkasten	ammunition box.
Patronenkorb	shell basket (*fixed ammunition*).
Patronenlager	powder *or* cartridge chamber.
Patronenmunition	fixed ammunition (*gun*).
Patronensperre	cut-off (*of rifle*).
Patronentasche	cartridge pouch.
Patronenwagen	small arms ammunition (S.A.A.) wagon.
Patrouille	patrol; party.
Patrouillenangriff	⎫
Patrouillengang	⎬ raid.
Patrouillenunternehmung	⎭
Patte	patch (*on lapel, sleeve, collar, &c.*).
Pauke	kettle drum.
Pauker	kettle drummer.
Pause	tracing.
Pause (Feuer-)	pause *or* interval in firing.
in Pausen	intermittently.
Pauspapier	tracing paper.
Pechkranz	pitch ring (*for incendiary purposes; also used for indicating the line reached by troops*).
Peilen	to sound, measure; to intercept (*wireless*).
Pelerine	cape.
Pelzmütze	fur cap, hussar busby.
Pendelkarte	map showing progress of construction work, &c.
Pendeln	to oscillate; to go to and fro between two points.
Pension(-iert)	pension(-ed).
Perlen	" pearls " (*light-signal*).
Personenkraftwagen	touring-car.
Personal	personnel.
Personalgeschütz	close-range gun.
Pfadfinder	scout; boy scout.
Pfahl	picket, pile.
Pfahlbrücke	pile bridge.
Pfahljoch	pile trestle.
Pfahlwerk	palisade.
Pfalz	the Palatinate; *also a type of German aeroplane.*

Pfeil	arrow; picket; upright *or* leg (*mining*).
Pferd	horse.
Chargenpferd	officer's charger.
Dienstpferd	troop horse.
gedrücktes Pferd	horse with saddle galls.
Handpferd	led horse, off horse.
Lastpferd	pack horse, heavy draught horse.
Mittelpferd	centre horse.
Reitpferd	riding horse.
Sattelpferd	saddle horse (*also* near horse).
Saumpferd	pack horse.
Stangenpferd	wheel horse.
Vorderpferd	lead horse.
Vorratspferd	spare horse.
Zugpferd	draught horse.
Pferdeappell	horse inspection.
Pferdearzneikasten	veterinary chest.
Pferdeaushebungskommissar	horse requisitioning authority.
Pferdebahn	(40 *cm. gauge*) trench tramway (*animal traction*).
Pferdebespannt	horse-drawn.
Pferdebestand	stock of horses.
Pferdedepot	remount depôt.
Pferdefeldbahn	(40 *cm. gauge*) trench tramway (*animal traction*).
Pferdegasmaske	horse respirator (*gas*).
Pferdepflege	horsemastership, care of horses.
Pferdelazarett	veterinary hospital.
Pferdestall	stable (*for horses*).
Pferdetränken	watering horses.
Pferdewärter	groom.
Pferdezucht	horse breeding.
Pflaster	plaster; pavement.
gepflasterte Strasse	paved road.
Pflichtvergessener	defaulter.
Pflock	peg, stake, picket.
Pflugschar	ploughshare.
Pfosten	post, picket.
Phosgengas	phosgene gas.
Phosphor	phosphorus.
Photogrammetertrupp	photographic survey section.
Picke	pick, pickaxe.
Pickelhaube	spiked helmet.
Pickeln	to work with pickaxes.
Pille	primer (*explosive*).

Pilot ...	pilot (*aviation*).
Pilotenprüfung ...	the first examination for airmen; pilot's examination.
Pinne ...	peg, pivot.
Pionier ...	pioneer, engineer.
Pionier-Abteilung ...	pioneer detachment.
Pionier-Belagerungs-Train ...	pioneer siege train.
Pioniergerät ...	pioneers' tools.
Pionier-Hauptdepot ...	pioneer main depôt.
Pionier-Kompagnie ...	pioneer company.
Pionier-Korps ...	the Corps of Pioneers.
Pionier-Mineur-Kompagnie ...	pioneer mining company.
Pionier-Park-Abteilung ...	pioneer park detachment.
Pionierstand ...	pioneer dug-out.
Pionier-Zwischendepot ...	pioneer intermediate depôt or dump.
Pistole ...	pistol.
gesicherte Pistole ...	pistol at safety.
Selbstladepistole ...	automatic pistol.
Pistolentasche ...	pouch.
Pivotlager ...	trunnion bearing (*gun*).
Pivotzapfen ...	trunnions (*gun*).
Piwumba (Pionier Waffen-und Munitions-Beschaffungsamt)	Pioneer Munitions Department of the War Ministry.
Plan ...	plan, map.
Plankammer ...	map office.
Plänkler ...	skirmisher.
Planlosigkeit ...	want of method.
Planmässig ...	methodical, according to plan regulation.
Planmaterial ...	topographical information, maps.
Planpause ...	tracing of a map.
Planquadrat ...	map square *or* co-ordinate (*on squared map*).
Planschiessen ...	shooting by the map (*artillery*).
Planübergang ...	level crossing.
Planunterlage ...	battery board.
Planwagen ...	ladder-sided wagon.
Platte ...	plate, platform.
Platzen ...	to burst (*of shrapnel*).
Platzpatrone ...	blank cartridge.
Plombe ...	lead seal (*e.g., of gas mask drum*).
Plündern ...	to plunder, pillage.
Pneumatikreifen ...	pneumatic tyre.
Polster ...	cushion.
Pontonbrücke ...	pontoon bridge.
Pontonier-Vorschrift ...	Manual of Pontoon Bridging.

Pontonwagen	pontoon wagon.
Portepee	officer's sword-knot, *worn also by certain other ranks* (*see below*).
Portepeeträger	a rank which includes "*Offizier-Stellvertreter*," "*Feldwebel*," "*Vizefeldwebel*" and some officials.
Portion	ration for a man (*as opposed to* "*Ration*" *or forage ration*).
eiserne Portion	iron ration.
Kriegs-Portion	field service ration.
laufende Portion	ordinary ration.
Positionswinkel	angle of sight (*gunnery*).
Posten	sentry.
patrouillierender Posten	visiting patrol.
Posten ablösen	to relieve sentries.
Posten aufstellen	to post a sentry.
Posten stehen	to be on sentry duty.
Posten vor Gewehr	sentry over arms.
Postenfeuer	infantry fire.
Postenhund	sentry dog.
Postenschüsse	infantry fire.
Postenstand	sentry post.
Postieren (sich)	to take up one's stand.
Postierung	sentry.
Post-Pferde und Wagen-Depot	post office horse and van depôt.
Postprüfungsstelle	postal censor's office.
Postsperre	interruption, stoppage of the postal services.
Poststempel	postmark.
Postüberwachungsstelle	postal censor's office.
Postwagen	postal van.
Postzeichen	postmark.
Prallschuss	ricochet.
Präsentiert das Gewehr!	Present arms!
Präsenzstärke	(*see* "*Friedenspräsenzstärke*").
Präzisionsschiessen	extremely accurate shooting.
Präzisionstelephon	detectophone.
Preisgeben	to abandon, give up.
Prellbock	buffer stop (*railway*).
Pressfutter	compressed forage.
Pressluftanlage	air compressor.
Pressluftminenwerfer	pneumatic *Minenwerfer*.
Priester-Granate	Priester bomb (*fired from a* "*stick*" *bomb-thrower*).
Priester (Werfer)	Priester bomb-thrower.
Pritsche	bed (*of boards*).
Probe	**test.**
auf die Probe stellen	**to test.**

Probealarm	practice alarm.
Probeflug	trial flight.
Probeschuss	trial shot.
Profil	profile.
Progressivdrall	increasing twist.
Projektion (horizontale)	horizontal equivalent.
Protokoll führen	to keep the minutes (*of a meeting*).
Protze	limber.
Protzachse	limber axle.
Protzhaken	limber hook.
Protzkasten	limber box.
Protzöse	trail eye (*on gun carriage*), limber eye (*on gun limber*), perch eye (*on ammunition wagon*).
Proviantamt	supply office *or* depôt.
Proviantkolonne	supply column.
Proviantlager	supply depôt.
Proviantmeister	director of a supply depôt.
Proviantwagen	supply wagon.
Prüfung	test, examination, check.
Prügel	stick; *also used for* code *or* cipher key.
Prügelweg	corduroy road.
Puffer	buffer (*railway*).
Pulswärmer	wristlet.
Pulver	powder (*usually black powder*).
rauchloses Pulver	} smokeless powder.
rauchschwaches Pulver	
Schwarzpulver	black powder.
Pulverfabrik	powder factory.
Pulverladung	charge of black powder.
Pulversatz	powder train.
Pulvertreibladung	propelling charge of black powder.
Pumpe	pump.
Punkt	point, full stop.
Punkt (im Gelände)	topographical feature.
O-Punkt	aiming point, reference point.
Punktfeuer	fire concentrated on one point.
Punktnetz	skeleton (*triangulation*).
Punktschiessen	fire directed on a single point.
Puppen	dummies.
Putzen	to clean, groom.
Putzlappen	cleaning rags.
Putzwerg	tow for cleaning, waste.
Putzzeug	cleaning materials.
Putzzeuggeld	allowance for cleaning materials.
Pyramiden ansetzen	to pile arms.

Q.

Quadrat	square (*on squared map*)
Quadratmeter	square metre.
Quadratnetz	square (*on squared map*).
Quartier	billet, quarters.
Quartiermacher	officer *or* N.C.O. in charge of billeting party.
Quartiermeister	quartermaster.
Quartierwechsel	change of billeting area *or* quarters.
Quartierwirt	inhabitant on whom troops are billeted.
Quartierzettel	billeting paper.
Quaste	tassel.
Quellbrunnen	fountain, well, spring.
Quellenmässig	on good authority, authentic.
Quellgrund	ground full of springs, quagmire.
Quer	oblique, across.
Quer ab von	abreast of.
Querbalken	bar, cross beam.
Querbolzen	cross bolt.
Querhindernis	obstacle perpendicular to the front.
Querschnitt	profile or section (*e.g., of trench*).
Quersteuer	aileron (*aeroplane*).
Querstollen	transverse gallery (*mining*).
Querstrasse	cross road.
Quetsche	tool for crushing *or* squeezing.
Quetschen	to blow in (*mining*).
Quetschladung	⎫
Quetschmine	⎬ camouflet.
Quetschung	⎭
Quittieren	to receipt, to give a receipt.
Quittungsschein	receipt.

R.

Rabatte	plastron (*of lancer's tunic*).
Racheschiessen	retaliatory fire.
Radau	row, noise, shouting (*colloquial*).
Räderbahre	wheeled stretcher.
Radfahrer	cyclist.
Radfahrerbataillon	cyclist battalion.
Radfahrerbrigade	cyclist brigade.
Radfahrerkompagnie	cyclist company.
Radgürtel	"wheel belt."
Radlafette	wheeled carriage (*of gun*).
Kanone in Radlafette (K. i. R.L.)	gun on wheeled carriage.
Radunterlage	platform (*gun*).
Rahmen	frame, case.
Rahmenflagge	signalling panel.
Rahmenmaske	frame mask (*gas mask, with special type of edging*).
Rahmenschild	parapet shield.
Rahmenstütze	shield support.
Rakete	rocket.
Fallschirmrakete.	parachute light.
Leuchtrakete	light rocket.
Rauchrakete	smoke rocket.
Rampe	ramp, slope.
Kopframpe	end-loading ramp.
Notrampe	extemporized ramp.
Seitenrampe	side-loading ramp.
Rand	edge, rim *or* lip (*of crater*), crest (*of height*).
Rang	rank, grade.
Rangabzeichen	badges of rank.
Rangieren	to shunt (*railway*).
Rangiergleise	siding (*railway*).
Rangliste	army list.
Rangstufen	degrees of rank, grades.
Rasantes Feuer	flat trajectory fire.
Rasen	sods, turf.
Rasenabdeckung	⎫ layer of sods.
Rasenplacke	⎭
Rasenstück	sod.
Rast	halt, rest, stay.
Rat	councillor; advice, council.
Ration	forage ration (*as opposed to "Portion," or ration for man*).
eiserne Ration	"iron ration" of forage.

Rations-Sätze	scale of rations.
Raubzug	marauding raid.
Rauchlos	smokeless (*powder*).
Rauchmeldepatrone	smoke indicator (*used in dropping messages from aeroplanes*).
Rauchrakete	smoke rocket.
Rauchschleier	smoke cloud *or* screen.
Rauchschwach	smokeless (*powder*).
Rauchschwaden	smoke clouds, drifts of smoke.
Räude	mange.
Räudestation	mange isolation hospital.
Raufe	hay rack (*stable*).
Raum	space, frontage, room.
Räumen	to evacuate.
Raumlöffel	scoop, scraper (*mining*).
Raummeter	cubic metre.
Räumung	evacuation.
Rea (Riesen-Ersatz-Abteilung)	giant aeroplane training depôt.
Rechnungsfehler	miscalculation.
Rechts um !	Right turn !
Rechtwinkliger Trichter	two-lined crater (*mining*).
Rege	lively, active, intense.
Regeln	to regulate, control.
Regiment	regiment.
Regimentsarzt	regimental medical officer.
Regimentsbagage	regimental transport.
Regimentsbefehl	regimental order.
Regimentsgefechtsstand (Stelle)	regimental battle H.Q.
Regimentskommandeur	regimental commander.
Regimentsstab	regimental staff.
Regimentsstapelplatz	regimental dump.
Regimentstambour	regimental drummer.
Reglement	regulations, text book, manual.
Regler	corrector (*artillery*).
Reglerkorrektur	correction (*artillery*).
Reglerteilung	correction scale (*on gun sight*).
Reibsatz	fulminate.
Reibung	friction.
Reibzünder	friction lighter.
Reibzündschraube	friction tube.
Reichsformat, auf	on foolscap paper.
Reichweite	range.
Reifen	rim of wheel ; tyre of wheel.
Reih und Glied	rank and file.
Reihen (in)	in file.
Reihenbild	mosaic (*aeroplane photographs*).

Reihenbildner	cinematograph camera (*used in aerial reconnaissances; sometimes* aeroplane *fitted with this camera*).
Reihenbildtrupp	section for making mosaics.
Reihenbildzug	mosaic section (*aviation unit*).
Reihenfeuer	bursts of fire (*artillery and machine guns*).
Reihenfolge	order of succession.
Reihenkolonne (in)	in file.
Reisegebührnisse	} travelling allowance.
Reisekosten	
Reisemarsch	march route.
Reisequartier	march billet.
Reisetag	date of journey (*e.g., on a movement order*).
Reisigbündel	brushwood, fascine, faggot.
Reissleine	lanyard.
Reitende Artillerie	horse artillery.
Reitende Batterie	horse artillery battery.
Reitendes-Feldjäger-Korps	King's Messengers.
Reiter	trooper, horseman.
Schwerer Reiter	trooper (*of heavy cavalry*).
Spanische Reiter	" knife-rests " (*wire entanglement*).
Reiter-Regiment, Schweres	not translated; heavy cavalry regiment (*Bavarian or Saxon*).
Reithose	pantaloons.
Reitpferd	riding horse.
Reitzeug	saddle and bridle.
Reizgeschoss	gas shell, tear shell, lachrymatory shell.
Reizpatrone	gas cartridge (*for testing gas masks*).
Reizraum	gas chamber (*a room for testing gas masks*).
Reizstoff	irritant substance (*lachrymator*).
Reklamiert	exempted, claimed for industry.
Rekrutendepot	recruit depôt.
Relais	chain of men.
Relaisposten	relay posts.
Relaisverbindung	connecting files.
Remontedepot	remount depôt.
Remontewesen	remount service.
Repartieren	to distribute.
Repressalien	reprisals.
Reserve	reserve (*also* " Reserve " *as opposed to* " Active ").
Reveille	reveille.

Revier ...	barrack room (*sometimes*, **medical** inspection room).
Revier bekommen ...	to be put on the sick list.
Revierkranken ...	men who are sick (*light duty*).
Revierkrankenstube ...	regimental sick and inspection room.
Revolver ...	revolver.
Revolverkanone ...	revolver-gun.
Revolverkanonen-Abteilung...	revolver-gun detachment.
Revolvertrommel ...	cylinder of revolver.
Rfla (Riesen-Flugzeug-Abteilung)	giant aeroplane flight.
Richtbaum ...	traversing lever (*on trail of field gun*).
Richtbogen ...	clinometer.
Richtempfängertrupp ...	wireless compass detachment.
Richtempfangsstation ...	wireless compass station.
Richten ...	to lay (*a gun*).
Richtfläche ...	clinometer plane.
Richtgerät ...	laying gear, aiming mechanism.
Richthebel ...	elevating lever.
Richtkanonier ...	gun layer.
Richtkreis ...	director (*gunnery*).
Richtkreisdiopter ...	"flash spotter."
Richtkreiskorrektur ...	corrections for displacement (*gunnery*).
Richtkreiszahlen ...	"director" readings.
Richtlatte ...	aiming post.
Richtmaschine ...	elevating or traversing handwheel.
Richtschraube ...	elevating screw.
Richtschütze ...	the man who aims and fires the machine gun; "No. 1." (*In the German Army he is* "*No. 2.*").
Richtstäbchen ...	aiming post.
Richtsitz ...	layer's seat.
Richtungshörer ...	direction finder (*sound*).
Richtungsstabilität ...	directional stability (*aeroplane*).
Richtungswinkel ...	angle of direction.
Richtvorrichtung ...	laying gear (*artillery*).
Riegel ...	bolt (*on door, &c.*); switch trench.
Riegelgraben ...	switch trench.
Riegelstellung...	switch line.
Riemen...	strap, sling (*of rifle*).
Riesen-Ersatz-Abteilung ...	giant aeroplane training depôt.
Riesen-Flugzeug-Abteilung ...	giant aeroplane flight.
Rillen-Munition ...	} R-ammunition (*ordinary S.A.A. with groove round base of bullet*).
R.-Munition ...	
Ringel ...	loop, coil.

Ringkanone (R.K.)	gun with chase rings.
Ringkragen	gorget.
Ringscheibe	ring target (*bull's eye target with rings*).
Rinne	gutter (*of trench*).
Rittmeister	Captain (*of cavalry or train*).
Rock	coat, jacket.
Waffenrock	tunic, field service jacket.
Rödelung	rack-lashing (*bridging*).
Rohr	bore; gun (*artillery*).
Rohrbremse	buffer (*of gun carriage*).
Rohrdetonierer	burst in the bore.
Röhrenbündel	cartridge bag (*gun ammunition*)
Röhrenleitung	pipe line.
Rohrhalter	breech lug (*of gun*).
Rohrjacke	jacket (*of gun*).
Rohrkimme	fixed sight (*on field gun*).
Rohrklaue	guide ring (*on gun*).
Rohrkrepierer	burst in the bore.
Rohrmündung	muzzle (*gun*).
Rohrrücklauf	gun recoil.
Rohrrücklaufgeschütz	gun which recoils in its carriage.
Rohrrücklauflafette	gun-recoil carriage.
Rohrwagen	travelling carriage (*for 21 cm. mortar*).
Rohrwand	bore (*gun*).
Rohrwiege	cradle (*of a gun carriage*).
Rohrzerscheller Rohrzerspringer	} burst in the bore.
Roland	*a type of German aeroplane.*
Rollbahn	trench tramway (50 *cm. gauge*).
Rolle	roll; pulley; rôle.
Rollendes Material	rolling stock.
Rollwagen	lorry (*fortress searchlight section*).
Ronde	"Rounds."
Ronde-Offizier	Officer of the "Rounds."
Rossarzt	veterinary surgeon.
Rost	trench boarding, "duck boards;" gridiron, grate; rust.
Rösten	to roast.
Rosten	to rust.
Rote Kreuz, das	the Red Cross.
Rotte	file.
blinde Rotte	blank file.
gerade Rotten	even files.
halbe Rotte	blank file.
ungerade Rotten	odd files.

Rotz	glanders.
Rückbau	reconstruction.
Rückbeförderung	evacuation (*of wounded, etc.*).
Rücken	to march, move; *also* back, rear.
Rückenfeuer	reverse fire.
Rückenwehr	parados.
Rückfahrt	return journey.
Rücklauf	recoil (*of a gun*).
Rücklaufgraben	" down " trench.
Rückleitung	return (*of electric circuit*).
Rückmarsch	march back, return march.
Rückmeldung	reply.
Rücksack	knapsack.
Rückschlag	defeat, reverse.
Rückstand	residue.
Rückstoss	repulse, recoil.
Rückstossverstärker	recoil intensifier (*on machine gun*).
Rückwärtig	behind the lines, rearward, back, rear, retired.
Rückwärts	backwards, to the rear.
Rückzug	retreat, retirement.
Ruder	oar.
Steuerruder	rudder.
Ruf	shout, call, hail, cry; reputation, repute.
Rufzeichen	call signal (*wireless*).
Ruhe	rest, calm, quiet.
Ruhebataillon	battalion resting.
Ruhelager	rest camp.
Ruhequartier	rest billets.
Ruhiges Feuer	deliberate fire (*artillery*).
Rühren	to move.
Rührt Euch !	Stand (or march) at ease!
Rumpf	body *or* fuselage (*of aeroplane*).
Rumpfboot	nacelle (*of aeroplane*).
Rumpler	*a type of German aeroplane.*
Rundballon	spherical balloon.
Rundbild	panorama.
Rundblickfernrohr	panorama sight.
Runde	"Rounds."
Russenwache	guard for Russian prisoners of war.
Rüsten	to prepare, equip, arm.
Rutschbahn	inclined plane for sliding material down, haulage apparatus (*mining*).
Rutschung	falling away of earth (*e.g., in a trench*).

S.

Säbel	sabre (*mounted troops*).
Säbelgriff	sword grip.
Säbelklinge	sword blade.
Säbelkoppel	sword belt.
Säbelschlaufe	frog (*of a bayonet, &c.*).
Säbeltasche	sabretache.
Säbeltroddel	sword *or* bayonet knot.
Sackgraben	block trench.
Sackgrube	saphead.
Säge	saw, saw edge (*of bayonet*).
Sägewerk	saw mill.
Salve	salvo (*artillery*), volley (*rifle*).
Salve abgeben	to fire a volley *or* salvo.
Salzdecke (*contraction for "Schutzsalzdecke"*)	anti-gas cover.
Salzsäure	hydrochloric acid.
Salz-Verladung	flash reducer (*for guns; sometimes used instead of "Vorlage"*).
Sammelkompagnie	salvage company.
Sammeln!	the "Assembly" (*infantry*).
Sammeln	to collect, rally, gather.
Sammelort	dump.
Sammelplatz	place of assembly, collecting station.
Sammel-Sanitäts-Depôt	medical stores collecting station.
Sammelstation	collecting station, salvage dump.
Sammelstelle	collecting station, salvage dump.
Sandgrube	sand pit.
Sandsack	sandbag.
Sandsackunterlage	a pedestal built up of sandbags.
Sandschutzbrillen	sand goggles.
Sanitäts-Departement	Medical Department (of War Ministry).
Sanitätsdienst	Army Medical Service.
Sanitätsinspektion	Medical Inspectorate.
Sanitätskasten	medical and surgical panniers.
Sanitätskolonne	ambulance column.
Sanitätskompagnie	bearer company, medical company.
Sanitätskorps	Medical Corps.
Sanitätskraftwagen-Abteilung	motor ambulance detachment.
Sanitätskraftwagen-Kolonne	motor ambulance convoy.
Sanitätsmannschaften	medical orderlies, men of the Medical Corps.
Sanitäts-Offizier	medical officer.
Sanitäts-Offizierdiensttuer	*medical student temporarily commissioned as medical officer or as medical officer with warrant rank.*

Sanitätspersonal	medical personnel.
Sanitätspflege, freiwillige	voluntary aid.
Sanitätssoldat	hospital orderly.
Sanitätsstaffel	bearer detachment.
Sanitätstasche	medical wallet.
Sanitätstornister	medical knapsack.
Sanitätsunterstand	field dressing station in a dug-out, medical dug-out.
Sanitätsverbandzeug	bandage, field dressing.
Sanitätsvorratswagen	medical store wagon.
Sanitätswagen	ambulance wagon.
Sanitätswesen	medical service.
Sappe	sap.
Sappenkopf	saphead.
Sappenposten	listening post in sap.
Sappenspitze	saphead.
Sattel	saddle; col (*topography*).
Sattelbaum	saddle tree.
Satteldecke	saddle cloth.
Sattelgurt	girth.
Sattelknopf	pommel.
Sattelpferd	riding horse (*also* near horse).
Sattelseite	near side.
Satteltasche	saddlebag.
Sattelzeug	saddlery.
Sattler	saddler.
Satz	jump, bound; ingredients, composition (*e.g.*, "*Zündsatz*" *or detonating composition*); sentence (*grammatical*).
Säuberung	clearing (*of trenches, &c.*).
Sauerstoff	oxygen.
Sauerstoffeinatmungsgerät	oxygen breathing (inhalation) apparatus.
Sauerstoff-Sirene	siren operated by compressed oxygen.
Saugpumpe	suction pump.
Schablonieren	to stencil.
Schacht	shaft (*mining*).
Schachtel	packet (*e.g., of cartridges;* 3 *clips of* 5).
Schaffen	to create, construct, arrange; to do; to convey.
nach vorne schaffen	to carry to the front.
Schaft	stock (*of rifle*); shaft (*of lance*); top (*of top boot*).
Schall	sound.
Schallmesstrupp	sound ranging section.

Schallmesszentrale	sound ranging central station.
Schallquelle	source of sound.
Schallrichten	sound ranging.
Schallsignal	sound signal.
Schallwelle	sound wave.
Schaltbrett	electrical switch board.
Schalter	switch (*electricity*).
ausschalten	to switch off.
einschalten	to switch on, to intercalate, to interpose.
Schalthebel	switch (*electricity*).
Schalung	revetment (*of a trench*).
Schandeck	gunwale (*pontoon*).
Schanzarbeiten	entrenching works.
Schanzbataillon	entrenching battalion.
Schanze	a field work.
Schanzen	to dig, entrench.
Schanzgeräte	entrenching tools (heavy).
Schanzkorb	gabion.
Schanzkorbbrücke	gabion bridge.
Schanztätigkeit	trenchwork, entrenching.
Schanz- und Werkzeugwagen	entrenching and tool wagon (*pioneers*).
Schanzzeug	entrenching tools (light).
Schanzzeugdepot	engineer dump.
Schanzzeugwagen	entrenching tool wagon (*infantry*).
Schapska	see "Tschapka."
Scharf	sharp; "live" (*of a grenade, &c.*).
Handgranate scharf machen	to insert a detonator in a grenade.
Scharfpatrone	ball cartridge.
Scharfschiessen	to fire with ball ammunition.
Scharfschiesser	sniper.
Scharfschütze	marksman, sniper.
Scharfschützenfeuer	independent fire.
Scharmützel	skirmish.
Schärpe	officer's sash.
Scharte	fissure, gap; loophole, embrasure.
Schartenblende	shutter of loophole plate.
Scharfschützen Abteilung (M.G.)	machine gun marksman detachment.
Schartenklappe	loophole shutter (*of infantry shield*).
Schartenplatte	loophole shutter.
Schartenschlitz	loophole.
Schartensohle	lower edge of loophole.
Schartenweite	width of loophole.
Schattenwirkung	shadow effect.
Schattierung	shading (*on map*).

Schätzen	to judge (*distance*), estimate, value.
Schaufel	shovel.
Scheibe	target.
Brustscheibe	head and shoulders target.
Figurscheibe	figure target.
Kniescheibe	kneeling figure target.
Kopfscheibe	head target.
Ringscheibe	ring target (*bull's eye target with rings*).
Scheibenstand	butts (*musketry*).
Scheide	scabbard.
Scheinangriff	feint attack.
Scheinanlage	dummy trench *or* defensive work.
Scheinbatterie	dummy battery.
Scheinbeobachter	dummy observer.
Scheinbesatzung	dummy garrison.
Scheinflankierung	dummy flanking position.
Scheingefecht	sham fight.
Scheingraben	dummy trench.
Scheinschulterwehr	dummy traverse.
Scheinstellung	dummy position.
Scheinunternehmung	feint attack.
Scheinwerfer	searchlight.
Scheinwerferzug	searchlight section.
Scherenfernrohr	stereo-telescope, " scissors " telescope.
Halbschere	the half scissors (*represents half the " scissors " telescope*).
Schicht	shift (*mining, &c.*) ; course. layer.
Schutzschicht	protecting course (*e.g., in roof of dug-out*).
Schichthöhe	vertical interval of contours.
Schichtlinie	contour.
Schiebbahn	trolley line.
Schieber	corrector (*to regulate the height at which shrapnel explodes*).
Schieber zum Auswerfer	extractor slide (*breech action of light field howitzer*).
Schiebetür	sliding door.
Schiebkarren	wheelbarrow.
Schiebwagen	hand trolley.
Schiedsrichter	umpire.
Schiene	rail (*railway*) ; splint (*surgical*).
Schienendecke	layer of rails.
Schienenlage	layer of rails (*e.g., to protect a saphead, etc.*).
Schienenstuhl	chair (*railway*).

Schiessanweisung	instructions for gunnery or musketry.
Schiessbaumwolle	guncotton.
Schiessbeispiel	example of ranging.
Schiessbuch	book containing record of the marksmanship of an individual soldier.
Schiessdienst	musketry duty.
Schiessen (beginnen, das)	to open fire.
Schiessen mit wechselnder Seitenrichtung	to open traversing fire.
Schiessfrei	out of range.
Schiessgas	gas from gas shell.
Schiessgerüst	stand (*for machine gun, (&c.)*).
Schiesslistenbuch	register of firing of a battery.
Schiessplatz	artillery range.
Schiessscharte	} loophole.
Schiessschlitz	
Schiessschule	School of Musketry.
Schiessschule (Artillerie-)	School of Gunnery.
Schiessstand	rifle range.
Schiesstafel	range table.
Schiessübung (jährliche)	annual musketry course.
Schiessverfahren	fire procedure, fire tactics.
Schiessverhau	barricade *or* abatis of trees.
Schiessvorschrift	regulations for gunnery *or* musketry.
Schiessweite (in)	within range.
Schiffbrücke	bridge of boats.
Schild	shield.
Schildbatterie	shielded battery.
Schildklappe	folding shield.
Schildlager	trunnion bearing.
Schildwache	sentry.
Schildzapfen	trunnion.
Schirmeindecker	parasol monoplane.
Schilf	reeds.
Schirmlafette	overhead shield (*of gun*).
Schirmmütze	peaked cap.
Schirren	to harness.
Schirrmeister	storekeeper (N C O.); pigeon-loft attendant.
Schlacht	battle.
Schlachtenflieger	low-flying battle machine.
Schlächterei	butchery.
Schlächtergerät	butcher's implements.
Schlachtlinie	line of battle.
Schlachtstaffel	battle flight (*aviation unit*).

Schlag	blow; pigeon loft; section *or* bay of trench.
Schlagartig	in sudden bursts (*artillery fire*).
Schlagbolzen	striker (*e.g., in a breech mechanism*).
Schlagen	to strike, beat, defeat; throw (*a bridge*); to submit (*proposals*).
Schlagfeder	striker spring.
Schlagfertigkeit	efficiency (*of troops*); rapidity of thought.
Schlagrohr	friction tube, friction igniter.
Schlagwort	code word.
Schlagzünder	percussion fuze.
Schlangenlinie	line with zig-zag trace.
Schlappe	reverse, check.
Schlauch	tube, hose.
Luftschlauch	inner tube of tyre.
Schlaufe	lifting band (*on lid of gun cartridge case*).
Schleichen	to crawl, creep.
Schleichpatrouille	reconnoitring patrol.
Schleier	screen (*e.g., cavalry, smoke, &c.*).
Schleifknoten	slip knot.
Schleiflatte Schleifleiste	} rubbing strake (*pontoon*).
Schlepparbeit	haulage work.
Schleppen	to haul, tow.
Schleppschacht	inclined gallery (*mining*).
Schleppseil	tow rope; guide rope.
Schlepptau	tow rope.
Schlepptrupp	hauling gang (*mining*).
Schleudergestell	catapult.
Schleudermaschine	bomb thrower.
Schleudern	to throw by means of a catapult.
Schleuse	sluice, lock.
Schliessende	supernumeraries (*on parade*).
Schlinge	sling, noose, trap.
Schlitten	sledge (*e.g., of a machine gun*).
Schlitz	slit, notch.
Schloss	lock (*e.g., of door, rifle, &c.*); castle.
Schlösschen	cocking piece.
Schlossgarde-Kompagnie	Castle Guard.
Schlossschützer	lock shield *or* protector.
Schlossteile	breech mechanism.
Schlucht	ravine.
Schlüpfung	slip (*of propeller*).
Schlüssel	key *or* spanner.
Schlüsselgraben	main trench (*which forms the key of the position*).

Schmal	narrow.
Schmalspurbahn	narrow gauge railway.
Schmiedewagen	forge wagon.
Schmierbüchse	grease-tin.
Schmieren	to grease, lubricate.
Schnalle	buckle; ribbon of an order.
Schnallen	to buckle, strap.
Schneehemd	white coat (*for snow*).
Schneemantel	white coat (*for snow*).
Schneeschuhläufer	skier.
Schneeschuhläuferbataillon	skiers' battalion.
Schneid	dash, smartness, spirit, energy.
Schneide	edge (*of a sword, &c.*).
Schneiden	to cut; to take bearings (*e.g., in survey work*).
Schneider	tailor.
Schneidig	sharp, smart, energetic, vigorous.
Schnellbrücke	temporary bridge.
Schnelldraht	} portable wire entanglement; concertina wire entanglement.
Schnelldrahthindernis	
Schnellfeuer	rapid fire.
Schnellfeuergeschütz	quick-firing gun.
Schnellhindernis	ready made obstacle, emergency obstacle.
Schnellladekanone	quick-firing (Q.F.) gun.
Schnelltelegraph	high-speed telegraph.
Schnellzündschnur	instantaneous fuze.
Schnitt	intersection, bearing.
Schnurbesatz	braid on hussar's tunic.
Schnurleine	small lashing.
Schnurschuhe	ankle boots, lace boots.
Schonen	to spare, preserve.
Schonungsbedürftige	*men who, it is considered, should not be employed in front line for various reasons, e.g., health, family reasons, &c.*
Schoss	skirt (*of a tunic*).
Schotter	road metal, ballast, broken stones.
Schraffieren	to hatch, hachure (*on a sketch*).
Schrägfeuer	oblique fire, flanking fire.
Schränkung	decalage (*aeroplane design*).
Schrapnel	shrapnel.
Schraube	screw, propeller.
hinterliegende Schraube	pusher screw.
vorn liegende Schraube	tractor screw.
Schraubanker	screw anchor bolt (*for obstac'es*).

Schraubenmutter	nut (*screw-threaded*).
Schraubenschlüssel	spanner.
Schraubenstrahl	race of a propeller (*aeroplane*).
Schraubenzieher	screw driver.
Schraubpfahl	screw post (*for wire entanglement*).
Schreiber	clerk.
Schreibstube	orderly room, office.
Schritt	pace.
Schroff	steep, abrupt.
Schubverringerung	slip (*of aeroplane propeller*).
Schuh	shoe, boot.
Schulschiessen	preliminary practices (*musketry, &c.*).
Schulschiessstand	practice (rifle or M.G.) range.
Schulterklappe	shoulder strap.
Schultermaschinengewehr	automatic rifle.
Schulterschnur	shoulder cord.
Schulterwehr	traverse.
Schuppe (*or* Schuppen)	shed, hangar.
Schurzholz	casing, *as opposed to* "*Getriebholz*," *frame and sheeting or lagging* (*trenches and mining*).
Schurzholznest	shelter.
Schuss	shot, round, rounds.
Bogenschuss	high-angle fire.
vereinzelte Schüsse	desultory fire.
Schuss!	Fire!
Schuss lag weit	"over." ⎫
Schuss lag kurz	"short." ⎬ (*of results of firing*).
Schuss lag gut im Ziel	"hit." ⎭
Schussbereit	ready to fire.
Schussbeschädigung	damage caused by gunfire.
Schussfeld	field of fire.
Schussrichtung	line of fire.
Schusssicher (*see also* "Bombensicher")	shell-proof (*against continuous bombardment by 6-in. guns*), *sometimes* "bullet-proof."
Schusstafel	range table.
Schussweite	range.
wirksame Schussweite	effective range.
Schusszahl	number of rounds.
Schusta (Schutzstaffel)	protective flight (*aviation unit*).
Schütte-Lanz	*a type of German airship.*
Schütten	to heap up, dam.
Schutz	protection, cover.
Schutzblech	protecting plate, mudguard (*bicycle*).
Schutzbrille	smoked spectacles, goggles.

Schütze	rifleman, sniper, marksman, skirmisher, private (*in all machine-gun units and in "Schützen" battalions*).
Schützenabzeichen	marksman's badge.
Schützenauftritt } Schützenbank	fire step.
Schützen-Bataillon	"Schützen" battalion (*not translated; corresponds to our "Rifles"*).
Schützenblende (aus Panzerstahl)	portable infantry shield.
Schützeneskadron	squadron of dismounted cavalry.
Schützenfeuer, langsames	deliberate independent fire.
Schützengefecht	skirmish.
Schützengraben	fire trench.
völlig eingeschnittener Schützengraben	trench without parapet.
geschlossene Schützengräben	closed works.
Schützengraben-Kanonen-Abteilung	trench-gun detachment.
Schützenhöhle	dug-out.
Schützenlinie	skirmishing line, extended order.
Schützenloch	rifle pit.
Schützennest	rifle pit.
Schützennische	recess (*in parapet*).
Schützenregiment	"Schützen" regiment (*not translated; corresponds to our "Rifles"*).
Schützenscharte	loophole.
Schützenschleier	covering party.
Schützenstand	rifle range.
Schützenstellung	position, infantry position.
Schutzflugzeug	protective machine, escorting aeroplane.
Schutzgerät	defensive appliances.
Schutzmaske	gas mask.
Schutzsalz	protective salts (*anti-gas*).
Schutzsalzdecke	anti-gas cover.
Schutzsalzlösung	protective salts solution (*anti-gas*).
Schutzschicht	protecting course (*e.g., in roof of dug-out*).
Schutzschild	armoured shield.
Schutzstaffel (Schusta)	protective flight (*aviation unit*).
Schutztruppen	The Protectorate Troops (*Colonies*).
Schwalbennester	bandsman's epaulettes.
Schwanken	to fluctuate, vary; to reel.
Schwanz (Lafettenschwanz)	trail (*of gun*); tail (*of aeroplane, &c.*).

Schwanzflosse	tail fin (*aeroplane*).
Schwanzkörper	fuselage (*of aeroplane*).
Schwanzsteuer	tail plane, rudder (*of aeroplane*).
Schwanzträger	boom (*of aeroplane*).
Schwanztute	bag at stern (*of kite balloon*).
Schwärmen	to extend (*line of skirmishers*).
Schwarzblech	black sheet iron.
Schwebebahn	suspension railway.
Schwefelkohlenstoff	carbon disulphide (*gas*).
Schwefla (schwere Flachbahn, *e.g.*, Batterie)	heavy, flat trajectory (battery).
Schweissapparat	welding apparatus.
Schweizer	dairyman.
Schwelle	threshold, sill; sleeper (*railway*).
Schwenken	to wheel.
Schwenkungswinkel	arc of traverse.
Schwere Artillerie des Feldheeres	Heavy Artillery of the Field Army.
Schwere Feldhaubitzbatterie	heavy field howitzer battery.
Schwere Funkenstation	heavy wireless field station (*mobile*).
Schwere Kolonnen-Brücke	heavy bridge for all arms.
Schwerer Reiter	trooper (*of heavy cavalry*).
Schwerer Rheinbrückentrain	Heavy Rhine Bridging Train.
Schweres Reiter-Regiment	*not translated;* heavy cavalry regiment (*Bavarian or Saxon*).
Schwerkraft	gravity.
Schwerpunkt	centre of gravity.
Schwimmer	float (*hydro-plane*).
Seebataillon	marine infantry battalion (*peace*).
Seeflieger-Abteilung	naval flying (hydroplane) squadron.
Seeflugzeug	hydroplane, seaplane.
Seele	soul; bore (*of a gun, &c.*).
Seelendurchmesser Seelenweite	} calibre.
Seewehr	" Seewehr " or naval reserve (*corresponds to* " Landwehr ").
Segeltuchtasche	canvas wallet.
Sehnenlänge	chord length (*plane of aeroplane*).
Sehnenriegel	switch line (*cutting off a salient*).
Sehnenstellung	line behind a salient.
Sehschlitz	observation loophole (*e.g., in a shield*).
Sehverbindung	visual communication.
Sehzeichen	visual signal.
Seilbahn	aerial railway.
Seilbahn-Abteilung	aerial railway detachment.
Seiltrommel	drum for brake rope (*field gun carriage*).

Seitenabstand	displacement (*gunnery*).
Seitenabweichung	error in line *or* direction (*gunnery*).
Seitendeckung	flank guard.
Seitenfeuer	enfilade fire.
Seitengewehr	side arm, bayonet.
Seitenhut	flank guard.
Seitenneigung geben	to bank (*an aeroplane*).
Seitenrampe	side-loading ramp.
Seitenrichtmaschine	traversing gear.
Seitenrichtung, schiessen (mit wechselnder)	to open traversing fire.
Seitenschlag	branch gallery (*mining*).
Seitensteuer	rudder (*of aeroplane*).
Seitenstrang	siding (*railway*).
Seitenstreuung	lateral error (*in the shooting of a gun*).
Seitenstück	stanchion of a frame (*mining*).
Seitenverschiebung	displacement (*artillery*).
Seitliche Wirkung	lateral effect.
Sektion	section.
Selbständig	independent, self reliant.
Selbstkosten	cost price (*net price*).
Selbstlader	automatic (*pistol*).
Selbstretter	life-saving apparatus, *similar to* "Salvo Set"; oxygen breathing apparatus.
Selter	mineral water, Seltzer water.
Sendestation	transmitting station (*wireless, &c.*).
Senkloch	drain, sump pit.
Senkrecht	vertical, perpendicular.
Senkschacht	vertical shaft.
Senkung	depression (*topography*).
Sergeant	senior "Unteroffizier."
Sergeantenknopf	*button (large) worn on collar as badge of rank for serjeant-majors, &c.*
Setzwage	field level (*mining*).
Seuchenlazarett	hospital for infectious diseases.
Sichergestellung	detailing (*of a man*).
Sicherheitsbesatzung	emergency garrison.
Sicherheitsdienst	service of protection.
Sichern / Sicherstellen	to cover, protect; place at "safe" (*of a rifle*).
Sicherung	protection, covering party; safety catch (*on rifle*).
Sicherungsband	safety band (*of a grenade*).
Sicherungsfeder	safety spring.

Sicherungsflügel	protective flank.
Sicherungsklinke	safety catch (*breech action of light field howitzer*).
Sicherungslinie	switch line.
Sicherungsriegel	switch trench.
Sichtzeichen	ground signal (*for signalling to aeroplanes*).
Sieb	sieve ; gauze.
Siebseite	gauze side (*of gas mask drum*).
Siegen	to be victorious.
Sielengeschirr	set of harness (*with breast-band instead of collar*).
Signalapparat	signalling apparatus.
Signalflagge	signalling flag.
Signalgeschoss	flare signal.
Signalgranate mit Leuchtstern	star shell.
Signalhupe	signal horn, syren.
Signallampe	signal lamp.
Signalmast	signal (*railway*).
Signalpatrone	light-signal cartridge.
Signalspruch	signal message.
Signaltrupp	signalling troop (*cavalry*).
Signalwerfer	signal-thrower.
Signalzeichen	ground signal (*for signalling to aeroplanes*).
Signatur	conventional sign (*topog.*).
Simulieren	to malinger.
Sitz	seat.
Sitzstufe	step (*of trench*).
Skizze	sketch.
S-Munition	*see " Munition."*
S. m. K.-Munition	armour-piercing ammunition (*rifle and machine gun*).
Sockel	pivot, pedestal.
Sockel-Flak	anti-aircraft gun on pivot mounting.
Socken	socks.
Sohlbreite, Sohlenbreite	width at bottom (*e.g., of a trench*).
Sohle	sole (*of trench, &c.*).
Soldat	soldier, private.
Soldbuch	pay book.
Sollstand und Iststand, Sollstärke und Iststärke	establishment and strength.
Sonderleitung	special circuit.
Sondiernadel	*iron rod, 3 ft. long, used when searching for land mines.*

Späher	scout.
Spähoffizier	scout officer.
Spähtrupps	special reporting detachments.
Spalte	split, crack; column (*of a tabular statement*).
Spange	clasp, buckle.
Spanische Reiter	"knife rests" (*wire entanglement*).
Spannen	to stretch, strain, bridge; to cock (*a rifle*).
Spannhaken	dog (*engineering*).
Spannkabel	stay (*of an aeroplane*).
Spannkette für den Unterschild	chain supporting lower shield (*of field gun*).
Spannschiene	brake bar (*field gun carriage*).
Spanntau	span lashing (*bridging*); spread (*aeroplane*).
Spannturm	cabane (*of an aeroplane*).
Spannung	tension, strain, anxiety, suspense; span.
Spannweite	span (*bridging*).
Spaten	spade.
S–Patrone	see "S–Munition" under *Munition*.
Speiche	spoke (*of wheel*).
Speiseträger	food carrier.
Speiseträggestelle	ration carrier (*for use in heavy fighting*).
Sperre	barricade, block; blockade.
Sperrfall	case calling for barrage fire.
Sperrfeuer	barrage, barrage fire, curtain fire.
Sperrfeuer anfordern ...	to request barrage fire.
Sperrfeuer ausführen ...	to form a barrage.
Sperrfeuer auslösen ...	to employ barrage fire, form a barrage, open barrage fire.
Sperrfeuer einsetzen ...	to begin, open barrage fire.
Sperrfeuer einstellen ...	to cease barrage fire.
Sperrfeuer verstärken ...	to intensify barrage fire.
Sperrfeuerposten	barrage sentry.
Sperrfeuerraum	barrage area.
Sperrfeuersignal	signal for barrage fire.
Sperrfeuerskizze	barrage sketch plan (*sketch showing the arrangements for barrage fire*).
Sperrfeuerstreifen	barrage lane.
Sperrfeuerzeichen	signal for barrage, barrage signal.
Sperrflieger	aeroplane on line patrol.
Sperrseil	rope barrier.
Sperrstück	stop.
Sperrtrupp	**blocking party.**

Sperrung	barricade, blocking.
Spiegel	mirror, *sometimes* periscope; bull's-eye.
Spiegelapparat	periscope.
Spiegelbeobachtung	observation by periscope.
Spielmann	bandsman, musician.
Spielleute	bandsmen.
Spieren	rigging (*of aeroplane*).
Spindel	pinion.
Spion	spy.
Spionage-Dienst	espionage service.
Spitze	face, head of a gallery (*mining*); point (*cavalry or advanced guard*); spike (*of helmet*).
Spitzenfahrer	lead driver (*artillery*).
Spitzenkompagnie	point company.
Splitter	splinter.
Splittermunition	ammunition designed for splinter effect.
Splittersicher	splinter-proof.
Splitterwirkung	splinter effect, fragmentation.
Splitzmaschine	cutting machine.
Sporn	spur; spade (*on trail of gun*).
Spornrädchen	rowel (*of spur*).
Sprachkundiger	linguist.
Sprachrohr	speaking tube.
Sprechtrichter	mouthpiece of transmitter (*telephone*).
Spreize	strut (*mining*).
Sprengbuch	register of mine explosions (*mining*).
Sprengen	to blow up, fire a charge, to "blow" (*mining*).
Sprengfertig	ready for firing (*of a mine*).
Sprenggas	explosive gas.
Sprenggehe	radius of disturbance (*mining*).
Sprenggranate	high explosive (H.E.) shell.
Sprengherd	centre of disturbance caused by explosion of a mine.
Sprenghöhe	height of burst (*of a shell*).
Sprengkammer	mine chamber.
Sprengkapsel	detonator.
Sprengkommando	demolition detachment.
Sprengkörper	slab of explosive.
Sprengladung Sprengmasse	} explosive charge.

Sprengmine	Minenwerfer H.E. shell.
ganze schwere Sprengmine	full-sized heavy *Minenwerfer* H.E. shell.
halbe schwere Sprengmine	half-sized heavy *Minenwerfer* H.E. shell.
viertel schwere Sprengmine	quarter-sized heavy *Minenwerfer* H.E. shell.
leichte Sprengmine	light *Minenwerfer* H.E. shell.
mittlere Sprengmine	medium *Minenwerfer* H.E. shell.
Sprengmittel	explosives (*including detonators*).
Sprengmunition	regulation explosive.
Sprengöl	nitro-glycerine.
Sprengpatrone	explosive charge.
Sprengpulver	blasting powder.
Sprengpunkt	burst (*of a shell*).
Sprengstoff	explosive.
Sprengstoffgehalt	bursting charge.
Sprengstück	splinter.
Sprengtrichter	mine crater.
Sprengung	explosion, blow.
Sprengvorschrift	Demolition Manual.
Sprengweite	zone covered by the burst of a shell.
Sprengwirkung	explosive effect.
Springen	to jump, leap, spring.
Spritze	squirt, syringe; face (*mining*).
Spritzweite	spraying distance, range of spray (*of a " Flammenwerfer "*).
Spruch	sentence (*legal*).
Sprungweise	by rushes (*of an advance*).
Spule	coil.
Spur	track, trace.
Spurweite	gauge (*railway*).
Stab	Staff, headquarters.
Stabsapotheker	pharmacist officer (*ranking as captain*).
Stabsarzt	Captain (*medical*).
Stabshoboist	band-serjeant.
Stabshornist	serjeant-bugler.
Stabs-Nachrichten-Abteilung	headquarters signal detachment.
Stabsoffizier	field officer.
Stabsoffizier der Fliegertruppen (Stofl)	Staff Officer for Aviation (*at Army H.Q.*).
Stabsordonnanz	headquarters orderly.
Stabsquartier	Headquarters.
Stabstrompeter	serjeant-trumpeter.
Stabsveterinär	Captain (*veterinary*).
Stabswache	staff guard *or* escort.
Stacheldraht	barbed wire.

Stafette	despatch rider.
Staffel	échelon, wagon line (*artillery*).
Staffelförmig aufstellen / Staffeln	} to form up in several lines.
Staffelgebiet	back billeting area.
Staffelstab	divisional train échelon.
Staffelweise	in échelon.
Stahlblech	steel plate.
Stahlblende	steel loophole plate.
Stahlfutter	steel bush.
Stahlguss	cast steel.
Stahlhelm	steel helmet.
Stahlkartusche	steel cartridge case.
Stahlkerngeschoss	armour-piercing bullet.
Stahlmantel	steel jacket (*of a gun*).
Stahlmassband	steel tape.
Stahlrohrlanze	steel lance.
Staken	boat hook.
Stalldienst	stable duty.
Stallhalfter	head-rope.
Stallleine	picket line.
Stammrolle	register of recruits, nominal roll (*of a company, &c.*).
Stammrollenauszug	extract from the recruit register *or* nominal roll.
Stammrollenummer	serial number allotted to each man in a company.
Stand	occupation, profession; state, condition, class.
in Stand setzen	to repair.
ständig	permanent.
Standgericht	Regimental Court Martial (R.C.M.).
Standmotor	stationary engine (*of an aeroplane*).
Standort	position, place where an individual or unit is quartered.
Standortswechsel	change of position, change of garrison.
Standsack	hand grenade bag.
Stange	pole.
Stangenpferd	wheel horse, wheeler.
Stangenvisier	tangent sight.
Stapel	heap, pile, dump; stocks, slip (*shipbuilding*).
Stapelmaterial	dunnage.
Stapeln	to pile up, stack (*shell, cartridges, &c.*)
Stapelplatz	depôt, dump, dumping place.
Stärke	strength, forces.

Stärkeausweis	return of fighting strength.
Stärkebestand	actual strength.
Stärkenachweis	} list *or* statement showing strength
Stärkenachweisung	*or* establishment.
Stärkeverhältnis	comparative strength.
Starkstrom-Abteilung	electric power detachment.
Starkstromanlage	electric power installation.
Start	start (*of aeroplanes, &c.*).
Starten	to start (*aeroplane, &c.*).
Stationsanruf	} station call (*wireless*).
Stationsruf	
Stativ	stand, tripod (*for telescope or camera*).
Stauen (sich)	to stand fast, resist.
Steckhülse	projecting rod (*inserted in point of instantaneous fuzes*).
Steg	footpath, footbridge.
Stegladen	gangway.
Stehende Heer (Das)	the Standing Army.
Steigbügel	stirrup iron.
Steigfähigkeit	} lifting power, climbing capacity
Steigkraft	(*aeroplane*).
Steigriemen	stirrup leather.
Steigung	gradient.
Steilbahngeschütz	howitzer.
Steilfeuer	high-angle fire.
Steilfeuergeschütz	howitzer.
Steilhang	steep bank, declivity.
Steinbruch	quarry.
Steinschlag	shower of stones.
Steinschotterung	road-metalling.
Stelle	position.
auf der Stelle treten	to mark time.
Stellen	to place; to set (*a fuze*).
zur Verfügung stellen	to place at the disposal of.
Stellmacher	wheelwright.
Stellmacherkasten	box of wheelwright's tools.
Stellring	setting ring (*on time fuze*).
Stellschlüssel	fuze key.
Stellung	position; line; emplacement trenches.
erste, zweite Stellung	1st, 2nd line position.
offene	exposed or open position.
vorgeschobene	advanced position.
verdeckte Stellung	covered position.
Zwischenstellung	intermediate position.
Stellungsbau	field fortification, construction of defences.

Stellungsdivision	front line division, division in line.
Stellungskämpfe	} trench warfare, position warfare.
Stellungskrieg	
Stellungskriegsverwendungsfähig	fit for employment in trench warfare.
Stellungswechsel	change of position (*e.g., of a battery*).
Stellvertretend (-er, -e, -es)	acting *or* deputy.
Stellvertretender Chef des Generalstabes	Chief of the Acting General Staff (*in Germany during war*
Stellvertretendes General-Kommando	H.Q. of Army Corps District (*in Germany during war*).
Stempel	stamp; strut, prop.
Steuerung	steering gear (*airship*).
Steuerungseinrichtungen	controls (*of aeroplane*).
Stich	thrust.
im Stiche lassen	to leave in the lurch.
Stichprobe	inspection; a test made at random.
Stichwort	code word, pass word.
Stichwörterverzeichnis	code.
Stickoxyde	oxides of nitrogen.
Stickstoff	nitrogen.
Stiefelhose	pantaloons.
Stiel	handle; stay (*aeroplane*).
Stielhandgranate	cylindrical grenade with handle, stick grenade.
Still gestanden!	Attention!
Still sitzen!	Attention! (*cavalry*).
Stinkkammer	gas chamber (*for testing masks*).
Stinkpatrone	testing cartridge (*for gas masks*).
Stinkraum	gas chamber (*a room for testing gas masks*).
Stirnblech	front plate of trail (*of light field howitzer*).
Stirnrampe	end-on ramp.
Stirnwiderstand	head-resistance (*aeroplane*).
Stirnschutzschild	protection plate for forehead.
Stockung	check, block.
Stockwerksfeuer	tiers of fire.
Stoff	material, cloth.
Stollen	deep dug-out; gallery (*mining, &c., sometimes a main gallery with its branches*).
Abwehrstollen	defensive gallery.
einen Stollen bauen	to mine a gallery or dug-out.
flacher Stollen	shallow gallery.
Zweigstollen	branch gallery.

Stollenbaukommando	...	tunnelling party.
Stollenbaukompagnie...	...	tunnelling company.
Stollenbrust	...	face of a gallery (*mining*).
Stolleneingang	...	mineshaft, shaft incline.
Stollentreppe	...	shaft opening.
Stolperdraht ... Stolperdrahthindernis	}	trip-wire.
Stolperdrahtmine	...	trip-wire mine.
Stoppelfeld	...	stubble field.
Stoppen	...	cease fire !
Stoppuhr	...	stop watch.
Stöpsel	...	plug (*telephone*).
Stöpselloch	...	plug-hole (*telephone*).
Störung	...	hitch, stoppage, interruption, breakdown.
Störungsfeuer	...	harassing fire.
Störungstrupp	...	breakdown squad, linemen (*telephone, &c.*).
Stoss	...	attack, raid, thrust ; side wall (*mining*).
Stossbalken	...	butt plate (*for road bearers of bridge*).
Stossboden	...	breech block.
Stoss-Division	...	counter-attack division.
Stosskompagnie	...	counter-attack company.
Stosssicher	...	proof against shock.
Stosstaktik	...	shock tactics.
Stosstrupp	...	assault detachment.
Strafen	...	to punish.
eine Strafe aufheben	...	to cancel a punishment.
Straffeuer	...	retaliation fire.
Straffheit	...	strictness, strict discipline.
Strandbatterie	...	shore battery.
Strapazen	...	hardships, sufferings.
Strasse	...	road, high-road.
eingeschnittene Strasse	...	sunk road, road in a cutting.
Strassenbaukompagnie	...	road-making company.
Strassenkreuzung	...	cross roads.
Strassenlager	...	road side camp.
Strassensperre	...	barricade.
Strauchbündel	...	fascine.
Strauchwerk	...	brushwood (*in revetment, &c.*).
Strebe	...	strut (*mining*) ; strut, stay (*aeroplane*).
Streckbalken	...	road bearer (*bridging*).
Strecke	...	stretch, length (*of trench, &c.*) ; section (*of railway line*) ; gallery (*mining*) ; bay (*of pontoon bridge*).

Streckenarbeiter	platelayer.
Streckenbau	railway construction.
Streichen	to extend; to stroke, graze; to cancel.
Streifabteilung	raiding party.
Streifen	to graze; row, band, strip, sector, zone, lane.
Streifkommando	flying column; *sometimes* raiding party.
Streifkugel	grazing bullet.
Streifpatrouille	long distance patrol.
Streifschuss	graze, grazing shot.
Streifzug	raid.
Streu	straw litter.
Streuen	to open searching and sweeping fire.
Streufeuer	searching and sweeping fire (*artillery and machine gun*).
Streukegel	cone of dispersion.
Streuschiessen	searching and sweeping fire.
Streuung	dispersion, irregular shooting, searching and sweeping.
mit geringer Streuung	known to shoot accurately.
Seitenstreuung	lateral error.
Streuung des Geschützes	error of the gun.
Tiefenstreuung	error in range; vertical searching fire.
Streuungsbereich	zone of dispersion.
Streuungsfeuer	searching and sweeping fire (*artillery and machine gun*).
Streuungsgarbe	cone of dispersion, cone of fire
Streuungsverhältnisse	"the 50 per cent. zone."
Strich	stroke, graduation (*on sight, &c.*).
Strichplatte	graticuled field (*optical instruments*).
Strichschiessen	accurate shooting.
Strickleiter	storming ladder.
Strohkraftfutter	composite forage.
Strohsack	paillasse.
Strom	stream; electric current.
Stromkreis	} circuit (*electric*).
Stromlauf	
Stromlinienform	stream-line shape (*aeroplane, &c.*)
Stube	room, barrack room.
Stück	piece, gun.
Stufe	step.
Stuka (Sturm-Panzer-Kraftwagen-Abteilung)	tank detachment.
Stumpfwinklige Trichterladung	overcharged mine (*mining*).

Sturm	assault.
Sturm-Abteilung	assault detachment.
Sturmabwehr	repelling an assault.
Sturmabwehrgeschütz	gun for repelling an assault.
Sturmanlauf	rush, assault.
Sturmanzeichen	sign for an attack.
Sturmausgangsstellung	departure trench, jumping off trench.
Sturm-Bataillon	assault battalion.
Sturmgasse	gap *or* passage for the assault (*through wire, &c.*).
Sturmgepäck	assault kit.
Sturmgestell	assault mounting, light support (*i.e., for a machine gun during an attack*).
Sturmkolonne	assaulting column; raiding party.
Sturmlafette	assault *or* auxiliary mounting (*machine gun*).
Sturmleiter	storming ladder.
Sturmlücke	breach.
Sturmmarsch	quickened step for assault.
Sturmpanzerkraftwagen	armoured car, "tank."
Sturmreifmachen Sturmreifschiessen	to prepare for the assault, heavy bombardment immediately preceding an assault.
Sturmriemen	chin strap of steel helmet.
Sturmsignal	the "charge."
Sturmstellung	position from which an assault is made.
Sturm-Trupp	assault detachment.
Sturmvorbereitungsfeuer	preparatory bombardment.
Sturm steht bevor!	Enemy about to attack!
zum Sturm auf!	Charge!
Sturmwelle	line *or* wave of assault.
Sturzflug	nose dive (*aeroplane*).
Stute	mare.
Stütze	strut (*of an aeroplane*).
Stützpunkt	strong point; supporting point.
Stützpunktlinie	line of strong points.
Subaltern-Offiziere	subaltern officers.
Summen	to buzz.
Summer Summerapparat Summerbrett	buzzer (*telegraphy*).
Summertaster	buzzer-key.
Sumpf	marsh; sump (*mining*).
System	system; face (*mining*).

T.

Tafel	table; signalling panel.
Tagebau	cut and cover construction.
Tagebuch	order book; file of orders; diary.
Tagesanbruch	daybreak.
Tagesbefehl	Order of the Day.
Tageseinfluss	error of the day (*artillery*).
Tagesrate	ordinary daily allotment (*of gun ammunition*).
Tagwasser	surface water.
Täglicher Dienst	routine.
Talbegleitung	side of a valley; a road which follows a valley.
Talhänge	slopes of a valley.
Talmulde	basin shaped valley, hollow.
Talsohle	bottom of valley.
Tambour	drummer.
Bataillonstambour	battalion serjeant-drummer.
Tambourmajor	drum-major.
Tank	tank, reservoir; *sometimes "Tank," for which, however, the usual word is "Panzerkraftwagen" or "Sturmpanzerkraftwagen."*
Tankabwehrgeschütz	anti-tank gun.
Tankstelle	petrol depôt.
Taschenmunition	small arms ammunition in pouches.
Taster	key (*electricity*); feeler, antenna.
Tätigkeit	action, activity.
Taube	pigeon; "Taube" (*a make of aeroplane*).
Tauglich	fit for service.
Täuschungsangriff	feint attack.
Täuschungsfeuer Täuschungsschiessen	} feint bombardment.
Teile	elements, parties, details.
Teilkartusche	cartridge with adjustable charge (*e.g., howitzer cartridge*).
Teilkreis	graduated circle.
Teilstrich	unit of angular measurement or millième = $\frac{1}{6400}$ part of 360°, *i.e.*, 3·375 minutes (*for both field and foot artillery; formerly the unit for foot artillery was $\frac{1}{16}$ of a degree, i.e., 3·75 minutes*).
Teilstrichzahl	number of graduations.
Telefonstand	telephone station.
Telefonstelle	telephone station.

Telefontrupp (des Regiments)	(regimental) telephone squad.
Telegraphen-Abteilung ...	telegraph detachment.
Telegraphenstange	telegraph post.
Telegraphentruppen	telegraph troops.
Telegraphenwagen	telegraph wagon.
Tempo (Angriffs-)	pace of the attack.
Teppichhindernis	"Carpet" entanglement.
Termin	time at which a report, &c., should be handed in.
Tewumba (Telegraphen Waffen- und Munitions-Beschaffungsamt)	Telegraph Section of the Munitions Department of the War Ministry.
Theodolit	theodolite.
Tiefenfeuer	fire distributed in depth.
Tiefengliederung	distribution in depth.
Tiefenstreuung	vertical searching fire; error in range.
Tiefenstreuverfahren	searching fire.
Tiefgestaffelt	distributed in depth (*not "écheloned"*).
T-Munition	T-shell (*lachrymatory gas shell*).
Tischgeld	messing allowance.
Titular	brevet.
Tornister	knapsack, pack, valise.
Totschlage	club, life preserver.
Tracierband	tracing tape.
Tragbahre	stretcher.
Tragbalken	transom (*bridging*); beam.
Tragbar	portable.
Tragbare Station (Funken-) ...	portable (trench) wireless station.
Tragdeck	plane (*of aeroplane*).
oberes Tragdeck	upper *or* top plane.
unteres Tragdeck	lower *or* bottom plane.
Trage	stretcher.
Tragebaum	perch (*of ammunition wagon, &c.*).
Tragegestell	carrying apparatus (*e.g., for spherical hand grenades*).
Tragegurt	belt (*for carrying an infantry shield, &c.*).
Trageknüppel	support.
Träger	carrier, bearer; girder.
Trägerkommando	} carrying party.
Trägertrupp	
Tragetier	pack animal.
Tragfähigkeit	carrying capacity.
Tragfläche	plane (*of aeroplane*).
Tragvermögen, nutzbares ...	carrying capacity (*aeroplanes, &c.*); useful load.

Tragweite	range.
Train	Train (*not translated, corresponds to our A.S.C.*).
Traindepot	Train depôt.
Trainfahrer	driver of the Train.
Trainsoldat	private of the Train.
Tränenerregend	lachrymatory.
Tränenreiz	irritation of the eyes (*caused by lachrymatory shells*).
Tränke	watering place for horses.
Tränkeimer	water-bucket (*for horses*).
Tränken	to water (*horses, &c.*).
Transport	conveyance, transport; *sometimes* troop train.
Transportfähig	fit for transport, able to be evacuated (*wounded*).
Transportkommando	details to accompany wounded or prisoners.
Trasse	trace (*e.g., of a new trench*).
Trassierband	tracing tape.
Treibkraft	propelling power.
Treibladung	propelling charge.
Treibmaschine	propeller, motor.
Treibmine	floating mine.
Treibspiegel	base of cartridge case.
Treidelpferd	barge-horse.
Treffenweise	units disposed one in rear of the other.
Treffer	direct hit.
Trefferbild	plotting of the fall of shots.
Trefffähigkeit } Treffgenauigkeit	accuracy of fire.
Treffpunkt	point of impact.
Treffsicherheit	accuracy of fire.
Trense	snaffle.
Tresse	braid.
Treten	to tread.
Tretleuchtzeichen	flare alarm (*actuated by treading on a board*).
Tretmine	contact mine (*actuated by treading on it*).
Trichter	funnel; mine crater, shell hole, shell crater.
Trichterfeld } Trichtergelände	crater area.
Trichterladung, stumpfwinklige	overcharged mine (*mining*).

Trichterwirkung	crater effect.
Trigonometrisch	trigonometrical, by triangulation.
Trigonometrischer Punkt	trigonometrical point.
Trinkwasserbereiter	drinking water apparatus, water sterilizer.
Tritt	step.
Trittbrett	footboard (*railway*).
Trommelfeuer	intense *or* heavy bombardment.
Trompeter	trumpeter.
Tross	baggage, impedimenta of an army.
Trosswagen	baggage wagon.
Trümmer	ruins, débris.
Trupp	section, party, squad.
Truppe	regimental officers and men (*as compared with the staff*).
Truppen	troops.
Truppenbewegungen	troops on the move, troop movements.
Truppeneinteilung	distribution of troops, order of battle.
Truppenführer	commander.
Truppenkette	cordon.
Truppensammlung	concentration of troops.
Truppenteil	unit.
Truppenübungsplatz	training ground.
Truppenverband	formation.
Truppenverbandplatz	regimental aid post.
Truppenverpflegung	provisioning of troops.
Truppenverschiebungen	changes in the disposition of troops.
Truppenvorgesetzte	unit commanders, commanding officers.
Tschako	shako.
Tschapka	lancer cap.
T-Träger	T-girder.
Tuch	cloth, linen; cloth signal.
Tuchfühlung	close touch.
Tuchzeichen	cloth signal, ground signal (*for signalling to aeroplanes*).
Turm	tower, turret.
Turmhaubitze	howitzer in turret.
Turmkanone	gun in turret.
Turmlafette	turret mounting.
Turnübung	gymnastic exercise.
Tusche	Indian (Chinese) ink.
Typhus	typhoid (*not typhus*).

U.

Üben	to practise, train.
Überbank feuern	to fire over the parapet.
Überbleibsel	remainder.
Überbringen	to convey.
einen Befehl überbringen	to deliver an order.
Überbringer	bearer (*of order, &c.*).
Überbrücken	to bridge.
Überdeckung	cover.
Übereinstimmung (bringen in)	to synchronize (*watches*); agreement, accord, unanimity.
Überetatsmässig	surplus to establishment.
Überfall	raid, surprise attack.
Überflügeln	to outflank.
Überführung	crossing, passage over; bridge over the line (*railway*).
Übergabe	surrender, giving up.
Übergang	crossing, passage (*of a river*); level crossing (*railway*).
Übergangsstadium	state of transition.
Übergangsstation	transfer station (*on L. of C.*).
Übergehen	to change over to (*artillery fire*).
Überheben	to exceed an issue, to draw in excess of requirements.
Überläufer	deserter.
Überlegenheit	} superiority.
Übermacht	
Übernehmen	to take over (*e.g., a position*).
das Kommando übernehmen	to take command of.
die Verantwortung übernehmen	to assume responsibility for.
Überplanmässig	surplus, surplus to establishment.
Überrumpeln	to surprise.
Überrumpelung	"coup de main."
Überschauen	to overlook, survey.
Überschiessen	to fire over *or* beyond the target; to fire over.
Überschlagen	to upset, capsize.
Überschnallkoppel	belt worn outside the tunic.
Überschreiten	to cross, pass.
Überschrift	heading.
Überschütten	to overwhelm (*with fire, &c.*).
Überschwemmung	inundation.
Übersehen	to overlook, dominate; to omit.
Übersicht	survey, view.
Übersichtlich	clear.
Übersichtskarte	outline map.
Übersichtsskizze	general sketch of the neighbourhood.
Überspringen	to pass beyond.

Übersteigen	to surmount, cross, exceed.
Überstreichen	to pass over (*of a gas cloud*).
Überstürzen	to capsize.
Übertragen	to entrust, transfer.
Übertragung	gear (*on bicycle, car, &c.*).
Übertreten	to go over to; to come under (*the orders of*).
Übertretung	contravention, infringement.
Überwachungsballon	special observation balloon.
Überwachungsbatterie	battery in readiness to engage fleeting targets.
Überwachungsflieger	artillery patrol aeroplane.
Überweisung	allotment, transfer.
Überwiegend	predominating.
Überwinden	to conquer; to overcome (*an obstacle*).
Überzug	cover (*of helmet, &c.*).
Übung	training, practice, exercise.
Übungsgraben	practice trench.
Übungsgranate	practice shell.
Übungshandgranate	dummy hand grenade.
Übungsladung	practice charge.
Übungsmaske	practice mask (*gas*).
Übungsmunition	practice ammunition.
Übungsplatz	training ground.
Übungsreise	staff tour, staff ride.
Übungswerk	practice work.
Uferbalken	shore transom (*bridging*).
Uferhang	sloping bank (*of river, &c.*).
Ulan	Ulan (*lancer*).
Ulanen-Regiment	" Ulanen " regiment (*lancer regiment*).
Ulanka	lancer tunic.
Umbau (in)	in course of reconstruction.
Umbetten	to " slew " (*e.g., a trench mortar*); to re-inter.
Umdruck	copies for distribution (*orders, &c.*).
Umfang	circumference; extent.
Umfassen	to outflank.
Umfassungsbewegung	outflanking movement.
Umfüllpumpe	compression pump.
Umgang	détour; breeching (*harness*).
Umgeändert / Umgearbeitet	converted (*shells, &c.*); corrected.
Umgehängt	slung.
Umgehen	to turn (*a position*), envelop; to make a détour.
Umgehend	by return.
Umgehungsbewegung	turning movement.

Umhang	cape.
Umhängen	to take up packs.
Umlagerung	removal (*of ammunition, &c.*).
Umlauf, in	to be circulated (*often found at foot of orders*).
Umlaufmotor	rotary engine.
Umquartieren	to change quarters.
Umsatteln	to shift saddles.
Umschnallen	to put on (*equipment*), buckle on.
Umschreiben	to paraphrase, transliterate.
Umsicht	caution, discretion, wariness.
Umstand	circumstance.
Umstehend	as stated overleaf.
Umtausch	turnover (*of stores*).
Umzug	move, change of quarters.
Unabkömmlich	indispensable.
Unausgebildet	untrained.
Ungezieltes Feuer	unaimed fire.
Ungestaffelt	without stagger (*of aeroplanes*).
Uniform	uniform.
Uniform, dunkelblaue	"dark blue" uniform (*as opposed to "field service"*).
Uniform, feldgraue	field-grey field service uniform.
Uniform, graugrüne	grey-green field service uniform.
Uniformstück	article of uniform.
Unklare Elemente	suspects.
Unnachsichtig	relentless(ly), severe(ly).
Unschädlich machen	to render harmless (*of a hand grenade or shell*); to put out of action.
Untauglich	unfit.
dauernd untauglich	permanently unfit.
Unterabschnitt	sub-sector.
Unterabschnittskommandeur	sub-sector commander.
Unterarzt	*medical student ranking as warrant officer.*
Unterbinden	to stop, to neutralize (*an attack*).
Unterbleiben	to remain undone.
Unterbringen	to billet, accommodate, station.
Unterbringung	billeting; storage (*of ammunition, &c.*).
Unterführer	subordinate commander.
Unterführung	passage underneath, bridge below the line (*railway*).
Untergebener	subordinate.
Untergeordneter	
Untergestell	pivot.
Untergruppe	sub-group.
Untergurt	girth.

Unterhalten	to entertain ; to sustain, maintain.
ein heftiges Feuer unterhalten	to keep up a heavy fire.
Unterholz	undergrowth.
Unterkommandeur	subordinate commander.
Unterkunft	billet, accommodation.
Unterkunftslager	rest camp.
Unterlage(n)	basis, data ; support.
Unterlassen	cancelling (*of an attack*).
Unterliegen	to succumb, suffer defeat.
Unternehmen	to undertake.
Unternehmen ... ... Unternehmung ...	} enterprise, operation.
Unteroffizier	non-commissioned officer *also " under-officer " which is a special rank of N.C.O corresponding to our corporal.*
Unterricht	instruction.
Unterrichts-	instructional.
Unterschild	lower shield (*of gun carriage*).
Unterschlupf	shelter, " funk hole," recess (*under parapet*).
Unterschrieben	signed.
Unterschrift	signature.
Unterstand	dug-out, shelter.
Minierter Unterstand ...	mined dug-out.
Unterstandstreppe	steps leading down to a dug-out.
Unterstehen	to be subordinate to.
Unterstellen	to place under the orders of.
Unterstützen	to support.
Unterstützung...	support, assistance.
Unterstützungsgraben ...	support trench.
zur Unterstützung der Posten	to reinforce the sentries.
Unterstützungstruppen ...	reinforcements.
Untersuchen	to inquire, examine, test, inspect.
Untertreteraum	dug-out.
Unterveterinär	sub-veterinary surgeon (*warrant officer*).
Unterwasserschneide-Abteilung	river detachment.
Unverletzlichkeit	inviolability, immunity.
Unversehrt	intact, undamaged.
Urlaub	leave.
Urlauber	man on leave.
Urlaubsschein	pass *or* furlough.
Urlaubsüberschreitung ...	overstaying leave.
Urlauberzug	leave train.
Urschrift	original document.
Urteil	judgment, sentence of court-martial.

V.

Vauwumba (Waffen- und Munitions-Beschaffungsamt Verwaltung)	Munitions Department Administration.
Vedette	vedette.
Ventil	valve.
Verankerung	holding down; anchorage, mooring.
Veranlagung, körperliche	physique.
Verantwortung	responsibility.
Verästelung	shower (*of sparks from rocket*).
Verband	formation; surgical dressing.
Verbandabteilung	minor dressings section (*of main dressing station*).
Verbandpäckchen	first field dressing.
Verbandplatz	
Verbandraum	} dressing station, first-aid post.
Verbandstelle	
Verbandzeug	surgical bandage, dressing material.
Verbandzeugtornister	surgical haversack.
Verbindung	communication, connection, liaison.
Verbindungsbahn	junction railway.
Verbindungsdienst	communication, liaison service *or* duty.
Verbindungsgalerie	transversal gallery (*mining*).
Verbindungsgraben	communication trench.
Verbindungs-Offizier	liaison officer.
Verbindungsstollen	} transversal gallery (*mining*).
Verbindungsstrecke	
Verbindungsstrecke	junction; connecting line.
Verblenden	to screen lights; to camouflage.
Verbolzen	to bolt together.
Verbrauch	consumption, expenditure (*e.g., of ammunition*).
Verbrechen	crime.
Verbringen	to dispose of.
Verbummeln	to lose by carelessness; to forget; to loiter.
Verbündeten (die)	the Allies.
Verdämmen	to tamp (*mining*).
Verdeck	deck; hood.
Verdecken	to mask (*fire*).
Verdienstorden	Meritorious Service Order.
Vereinbarung	co-operation, arrangement, agreement.
Vereinslazarett	auxiliary hospital.
Verfahren	procedure, method, system, action.
Verfeuern	to fire off, fire away.
Verfolgen	to pursue.

Verfügbar	available.
Verfügen über	to have at one's disposal.
Verfügungen	instructions.
zur Verfügung	available.
zur Verfügung stellen	to place at the disposal of.
Verfügungstruppen	reserves, troops remaining at disposal.
Vergasen	to gas; to bombard with gas shell.
Vergaser	carburettor.
Vergehen	offence (minor).
Vergeltungsfeuer	retaliatory fire.
Vergossen	grouted (*with cement*).
Vergütung	compensation.
Verhalten	behaviour, action, procedure.
Verhältnis	circumstance; proportion, relation.
Verhandlung	negotiation; trial.
Verhau	abatis.
Verheeren	to ravage, devastate.
Verheimlichen	to conceal.
Verhör	cross-examination.
Verhören	to examine (*prisoners*).
Verkehr	traffic, communication.
Verkehrsamt	transportation traffic office (*railway*).
Verkehrsgraben	supervision *or* lateral communication trench.
Verkehrsmittel	means of transport.
Verkehrsoffizier vom Platz	fortress communication officer.
Verkehrstruppen	communication troops.
Verkehrswesen	Communication Service.
Verkleiden	to disguise, mask; to revet.
Verkleidung	revetment.
Verladeort	place of entrainment.
Verladerampe	entraining platform *or* siding.
Verladestelle	entraining point.
Verlade-Kommando	loading detachment (*at docks, etc.*).
Verlauf	course, development; trace (*of a trench*).
Verläufer	straggler.
Verlautbaren	to proclaim.
Verlegen	to transfer.
Feuer rückwärts verlegen	to shorten range.
Feuer vorwärts verlegen	to lengthen range.
Verlegung	relaying (*of a telephone circuit*).
Verletzung	injury.
Verletzungsliste	casualty list.
Verluste	losses, casualties.
Verlustliste	casualty list.
Vermessung	survey.
Vermessungs-Abteilung	survey section.

Vermisste	missing, stragglers.
Vermittlung Vermittelung	} telephone exchange ; intervention.
Vermittlungsstation	transmitting station (*telegraph &c.*).
Vermorel-Apparat	Vermorel sprayer.
Vernehmung	examination (*e.g., of prisoners*).
Vernehmungsoffizier	intelligence officer at Corps H.Q. (*for the examination of prisoners*).
Vernichtung	annihilation, destruction.
Vernichtungsfeuer	annihilating fire.
Vernichtungstrupp	" mopping up " party.
Vernickelt	nickel-plated.
Verordnungsblatt (Armee-)	Army Orders.
Verpassen	to test; to adjust (*e.g., a gas mask*).
Verpassungsraum	gas testing chamber.
Verpflegung	supply (*food*), rationing.
Vorbringen der Verpflegung	carrying up rations.
Konserven-Verpflegung	tinned rations.
Verpflegungsabteilung	supply section of the Intendance.
Verpflegungsgebühr	scale of rations.
Verpflegungskolonne	supply column.
Verpflegungsmittel	rations.
Verpflegungsnachschub	supply of rations, bringing up rations.
Verpflegungs-Offizier	supply officer.
Verpflegungsstärke	ration strength.
Verpflegungstruppen	supply troops.
Verpflegungszug	supply train (*railway*).
Verproviantieren (eine Festung)	to provision (a fortress).
Verraten (eine Stellung)	to disclose (a position); to betray.
Verriegelung	barricade of timber used in tamping (*mining*).
Versagen	to miss fire; to break down.
Versager	a misfire, " blind " (*shell*).
Versammlungsformation	assembly formation.
Versammlungsgraben	assembly trench.
Verschalbretter	boards for revetting.
Verschalung	revetting.
Verschanzung	entrenchment.
Verschanzung aufwerfen	to throw up an entrenchment.
Verschieben	to move (*troops, &c.*).
Verschiessen	to fire away, expend (*ammunition*).
Verschleierung	masking, concealment, screen.
Verschluss	breech (*of gun or rifle*).
unter Verschluss	under lock and key.
Verschlussbolzen	locking bolt (*breech mechanism of field gun*).
Verschlusshebel	crank handle (*machine gun*).
Verschlusskappe	cap of fuze.
Verschlusskeil	breech block, wedge.

Verschlusskurbel	... ...	crank of breech (*Krupp guns*).
Verschlussschraube	... ...	locking screw (*of breech of gun*).
Verschlussstück	... ...	breech block.
Verschlussteile	... ...	breech fittings.
Verschlussüberzug	... ...	breech cover.
Verschmelzung	... ...	amalgamation.
Verschütten	... ...	bury alive; to block up (*e.g., with earth*).
Gräben werden leicht verschüttet		trenches soon fall in.
Verschüttung	... ...	collapse (*of a dug-out*).
Verschüttet	... ...	buried.
Versetzung	... ...	transfer.
Verspreizung	... ...	strutting (*mining, &c.*).
Versprenger	... ...	straggler.
Verständigung	... ...	hearing signals (*on telephone, &c.*).
Ist Verständigung gut?	...	Are signals good? (*on telephone, &c.*).
Verstärken	... ...	to strengthen, reinforce.
Verstärkung	... ...	reinforcement.
Versteifern	... ...	to strut (*mining, &c.*).
Verstreben	... ...	to brace (*e.g., the frames of a dug-out*).
Versuch	... ...	experiment, trial, test.
Versuchsanstalt	... ...	experimental laboratory *or* institute.
Verteidigen	... ...	to defend.
Verteidigungsanlagen	... ...	defences, defence works.
Verteidigungsfähig	... ...	capable of defence.
Verteidigungsstellung	...	defensive position.
Verteilung	... ...	distribution.
Verteilungstafel	... ...	switchboard (*on to which the leads for testing and firing mines are brought*).
Vertragsmacht	... ...	treaty power.
Vertretung (in)	... ...	"By order," "Signed for" (*above a signature on a document*).
Vervielfältigen	... ...	to reproduce (*e.g., by printing, hectograph, &c.*).
Vervollständigen	... ...	to complete (*entries, &c., on forms*).
Verwaltung	... ...	administration.
Armeeverwaltungs-Departement		Army Administrative Department.
Feldverwaltungs-Behörden		field administrative authorities.
Verwaltungsbeamte	... ...	administrative official.
Verwaltungsbehörden	...	administrative authorities.
Verweis	... ...	reprimand.
Verwenden	... ...	to use, employ, make use of.
Verwindung	... ...	warp (*wing of aeroplane*).
Verzeichnis	... ...	list.

Verzögerung	... ...	delay, delay action.
Veterinär	... ...	Second-lieutenant
Generalveterinär	... ...	Colonel
Korpsstabsveterinär		Major
Oberstabsveterinär		brevet Major
Stabsveterinär	... ...	Captain
Oberveterinär	... ...	Lieutenant

} *(veterinary)*.

Vieleck	... ...	polygon.
Viereck	... ...	quadrangle, square, rectangle.
Vierkantholz	... ...	squared timber.
Vierzöllig	... ...	4-inch.
Visier ...	... ...	sight (*of rifle*), *especially* back sight.
Visier einstellen	...	to adjust a sight.
Visieraufsatzstange	...	leaf of back sight.
Visierfernrohr ...	... ...	telescopic sight.
Visierklappe ...	... ...	flap (*covering loophole in shield of field gun*); leaf of backsight (*rifle*).
Visierschiebe ...	... ...	slide on back sight.
Visierwinkel ...	... ...	angle of elevation (*rifle*).
Vizefeldwebel ...	... ...	vice-serjeant-major.
Vizewachtmeister ...	...	vice-serjeant-major (*mounted troops*).
Vogelperspektive	...	} bird's eye view.
Vogelschau	... ...	
Völkerrecht	... ...	law of nations.
Vollbahn	... ...	standard gauge railway.
Voll-Geschoss ...	... ...	shot, as opposed to shell (*artillery*).
Vollkriegsfähig	... ...	fit for active service.
Vollsalve	... ...	complete salvo.
Vollspurbahn ...	... ...	standard gauge railway.
Vollstrecken ...	... ...	to carry out (*a punishment*).
Volltreffer	... ...	direct hit.
Vollzählig	... ...	in full strength.
Vollzug	... ...	execution of orders.
Vollzugsmeldung	... ...	report of execution of orders.
Vorbereitung ...	... ...	preparation.
Vorbereitungsfeuer ...	...	preparatory bombardment.
Vorbohrer	... ...	rimer.
Vorbringen (der Verpflegung)		carrying up (rations).
Vorderbracke	... ...	swingle-tree.
Vorderkaffe	... ...	bow (*of a pontoon*).
Vorderlader	... ...	muzzle loader.
Vordermann	... ...	front rank man.
Vorderpferd	... ...	lead horse.
Vorderwagen ...	... ...	limber.
Vordringen	... ...	to advance, press forward.
Vorfühlen	... ...	to endeavour to establish contact; to feel one's way forward.

Vorführen	to bring up, lead forward.
Vorgehen	to advance.
Vorgelände	foreground, " No man's land."
Vorgesetzter	superior.
Vorhanden	existing, available.
Vorholfedern	running out springs (*gun*).
Vorhut	advanced guard.
Vorkommando	advance party.
Vorlage	proposal; text; flash reducer (*gun ammunition*).
Vorlaufgraben	" up " trench.
Vorlegen (Feuer)	to lengthen range.
Vormarsch	advance.
Vornewand	face (*of a mine*).
Vorposten	outpost.
Vorposten ausstellen	to throw out outposts.
Vorpostengefecht	affair of outposts.
Vorpostenkette	chain of sentries.
Vorpostenkommandeur	outpost commander.
Vorpostenkompagnie	outpost company.
Vorpostenlinie	outpost line.
Vorrat	supply; spare (*in distribution of orders, &c.*).
Vorratspferd	spare horse.
Vorratswagen	store wagon.
Vorraum (eines Unterstandes)	anteroom (to a dug-out).
Vorrichtung	device, arrangement, mechanism.
Vorschieben	to push forward, advance.
Vorschrift	regulations.
Vorschub	help, assistance.
Vorschub leisten	to afford assistance, lend a hand.
Vorsprung	salient.
Vorstand	directorate, managing committee.
Vorstecker	safety pin (*of fuze*).
Vorstellung	advanced position.
Vorstoss	attack, raid, thrust; piping, edging (*uniform*).
Vortrab	vanguard.
Vortreiben	to run out, drive (*a gallery*) (*mining, &c.*).
Vortrupp	vanguard.
Vortruppen	advanced troops.
Vorverlegen	to " lift " (*artillery fire*).
Vorwärts	forward.
Vorwerk	advanced work; farm; manor (" Vw." *on a military map*).
Vorziehen	to move up; to give preference to.

W.

Wache	guard, sentry.
Wachhabender	officer (N.C.O.) of the guard.
Wachposten	sentry.
Wachstuchmütze	waterproof cap (*worn by Landwehr*).
Wachtdienst	guard duty.
Wachthabender	officer (N.C.O.) of the guard.
Wachtmeister	serjeant-major (*of cavalry or field artillery*).
Wachtturm	watch tower (*topog.*).
Wadenbinde	puttee, legging.
Waffe	weapon, arm.
Waffen- und Munitions-Beschaffungsamt	Munitions Department of the War Ministry.
Waffengattung	arm of the service.
Waffenhaus	arsenal.
Waffenmeister	armourer serjeant; artificer.
Waffenmeisterkasten	artificer's tool chest.
Waffenmittelwagen	travelling repair shop.
Waffenrock	tunic.
Waffenruhe }{ Waffenstillstand	armistice.
Waffensammeloffizier	salvage officer.
Waffensammelstelle	salvage depôt.
Wagenburg	barricade of wagons.
Wagenfähre	ferry for wagons.
Wagengerassel	the rattling of carts or wagons.
Wagenhalteplatz	halting place for (ambulance) vehicles.
Wagenplan	awning, tarpaulin, cover, hood (*of a cart*).
Wagenstaffel	wagon line.
Wagenstütze	prop (*of ammunition wagon, &c.*).
Wagenunterverteilungsstelle	rolling stock distribution centre.
Wagerecht	horizontal.
Wahrnehmung	observation.
Waldstück	small wood.
Wall	rampart.
Wallgraben	moat, ditch of rampart.
Wallmeister	staff serjeant of fortifications.
Wallspiegel	trench periscope.
Walzblech	rolled iron plate.
Walzblei	sheet lead.
Walze (Draht-)	roller, cylinder (*e.g., of wire*).
Walzeisen	rolled iron.

Walzen	to roll, roll out.
Wand	wall.
Wandergeschütz	roving gun, mobile gun (*applied to A.A. gun*).
Wappen	armorial bearings.
Wassereimer	water bucket.
Wasserflugzeug	hydroplane, seaplane.
Wassergraben	drainage channel (*mining, &c.*).
Wasserkasten	water tin (*in which water to refill the barrel casing of a machine gun is carried*).
Wasserkessel	
Wasserleitung	water supply, aqueduct.
Wasserleitungsröhre	water pipe, conduit pipe.
Wässern	to irrigate.
Wassersack	canvas bucket.
Wasserschaufel	water scoop (*pontoon*).
Wasserstoff	hydrogen.
Wassertragesack	canvas water bucket.
Wasserversorgung	supply of water, water supply.
Wasserwage	water-level.
Wasserzapfstelle	stand pipe.
Wechselgetrieb	variable gear.
Wechselstand	alternative position (*machine gun*).
Wechselstellung	alternative emplacement.
Wechselstrom	alternating current (*electrical*).
Weckerapparat	magneto-ringing apparatus (*telephone*).
Weg	road, way, track.
Wegbündel	cross roads.
Wegeführer	guide (*e.g. in the trenches*).
Wegekarte	route map.
Wegekreuz	road junction, cross roads.
Wegekreuzung	
Weggabel	road fork, fork in the road.
Wegnetz	system of roads.
Wegsamkeit	practicability (*of a road*).
Wegverlegen	to " lift " (*artillery fire*).
Wegweiser	finger post, signboard.
Wehrmann	" Landwehrmann ", Landwehrman.
Wehrordnung	regulations dealing with conscription laws.
Wehrpflicht	liability for service.
Weiche	points (*railway*).
Weichen	to yield, give way, give ground.
Weissblech	tin plate.
Weisung	instructions.

Weit	"over" (*artillery*).
Weiterleitung	circulation (*of orders*).
Weiterleitungsstelle	forwarding office (*e.g., of Army Clothing Depôt*).
Wellblech	corrugated iron.
Wellblechdecke	corrugated iron cover.
Wellblechfeld	corrugated iron sheet.
Wellblechrahmen	corrugated iron section.
Wellblechschalung	corrugated iron lining.
Wellblechtafel	sheet of corrugated iron.
Welle	wave; shaft (*e.g., of propeller*).
Wellenlänge	wave length (*wireless, &c.*).
Wendeplatz	turntable, place for turning vehicles.
Wendepunkt	critical moment, turning point.
Wendesappe	wavy sap.
Wendung	turn.
Werfer	"thrower" (*bomber*).
Werfer	sometimes used for "*Minenwerfer*."
Werferführer	N.C.O. in charge of trench mortar.
Werferstand	trench mortar emplacement.
Werftkompagnie	aircraft repair company (*of training squadron*).
Werk	work, redoubt.
Werkstatt } Werkstelle }	workshop.
Werkzeugkasten	tool chest.
Werkzeugtasche	tool wallet.
Werkzeugwagen	tool wagon.
Wetter	weather.
unsichtiges Wetter	misty, hazy, weather.
Wetterbeobachtung	meteorological observation.
Wetterbericht	meteorological report.
Wetterdienst	meteorological service.
Wetterlage	weather conditions.
Wetterlotte	air pipe (*mining*).
Wewa (A.L.), Wetterwarte (am Luftschiffhafen)	meteorological station (at airship base).
Wickelgamasche	puttee.
Widerstand	resistance; electrical resistance.
Widerstandsfähig	capable of resistance.
Widerstandskraft } Widerstandsvermögen }	defensive power, resisting power.
Widerstreben	to oppose, resist.
Wiederherstellen	to repair.
Wiege	cradle (*e.g., of a gun carriage*).
Wiegenkappe	cradle cap (*gun carriage*).

Wimpel	streamer, pennant.
Windewagen	winch wagon (*balloon section*).
Windfächer	fan.
Windfähnchen	weather cock.
Windfahne	anemoscope (*flag*).
Windmesser	anemometer, wind gauge.
Windrosendarstellung	wind-compass card.
Windsbraut	gust of wind, squall.
Windschirm	wind screen.
Windstärkemesser	anemometer.
Windstoss	gust of wind.
Winkel	angle.
ausspringender Winkel	salient.
einspringender Winkel	re-entrant.
toter Winkel	dead ground.
vorspringender Winkel vorstehender Winkel	} salient.
Winkeleisen	angle iron.
Winkelfernrohr	periscope.
Winkelmesser	clinometer, goniometer.
Winker	flag signaller.
Winkerflagge	signalling flag.
Winkerstelle	flag signalling station.
Winkertrupp	flag signalling group (*all arms*).
Winkerverbindung	flag signalling communication.
Winkerzeichen	flag signal.
Wirksamkeit	efficacy.
Wirkung	effect.
Wirkungsbereich	effective range, sphere of operations.
Wirkungsfeuer	fire for effect.
Wirkungshalbmesser	radius of explosion (*mining*).
Wirkungsschiessen	effective bombardment, fire for effect.
Wirtschaftskompagnie	tradesman *or* works company.
Wischen	to wipe.
Wischer	pull-through (*rifle*); sponge (*gun*).
Wischfalte	cleaning fold (*of German gas mask*).
Wischstrick	pull-through (*rifle*).
Wohngraben	living trench.
Wohnunterstand	living dug-out.
Woilach	saddle blanket.
Wölbung	camber (*of wing of aeroplane*).
Wolfsgrube	"trou de loup."
Wortlaut	text of a message.
Wucht	weight (*of an attack*).
Wumba (Waffen- und Munitions-Beschaffungs-Amt)	Munitions Department of the War Ministry.

Wundtäfelchen	diagnosis tally (*on which the M.O. writes his diagnosis of the wound, &c.*).
Wurffeuer	trench mortar fire.
Wurfgeschwindigkeit ...	rate of fire.
Wurfgranate	trench mortar bomb (*fired from "Granatwerfer"*).
Wurfladung	propelling charge.
Wurfladung (Ladungsmine) ...	canister bomb.
Wurflinie	trajectory.
Wurfmine	*Minenwerfer* H.E. shell (*the modern term is "Sprengmine," q.v.*)
lange schwere (l.s.W.M.) ...	25 cm. heavy *Minenwerfer* (long H.E. shell).
kurze schwere (k.s.W.M.) ...	25 cm. heavy *Minenwerfer* (short H.E. shell).
mittlere gezogene (m.gez. W.M.)	17 cm. medium rifled *Minenwerfer* (H.E. shell).
mittlere glatte (m.gl.W.M.)	(?) 17 cm. medium smooth bore *Minenwerfer* (H.E. shell).
leichte gezogene (l.gez.W.M.)	7.5 cm. light rifled *Minenwerfer* (H.E. shell).
glatte leichte (Lanz) (gl.l. W.M. Lanz)	9.1 cm. light smooth bore Lanz *Minenwerfer* (H.E. shell).
Wurfweite	length of throw.

Z.

Zähigkeit	tenacity, obstinacy.
Zahl und Art	quantity and nature.
Zahlmeister	paymaster.
Zahnbogen	toothed arc (*elevating gear of gun*).
Zahnrad	cogged wheel.
Zange	pincers, tongs.
Zapfen	trunnions (*of gun*), pin, plug, pivot.
Zapfenlager	trunnion bed (*of gun*).
Zapfenstreich	tattoo, " retreat."
Zaum	bridle.
Zaumzeug	headgear.
Zaun	fence.
Zeche	pit-head (*of coal mine, etc.*).
Zeichen	sign, signal, distinguishing mark; conventional sign.
Zeichen-Erklärung	list of conventional signs; "reference."
Zeichenverbindung	communication by visual signals.
Zeichner	draughtsman.
Zeigefinger	index finger.
Zeiger	index, indicator; hand of a clock.
Zeit	time, period.
A-Zeit	period in front line.
B-Zeit	period in support.
C-Zeit	period in rest.
Nullzeit	zero time.
Zeitangabe	statement of date.
Zeiteinteilung	time table.
Zeitschnur	safety fuze.
Zeitweilig	intermittent.
Zelt	tent.
Zelt aufschlagen	to pitch a tent.
Zeltausrüstung	tent equipment.
Zeltbahn	tent square.
Zeltpflock	tent peg.
Zeltstange	tent pole.
Zementmörtel	cement mortar.
Zementsack	cement sack.
Zentner	$\frac{1}{2}$ quintal = 50 kg. = 110.23 lbs.
Zentral	central.
Zentrale	central, telephone exchange.
Zentralnachweisebureau	Central Information Bureau.
Zentrierwulst	shoulder of a shell.
Zermürben	to crush.
Zernieren	to invest, besiege, blockade.
Zersplittern	to splinter, break to pieces; to disperse (*e.g., troops, fire, &c.*).

Zersprengen	to cut up, rout.
Zerstören	destroy, demolish, cut (*wire entanglement*).
Zerstörung	demolition.
Zerstörungsfeuer	destructive fire.
Zerstreuen	to scatter.
Zertrümmern	to wreck, break in pieces.
Zetwumba (Zentral Waffen- und Munitions - Beschaffungsamt	Central Munitions Department.
Zeug	*prefixed to rank = ordnance.*
Zeug	material.
Zeugamt	Ordnance Department.
Zeugdepot	ordnance depôt.
Zeuge	witness.
Zeughaus	arsenal, armoury.
Zeugoffizier	ordnance officer.
Zeugpersonal	ordnance corps.
Ziegelei	brick-field, tile works.
Ziegelstein	brick.
Ziehen	to draw, move.
Ziehen (auseinander)	to keep extended.
Ziel	objective; target, aim.
Zielabschnitt	target sector, sector to be taken under fire.
Zielbezeichnung	designation of targets.
Zielen	to aim.
Zielerkundung	reconnaissance of a target.
Zielfernrohr	telescopic sight.
Zielpunkt	objective; point aimed at.
Zielscheibe	target.
Zielskizze	range card.
Zielspiegel	periscope.
Zielstation	destination; railhead.
Zielstreifen	target sector.
Zieltafeln	target tables.
Zielwechsel	change of target.
Zielzuweisung	indication of targets.
Zierat	ornaments (*on helmet, &c.*).
Ziffer (Ziff.)	paragraph; cipher; numeral.
Zimmermann	carpenter.
Zinnfolie	tinfoil.
Zirka	about (*circa*).
Zivilarbeiterbataillon	civilian labourers' battalion.
Zivilbevölkerung	civil population.
Zivilkleidung (*or* Zivil)	plain clothes.
Zollbeamter	customs official.

Zone	sector, zone, area.
Zubehör	accessories.
Zubehörkasten	box containing accessories.
Zubereiten	to prepare (*e.g., food*).
Zubereiter	fitter.
Zucht	discipline; breeding (*horses, cattle*).
Züchten	to breed.
Zudecken	to cover up; to overwhelm (*with fire*).
Zufahrtsweg	track leading up to a position, approach.
Zufallstreffer	chance hit.
Zuflucht	refuge, shelter; recourse.
Zufuhr	the bringing up of supplies.
Zufuhr abschneiden	to cut off supplies.
Zufuhrstrasse	approach.
Zu Fuss (Garde-Regiment)	Foot (Guards).
Zug	platoon, section, cavalry troop (*of 3 or more "Groups"*); train; rifling (*of a gun*).
Zugang	admission to hospital, &c.; access, approach.
Zugangsgraben	} communication trench, approach trench.
Zugangsweg	
Zugbrücke	drawbridge.
Zügel	rein, bridle.
Zugeteilt	attached to, allotted to.
Zugführer	platoon (section) commander.
Zugkolonne	column of platoons.
Zugloch	ventilator.
Zugpferd	draught horse.
Zugsbereich	platoon sector.
Zugschraube	tractor (*aeroplane*).
Zugtau	drag rope.
Zugweise	by platoons.
Zulage	extra pay; allowance.
Zulegen	to add to.
50 Meter zulegen!	Plus 50 metres! Lengthen range 50 metres!
Zündbolzen	percussion pellet (*fuze*).
Zünder	fuze, detonator.
Aufschlagzünder	percussion fuze.
Brennzünder	time fuze.
Doppelzünder	time and percussion fuze.
Innenzünder	internal fuze.
Kopfzünder	nose fuze.
kurzer Bodenzünder	short base fuze.
langer Bodenzünder	long base fuze.

Zünder stellen	to set a fuze.
Zünderschlüssel	fuze key.
Zünderstellmaschine	automatic fuze setter.
Zünderteller	ring of a fuze.
Zündfertig	ready for firing.
Zündglocke (Amboss der)	detonator cap.
Zündhütchen	percussion cap.
Zündkapsel	detonator.
Zündkasten	exploder (*mining*).
Zündladung	exploder (*in a shell*).
Zündloch	vent.
Zündmittel	means of ignition (*fuzes, detonators, &c.*).
Zündröhre	fuze, friction tube.
Zündsatz	detonating composition.
Zündschnur	fuze, safety fuze; lanyard.
Zündung	fuze, primer *and* detonator; *also* the firing of a charge.
Zur Disposition (z. D.)	on half pay (*of officers*).
Zureicher	*carrier in a bombing squad, the man who hands the grenade to the thrower.*
Zurrbrücke	housing bracket (*gun carriage*).
Zurrgriff	handle of clamping gear for travelling (*light field howitzer*).
Zurückstellen	to "put back" (*men liable to military service*).
Zuruf	call, verbal message.
Zusammenarbeiten	co-operation; to co-operate.
Zusammenfassen	to concentrate.
Zusammensetzen (Gewehre)	to pile (arms).
Zusammensetzung	composition.
Zusammenstoss	collision.
Zusammentreffen	to meet, encounter.
Zusammentreten	to stand to.
Zusammentritt	assembly, parade.
Zusammenwirken	co-operation, to co-operate.
Zusammenziehen (Truppen)	to assemble, concentrate.
Zusatz	supplement.
Zusatzladung	super-charge, additional charge (*gun ammunition*).
Zuschuss	allowance.
Zusprechen	to adjudge.
Zuständige Stelle	the proper authority.
Zustellen	to transmit, deliver, convey.
Zurückgehen	to retreat, retire, fall back.
Zurückhaltung	reticence, reserve.

Zurücklaufen	to recoil (*gun*).
Zurückschlagen	to beat off, repulse.
Zurückweichen	to recoil, fall back.
Zuteilen	to attach; to allot to.
Zuteilung	allotment; attachment.
Zuverlässig	reliable.
Zuweisung	allotment.
Zuwiderhandlung	infringement, violation, contravention.
Zweck	objective, purpose, object.
Zweidecker	biplane.
Zweigstellung	switch line.
Zweigstollen	branch gallery (*mining*).
Zwickzange	tweezers.
Zwieback	biscuit.
Zwillingszüge	trains run in two portions.
Zwischendepot	intermediate dump *or* depôt.
Zwischengelände	intervening country *or* ground.
Zwischenlandeplatz	advanced landing ground (*aviation*).
Zwischenpark	intermediate park.
Zwischenpolster	intermediate cushion (*e.g.*, *of earth over a dug-out*).
Zwischenposten	intermediate posts (*on lamp signal line, &c.*).
Zwischenraum	interval.
in Zwischenräumen	intermittently (*artillery fire*).
Zwischenstellung	intermediate position.
Zwischenzeit	meantime.
Zwischenzeiten	pauses.
mit Zwischenzeiten	intermittently (*artillery fire*).
Zylinderkappe	cap of buffer cylinder (*field gun*).

ABBREVIATIONS.

Method of using Abbreviations in Orders.

In the German Field Service Regulations, 1908, paragraph 105, the following examples are given of the employment of abbreviations in orders, reports, &c. :—

I. R. 130	130th Infantry Regiment.
St. I. u. 1I/27, or I.R. 27 St. I. II.	Staff, and 1st and 2nd Battalions, 27th Infantry Regiment; or 27th Infantry Regiment, Staff, 1st and 2nd Battalions.
I.R. 67 (ohne 11.)	67th Infantry Regiment (less the 11th Company).
Jäg. 3	3rd *Jäger* Battalion.
M.G.A. 1	Machine Gun Detachment No. 1.
St. 1. 3. 4./Ul. 14 or Ul. 14 (ohne 2.)	Staff, 1st 3rd and 4th Squadrons, 14th *Ulanen* Regt.; or 14th *Ulanen* Regt. (less the 2nd Squadron).
St. u. R/F. A. 34 or F.A. 34 St. u. R.	Staff and Horse Artillery *Abteilung*, 34th Field Artillery Regiment; or 34th Field Artillery Regiment, Staff and Horse Artillery *Abteilung*.
II (F)/F.A. 4	2nd *Abteilung* (field howitzer) of 4th Field Artillery Regiment.
St. u. I (s. F.H.)/Fuss-A. 4	Staff and 1st (heavy field howitzer) Battalion of 4th Foot Artillery Regiment.
II (Mrs.)/Fuss-A.5	2nd Battalion (mortar) of 5th Foot Artillery Regiment.
1./Pi. 3	1st Company, 3rd Pioneer Battalion.
S.K. 2	2nd Bearer Company.
K. Tel. A.	Corps Telegraph Detachment.

ABBREVIATIONS.

Abbreviation.	Signification.	English Equivalent.
	A	
A.	Abteilung	"Abteilung"; (*sometimes* "*detachment*").
A.	Abwehr	defence.
A.	Abschnitts-	sector.
A.	Amt	office.
A.	Anordnungen	instructions.
A.	Arbeiter (Arbeits-)	labour (*adjective*).
A.	Arendt	Arendt (*a type of power buzzer and also of listening set*).
A.	Armee	Army.
A.	Art	pattern.
A.	Artillerie	artillery.
A.A.	Armee-Abteilung	Army Detachment (*equivalent to an Army*).

Abbreviation.	Signification.	English Equivalent.
a/A.	alter Art	old pattern.
A. Abt.	Armee-Abteilung	Army Detachment.
A. Abt.	Artillerie-Abteilung	artillery "Abteilung."
a.a.O.	an anderen Orten	in other places, elsewhere.
a.a.O.	am angeführten Orte	*loco citato.*, in the passage quoted.
a. B.	auf Befehl	"By order," "Signed for ", (*above a signature in a document*).
A.B.	Armee-Befehl	Army Order.
ab.	abgegangen	dispatched.
A.B.d.B.K.	auf Befehl des Bataillon-Kommandeurs	by order of the battalion commander (*in front of a signature*).
abds.	abends	in the evening, p.m.
Abs.	Absender	sender.
Abst.	Abstand	distance.
Abt. Abtlg. Abtl.	Abteilung	section, detachment, flight, &c.; "Abteilung" (*not translated in the case of field artillery, when it is a group of 3 batteries*).
A.B. zur Fp.D.O.	Ausführungs-Bestimmungen zur Feldpost-Dienstordnung	Instructions for the Execution of the Regulations for the Field Post.
A.C. a.c.	anni currentis	of the current year.
A.D.	Allgemeines Kriegsdepartement	General War Department (*of Prussian War Ministry*).
a.D.	ausser Dienst	retired (*of officers*).
a.d.D.	an diesem Datum	on this date.
Adj.	Adjutant	adjutant.
A.E.G.	Allgemeine-Elektricitäts-Gesellschaft	(*A firm which manufactures aeroplanes, fuzes and other war material*).
A.Fe.A.	Armee-Fernsprech-Abteilung	Army telephone detachment.
A.Fe.Park	Armee-Fernsprech-Park	Army telephone park.
Aferna	Armee-Fernsprech-Abteilung	Army telephone detachment.
Afernpark	Armee-Fernsprech-park	Army telephone park.
Afl	Artillerie-Flieger	artillery aeroplane.
Afla	Artillerie-Flieger-Abteilung	artillery reconnaissance flight.
A.Fl.P. A.Flug-Park	} Armee-Flug-Park	Army aircraft park.
A.Fssa.Kr.P.	Armee-Fussartillerie-Kraftzug-Park	Army foot artillery tractor park.
Afunka	Armee-Funker-Abteilung	Army wireless detachment.
Afunkpark A.Fu. Park	} Armee-Funker-Park	Army wireless park.
A. Gr.	Artillerie-Gruppe	artillery group.
Agru	Arendt-Gruppe	listening set section.
A.H.Kw.	Armee-Hauptkwartier	} Army Headquarters.
A.H.Q. A.H. Qu.	Armee-Hauptquartier	
A.K.	Abschnitts-Kommandeur	sector commander.
A.K.	Armee-Korps	Army Corps, Corps.

Abbreviation.	Signification.	English Equivalent.
Aka	Artillerie-Kampf-Artillerie	counter-battery artillery.
A.K.D.	Allgemeines Kriegsdepartement des preussischen Kriegsministeriums	General War Department of the Prussian War Ministry.
A.K.K.	Armee-Kraftwagen-Kolonne	Army M.T. column.
A.K.O.	Allerhöchste-Kabinetts-Ordre	Order of His Majesty in Council.
Akofern	Armee-Fernsprech-Kommando (Kommandeur)	Army Telephone H.Q. (Commander).
Akofunk	Armee-Funker-Kommando (Kommandeur)	Army Wireless H.Q. (Commander).
A.K.P.	Armee-Kraftwagen-Park	Army M.T. park.
Akonach...	Armee-Nachrichten-Kommandeur	Army Signal Commander.
A.m.d.F.b. A.m.F.b.	augenblicklich mit der Führung beauftragt	temporarily in command.
A.M.K.	Artillerie-Munitions-Kolonne	artillery ammunition column.
A.M.Tr.	Artillerie-Messtrupp	artillery survey section.
A.M.W.Schule	Armee-Minenwerfer-Schule	Army trench mortar school.
an.	angekommen	arrived.
A.N.	Auslandesnachricht	information received from abroad (*on casualty lists*).
Ana A.N.A.	Nachrichtenmittel-Abteilung des Artillerie-Regiments	artillery regimental signalling detachment.
Anh.W.	Anhängewagen	trailer.
Anl.	Anlage	appendix.
Anm.	Anmeldung	report, notice.
Anm.	Anmerkung	remarks.
Anst.	Anstalt	establishment.
Anst.	Anstellung	appointment.
A.O.K.	Armee-Oberkommando	Army Headquarters (*Staff*).
A.O.v.Pl.	Artillerie-Offizier vom Platz	Fortress Artillery Officer.
A.P.K.	Artillerie-Prüfungs-Kommission	Ordnance Committee.
Ar.A. Ara Ar. Abtlg.	Arendt-Abteilung	listening set section.
Arko	Artillerie-Kommandeur	Divisional Artillery Commander.
Arm.	Armee	Army.
Arm.	Armee-Korps	Army Corps (*on identity disc*).
Arm.	Armierungs-	labour (*adjective*).
Arm. Batl.	Armierungs-Bataillon	labour battalion.
Art. Artl.	Artillerie	artillery.
Art.Kdo.	Artillerie-Kommando	Divisional Artillery Headquarters.
Art.Kdr. (vom Dienst)	Artillerie-Kommandeur (vom Dienst)	Divisional Artillery Commander (on duty).
Art.Mun.Kol.	Artillerie-Munitions-Kolonne	artillery ammunition column (*heavy*).
A.S.	Acetylen-Sauerstoff	oxyacetylene (*used in portable searchlight and signalling lamps*).
Asto	Arendt-Station	listening set.

Abbreviation.	Signification.	English Equivalent.
A.St.z.b.V.	Artilleriestab zur besonderen Verwendung	Special artillery staff (*Group H.Q.*).
Ata A.T.A.	Armee-Telegraphen-Abteilung	Army telegraph detachment.
A.T.A.	Arendt-Telegraphen-Abteilung *or* Erdtelegraphen-Abteilung	listening set section *or* power buzzer section.
A.T.-Station	Erdtelegraphen-Station	power buzzer station.
A.T.B.	Armee-Tages-Befehl	Army Order of the Day.
Aufgeb.	Aufgebot	ban (*of Landsturm or Landwehr*).
av.	Arbeitsverwendungsfähig	suitable for employment for labour.
A.V.B.	Armee-Verordnungs-Blatt	Army Orders.
A.V.D.	Armee-Verwaltungs-Departement	Army Administrative Department.
A.V.F.	Arbeitsverwendungsfähig im Felde	fit for labour employment in the field.
A.V.F.	Ausbildungsvorschrift für die Fusstruppen im Kriege	Manual of Infantry Training during war.
A.V.G.	Arbeitsverwendungsfähig in der Garnison	fit for labour employment in Germany.
A.V.O.	Artillerie-Verbindungs-Offizier	artillery liaison officer.
A.W.	Atemwiderstand	breathing resistance (*gas mask*)
A.W.	Aussenwache	outlying piquet.
Awumba	Artillerie-Waffen- und Munitions-Beschaffungsamt	Artillery Munitions Department of the War Ministry.
Az.	Aufschlag-Zünder	percussion fuze.

B.

Abbreviation.	Signification.	English Equivalent.
B.	Bach	stream, brook (*topog.*).
B.	Bäckerei	bakery.
B.	Grosse Bagage	baggage section of the train.
B.	Ballon	balloon.
B.	Bataillon	battalion.
B.	Batterie	battery.
B.	Bau	construction.
B.	Bay(e)risch	Bavarian.
B.	Befehl	order.
B.	Bekleidungs-	clothing (*adjective*).
B.	Belagerungs-	siege (*adjective*).
B.	Beobachtungs-	observation.
B.	Bereitschafts-	emergency, *sometimes* support.
B.	Betriebs-	traffic (*adjective*).
B.	Berg	hill, mountain (*topog.*).
B.	Bezirk	district.
B.	Brief	letter.
B.	Brigade	brigade.
B.	Brücke	bridge, bridging.
b.	bay(e)risch	Bavarian.
B.A.	Bekleidungsamt	clothing office *or* depôt.
B.Abt.	Bau-Abteilung	construction section.
Bäck. Kol.	(Feld-)Bäckerei-Kolonne	(field) bakery column.
B.A.K.	Ballon-Abwehr-Kanone	anti-aircraft gun.
B.A.K.	Bayrisches Armee-Korps	Bavarian Army Corps.

Abbreviation.	Signification.	English Equivalent.
B.A.K.(I)	1tes Bayrisches Armee-Korps	I. Bavarian Army Corps.
B.A.K.Z....	Ballon-Abwehr-Kanonen-Zug	anti-aircraft gun section.
Ballka	Ballonkampfgruppe	balloon battle group.
Ballongruko	Ballon-Gruppen-Kommandeur	Balloon Group Commander.
B.A.M.K.	Ballon-Abwehr-Maschinen-Kanone (?)	anti-aircraft automatic gun.
Baon.	Bataillon	battalion (*on official stamps*).
Bat.	Bataillon	battalion (*on official stamps*).
Bat.	Batterie	battery.
Batl.	Bataillon	battalion.
Batn.	Bataillon	battalion (*on official stamps*).
Batt. } Battr.	Batterie	battery.
Bay. } Bayr.	Bayerisch	Bavarian.
B.b.a.	Bahn-Beauftragter	Railway Representative (*at Army H.Q.*).
Bba.	Bataillonsbagage	battalion transport.
B. B. P.	Batterie-Bau-Park	battery construction park.
Bbv.	Bahnbevollmächtigter (bei den Linien-Kommandanturen)	(?)
Bd. G.	Brand-Geschoss	incendiary shell.
B.d.G.Ost.	Beauftragter des Generalquartiermeisters für den östlichen Kriegsschauplatz	Deputy of the Quartermaster-General for the Eastern Theatre.
B.d.G.West.	Beauftragter des Generalquartiermeisters Gr. H.Qu.	Deputy of the Quartermaster-General, G.H.Q.
b.d.Tr.	{ bei der Train bei der Truppe	in the Train. with the troops.
Bd. Z.	Boden-Zünder	base fuze.
B.E.B.	Brigade-Ersatz-Bataillon	Brigade Ersatz battalion.
Bedekaval	Beauftragter des Kriegs-Ministeriums in Valenciennes	Representative of the War Ministry at Valenciennes (*for requisitioning purposes*).
Bef.	Befehl	order.
bef.	befördert	sent on, dispatched.
Befhb.	Befehlshaber	commander, in command.
Begl.	Begleit-	accompanying, escort(-ing).
beh.	behelfsmässig	improvised.
Beil.	Beilage	annexe; enclosure; appendix.
Bekl.	Bekleidung	clothing.
Belag.	Belagerungs-	siege (*adjective*).
Bel. Pk.	Belagerungs-Park	siege park.
Bel. Tel. Abt.	Belagerungs-Telegraphen-Abteilung	siege telegraph detachment.
Bel. Tr.	Belagerungs-Train	siege train.
Beob.	{ Beobachter Beobachtungs-	observer. observation-.
Beob.St.	Beobachtungsstand	observation post.
Beob. W.	Beobachtungswagen	observation wagon.
ber.	beritten	mounted.
Ber.Büchse	Bereitschaftsbüchse	"alert" box (*gas*).
Bereitsch.K.	Bereitschaftskompagnie	support company.
Bes.A.	Besondere Anordnungen	special instructions.
Bes. K.	Besatzkompagnie	company in line.
besp.	bespannt	horsed.

Abbreviation.	Signification.	English Equivalent.
Besp. Abt.	Bespannungs-Abteilung	draught horse section.
betr.	betreffend / betreffs	concerning.
Betr.-Abt.	Betriebs-Abteilung	traffic department; operating section.
Betr.-K.	Betriebs-Kompagnie	traffic company, operating company.
Bez. Offz.	Bezirks-Offizier	district officer.
bez. bezl. bezüg. bezügl.	bezüglich	with reference to.
bezw.	beziehungsweise	or as the case may be.
Bfhb.	Befehlshaber	commander, General Officer Commanding.
Bfst.	Befehlsstelle	command post.
B.G.O.	Bataillons-Gas-Offizier	battalion gas officer.
Bhf.	Bahnhof	railway station (*topog.*).
Bh. Flak	behelfsmässige Flugabwehrkanone	anti-aircraft gun on improvised mounting.
Bivl	Beobachter in der vorderen Linie	forward observer.
B.K.	Brigade-Kommandeur	Brigade Commander.
Bkl.-O.	Bekleidungsordnung	Clothing Regulations.
B.K.O.	Brigade-Kommando-Ordnung (?)	Brigade Order.
Bl.	Blatt	sheet, leaf.
Bl.	blind	blind (*shell*).
Bllabw. K.Z.	Ballon-Abwehr-Kanonen-Zug	anti-aircraft gun section.
Blst.	Block-Station	block signal station (*railway*; *topog.*).
B.O. B. Off.	Beobachtungs-Offizier	observation officer.
Bogohl	Bomben-Geschwader der obersten Heeres-Leitung	Bombing Squadron under General Headquarters.
Bona	Ballon-Nachrichten-Abteilung	balloon intelligence section.
Br.	Brigade	Brigade.
Br.	Brücke	bridge.
Br.	Brunnen	well (*topog.*).
Brandgr.	Brandgranate	incendiary shell.
Br. B. Br. Bef.	Brigade-Befehl	Brigade Order.
Brck. Tr.	Brücken-Train	bridging train.
B.R.D.	Bayrische-Reserve-Division	Bavarian Reserve Division.
Brd. Gesch.	Brandgeschoss	incendiary shell.
Brg.	Brigade	Brigade.
B. Gef. Std	Brigade-Gefechts-Stand	Brigade Battle Headquarters.
Brig.	Brigade	Brigade.
Br. Mrs.	Bronze-Mörser	bronze mortar.
Br. St. Qu.	Brigade-Stabsquartier	Brigade Headquarters.
Br. Tr.	Brücken-Train	bridging train.
Br. T. Schlag	Brief-Tauben-Schlag	carrier pigeon loft.
Brück. Tr.	Brücken-Train	bridging train.
b. St.	beim Stabe	*not translated; it refers to officers who are attached to regimental H.Q.*

Abbreviation.	Signification.	English Equivalent.
B. St.	Beobachtungs-Stand Beobachtungs-Stelle	observation post.
B.T.K.	Bereitschafts-Truppen - Kommandeur	commander of the supports.
Btl. Btln.	Bataillon	battalion.
Btls.-Kdr.v.D.	Bataillons-Kommandeur vom Dienst	battalion commander on duty.
Btl. St.	Bataillons-Stab	battalion staff.
Btn.	Bataillon	battalion.
Bttr.	Batterie	battery.
Btr.	Betriebs-	traffic (*adjective*).
B.V.	Behelfsbrücken-Vorschrift	Manual of Extemporised Bridging.
Bva.	Bevollmächtigter Aufsichtsoffizier im Bereiche des Feldeisenbahnwesens	Deputy Supervising Officer of the field railway system.
Bvg.	Bevollmächtigter Generalstabsoffizier des Feldeisenbahnchefs	Deputy G.S.O., attached to the Director of Railways.
Bvg Wilhelm	Bevollmächtigter Generalstabsoffizier bei der Heeresgruppe Kronprinz des Deutschen Reichs	Deputy G.S.O. with the Group of Armies of the German Crown Prince.
Bvs	Bevollmächtigter der deutschen Schiffahrtsgruppe „Donau" beim bevollmächtigter Generalstabsoffizier Rumänien	Deputy for the German Inland Water Transport on the Danube attached to the Deputy G.S.O. Rumania.
B.W.	Bahn-Wärter	plate-layer's hut (*railway; topog.*).
bz.	bezahlt	paid.
Bz.	Brenn-Zünder	time fuze.
bzgl.	bezüglich	in reference to, concerning.
bzw.	beziehungsweise	or as the case may be.
Bz.	Brenn-Zünder	time fuze.

C.

C.	Celsius	Celsius, centigrade (*thermom.*).
C/92	Construction/92	1892 pattern (*ammn.*).
ca.	circa	about.
cbm.	Kubikmeter	cubic metre.
C.G.S.	Chef des General-Stabes	Chief of the General Staff.
Ch.d.St.d.F.H.	Chef des Generalstabs des Feldheeres	C.G.S. of the Field Army.
Chefkraft	Chef des Feldkraftfahrwesens	Director of Mechanical Transport in the Field.
Chev. Leg. Chevl.	Chevaulegers	"Chevaulegers" (Bavarian light cavalry).
Ch. Hs.	Chaussee-Haus	turnpike (*topog.*).
chi. chif.	chiffriert	enciphered.
cm.	Centimeter	centimetre.
Cyl.	Cylinder	cylinder.

Abbreviation.	Signification.	English Equivalent.
	D.	
D.	Departement	department.
D.	Depot	depôt.
D.	Deutsch	German.
D.	Dienst	service.
D.	Direktion	Directorate.
D.	Disziplinär	disciplinary.
D.	Division	division.
D.	Dragoner	dragoon.
d.	durch	through, by.
D.A.z.D.	Dienstanweisung zur Durchführung der Militärtransporte im Mobilmachungsfalle	Instructions for the carrying out of military transport in case of mobilization.
d.B.	durch Boten	by messenger.
D. Br .Tr.	Divisions-Brücken-Train	divisional bridging train.
D.d.G.	Dum-Dum Geschoss.	Dum-Dum bullet.
Deckbl.	Deckblatt	corrigendum, amendment.
D.F.P.	Deutsche Feld-Post	German Field Post.
Dep.	Depot	depôt.
Dewumba	Waffen- und Munitions-Beschaffungsamt Depot	Depôt of the Munitions Department of the War Ministry.
D.f.Gask.	Dienstvorschrift für den Gaskampf	Instructions for Gas Warfare.
D.F.W.	Deutsche Flugzeugwerke	German Aeroplane Works, Leipzig.
D.G.O.	Divisions-Gas-Offizier	Divisional Gas Officer.
d.Gr.	durch Granate	by shellfire (*of wounds*).
D.G.S.O.	Diensttuender Gasschutzoffizier	Gas Officer on duty.
D.G.St.	Divisions-Generalstab	General Staff of the Division.
dienstl.	dienstlich	official.
Difua	Divisions-Funker-Abteilung	divisional wireless detachment (*permanently allotted to a divisional sector: formerly "Fukla"*).
Dina	Divisions-Nachrichtenmittel-Abteilung	divisional signalling detachment.
Div.	Division	division.
Div.-Beob.-Stelle	Divisions-Beobachtungsstelle	divisional observation post.
Divferna	Divisions-Fernsprech-Abteilung	divisional telephone detachment.
Divfua Divfunka	} (see Difua, *which is the more us*ual abbreviation).	
Div.K.K.	Divisions-Kraftwagen-Kolonne	divisional M.T. column.
Divkonach	Divisions-Nachrichten-Kommandeur	Divisional Signal Commander.
Div.St.Qu.	Divisionsstabsquartier	Divisional H.Q.
Div. Verf.	Divisions-Verfügung	Divisional Order.
D.K.	Divisions-Kavallerie	divisional cavalry.
D.K.K.	Divisions-Kraftwagen-Kolonne	divisional M.T. column.
d.L.	der Landwehr	of the Landwehr, Landwehr.
Dl.T. D.L.T.	} Drahtlose Telegraphie	wireless telegraphy.
d.M.	dieses Monats	of this month, inst.
d.O.	der Obige	the above.
d.O.	durch Ordonnanz	by orderly.
Dopp. Z.	Doppel-Zünder	time and percussion fuze.

Abbreviation.	Signification.	English Equivalent.
D.P.	Doppelposten	double sentry post.
Dpp.	doppelt	double.
Dpp.-Zug. Dpp(Zg).	Doppelzug	detachment (divisional telephone).
Dr.	Dragoner	dragoon.
D.R.	Dragoner-Regiment	dragoon regiment.
d.R.	der Reserve	of the Reserve, Reserve.
Drawa	Drachenwarte	kite balloon meteorological station.
Dreh. Br.	Drehbrücke	swing bridge (*topog.*).
ds.	dieses Monats	of this month, inst.
D.-St.O.	Disziplinarstrafordnung	Disciplinary Regulations.
D.St.Q.	Divisionsstabsquartier	Divisional H.Q.
D.T.B.	Divisions-Tages-Befehl	Divisional Order of the Day.
D.U.	dauernd untauglich	permanently unfit.
D.V.	Divisions-Verfügung Divisions-Verordnung	Divisional Order.
D.V.E.	Druckvorschriften-Etat	Numbered Index of Official Publications.
D.W.M.	Deutsche Waffen- u. Munitionsfabrik	German Arms and Munitions Manufacturing Co.
Dz. D.Z.	Doppel-Zünder	time and percussion fuze.

E.

E.	eigene Truppen	our troops.
E.	Eisenbahn	railway.
E.	Ersatz	"Ersatz."
E.	Eskadron	squadron.
E.	Etappe	L. of C.
E.B.	Ersatz-Bataillon	"Ersatz" battalion.
E.B.K.	Eisenbahn-Bau-Kompagnie	railway construction company.
E. Bt. K.	Eisenbahn - Betriebs - Kompagnie	railway traffic company.
Ec.	Eisen-Centrierung	with rear driving band only (*shell*).
Efema	Feldmunitions-Anstalten	field ammunition depôts.
E.F.K.	Etappen-Fuhrpark-Kolonne	L. of C. supply park.
E.Flak	Eisenbahn-Flug-Abwehr-Kanone	anti-aircraft gun on railway mounting.
E.H. Btln.	Eisenbahn-Hilfs-Bataillon	auxiliary railway battalion.
E.H.O.	Etappen-Hauptort	L. of C. Main Depôt.
E.H.Z.	Empfindlicher Haubitz-Zünder	sensitive, *i.e.*, instantaneous, howitzer fuze.
E.I.	Etappen-Inspektion	L. of C. Inspectorate.
Einw.	Einwohner	inhabitant.
Eisb.	Eisenbahn	railway.
Eisb. Bau- Komp.	Eisenbahn-Bau-Kompagnie	railway construction company.
Eisb.Betr.Komp.	Eisenbahn-Betriebs-Kompagnie	railway traffic company.
Eisb. Tr.	Eisenbahntruppen	railway troops.
Eispark	Eisenbahn-Ersatz-Park	railway stores park.
Eis. Tr.	Eisenbahn-Truppen	railway troops.
E.K.	Eisernes Kreuz	Iron Cross.
E.K.	Ersatz-Kompagnie	"Ersatz" company.
E.K.K.	Etappen-Kraftwagen-Kolonne	L. of C. M.T. column.

Abbreviation.	Signification.	English Equivalent.
E.K.Z.	Empfindlicher Kanonen-Zünder	sensitive, *i.e.*, instantaneous gun fuze.
E.K.II.Kl.	Eisernes Kreuz zweiter Klasse	Iron Cross, Second Class.
E.M.	Ergänzungs-Mannschaften	drafts.
Entw.M.	Entwässerungs-Mühle	mill for draining ground (*topog.*).
E.O.bei	Eisenbahn-Offizier beim (A.O.K., etc.)	Railway Officer at (Army H.Q., etc.).
E.O.d.I.	Erkundungs-Offizier der Infanterie	infantry reconnaissance officer.
Erl.	Erlass	order, rescript.
erl.	erledigt	settled, finished.
Ers.	Ersatz	"Ersatz" (*see under* "*Ersatz*").
Ers.	Ersuchung	request, demand.
Ers.E.R.	Ersatz-Bataillon Eisenbahn-Regiments	Depôt Battalion of the Railway Regiment.
E.S.B.	Eisenbahn-Sockel-Batterie (?)	A.A. battery on railway mounting.
E.S.K.	Eisenbahn-Sonder-Kommando	special railway staff.
Esk.	Eskadron	squadron.
Et.	Etappen	Lines of Communication.
Et.	Etappe	L. of C.
Et.	Etat	establishment.
Etap.	Etappe	L. of C.
Et.B.K.	Etappen-Bäckerei-Kolonne	bakery column on the L. of C.
E.Tel.B.Tr.	Eisenbahn-Telegraphen-Bautrupp	railway telegraph construction detachment.
E.T.D. / E.Tel.Dir.	Etappen-Telegraphen-Direktion	L. of C. Telegraph Directorate.
Etelstation	Erdtelegraphen-Station	power buzzer station.
Etel / Erdtel	Erdtelegraphie	power buzzer.
Et.Fp.K.	Etappen-Fuhrpark-Kolonne	L. of C. supply park.
Et.G.u.P.Amt.	Etappen-Güter- und Paketenamt	L. of C. goods and parcels office.
Et.H.B.K.	Etappen-Hilfs-Bäckerei-Kolonne	auxiliary bakery column on the L. of C.
Et.H.K.	Etappen-Hilfs-Kompagnie	auxiliary company on the L. of C.
Et.H.W.St.	Etappen-Hilfs-Weiterleitungs-Stelle	auxiliary forwarding station on the L. of C.
Et.K.	Etappen-Kommandant	L. of C. Commandant.
Et.Ko.M.u.T.	Kommandeur der Etappen-Munitionskolonnen und Trains	Commander of Ammunition Columns and Trains on the L. of C.
Et.Mag.Verwaltg.	Etappen-Magazin-Verwaltung	administration of L. of C. depôts.
Et.Mun.Kol.	Etappen-Munitions-Kolonne	L. of C. ammunition column.
Et.Pf.D.	Etappen-Pferde-Depôt	L. of C. remount depôt.
Et.Tel.Dir.	Etappen-Telegraphen-Direktion	L. of C. Telephone Directorate.
Etra	Feldeisenbahnchef Eisenbahntransportabteilung (West, Ost, Südost)	Director of Field Railways, Railway Transport Department (Western, Eastern, South-Eastern Theatres).
Et.S.Komp.	Etappen-Sammel-Kompagnie	L. of C. salvage company.

Abbreviation.	Signification.	English Equivalent.
E.V.	Etappenverwendungsfähig	suitable for employment on the L. of C.
E.V.F.	Etappenverwendungsfähig im Felde	suitable for employment on the L. of C. in the field.
Ew.	Euer	Your (*e.g.*, *Your Excellency*).
Exempl.	Exempläre	copies.
Ex. Pl.	Exerzier-Platz	drill ground (*topog.*).
Exz.	Exzellenz	Excellency (*title given to Lieut.-Generals and senior ranks in the German Army*).

F.

F.	Fahrend	field (*as opposed to "horse" artillery*).
F.	Fahrenheit	Fahrenheit (*thermom.*).
F.	Feind	the enemy.
F.	feindlich	the enemy's, hostile.
F.	Feld-	field.
F.	Fernsprecher	telephone.
F.	Festung	fortress.
F.	Flieger	} usually "aircraft" or "aeroplane" *in compound words*.
F.	Flug	
F.	Flugzeug	aeroplane.
F.	Friedens-	peace (*adjective*).
F.	Fuhrpark	transport park.
F.	Funken-	wireless.
F.	Füsilier	fusilier.
F.	Fuss	foot (*adjective*).
(F)	Feld-Haubitze	*indicates a light field howitzer.* battery, ammunition column, &c.
f.	für	for.
F.A.	Feld-Artillerie	field artillery.
F.A.	Flug-Abwehr	anti-aircraft.
F.A.B.	Feld-Artillerie-Brigade	field artillery brigade.
Fabr.	Fabrik	factory.
F.A.Btl.	Fuss-Artillerie-Bataillon	foot artillery battalion.
Fähnr.	Fähnrich	ensign.
fahr.	fahrend	field (*as opposed to "horse" artillery*).
F.A.K.	Flug-Abwehr-Kanone	anti-aircraft gun.
F.A.M.	Friedrich August Medaille	Frederick Augustus Medal.
F.A.R.	Feld-Artillerie-Regiment	field artillery regiment.
Fb.	Fliehbolzen	centrifugal bolt (*in fuze, etc.*).
Fbba	Feld-Bahn-Betriebs-Amt	field railway traffic office.
F.B.D.	Feld-Bahn-Depot	field railway depôt.
F.B.K.	Feld-Bäckerei-Kolonne	field bakery column.
Fblt.	Festungsbauleutnant	2nd lieutenant in the fortress construction service.

Abbreviation.	Signification.	English Equivalent.
Fb. Off.	Festungsbau-Offizier	fortress construction officer.
Fbr.	Fabrik	factory (*topog.*).
f.Bttr.	fahrende Batterie	field artillery battery.
F.D.	Festungsdienstordnung	Fortress Service Regulations.
Fda. Fd.(Artl.).	Feld-Artillerie	field artillery.
F.d.b.D.K.	Für den befehlenden Divisions-Kommandeur	for the General Commanding the Division.
F.d.G.K.	Für das General-Kommando	for the Corps Commander.
fdl.	feindlich	hostile, the enemy's.
Fd. Laz.	Feld-Lazarett	field hospital.
f.d.R.	für die Richtigkeit	certified correct.
Fe.	ferme	farm (*on French maps*).
Fe.	Fernsprech	telephone.
F.E.A.	Flieger-Ersatz-Abteilung	training squadron (*aviation depot*).
Fe.A.A.	Fernsprechabteilung bei einem Armee-Kommando	telephone detachment at Army H.Q.
Feba	Feldbahn	field railway (*metre gauge*).
Fedrawa	Feld-Drachenwarte	field kite balloon meteorological station.
Fe.Dz.	Fernsprech-Doppelzug	divisional telephone detachment (*obsolete*).
feindl.	feindlich	hostile, the enemy's.
Feka	Fern-Kampf-Artillerie	long-range artillery.
Felda	Feld-Artillerie	field artillery.
Feldlaz.	Feld-Lazarett	field hospital.
Feldb. Betr. Komp.	Feldbahn-Betriebs-Kompagnie	field railway traffic company.
Fech. Zstl.	Chef des Feldeisenbahnwesens, Zentralstelle	Director of Military Railways, Central Office.
Feldeisenbahnchef	Chef des Feldeisenbahnwesens	Director of Military Railways.
Feldtelchef	Chef der Feldtelegraphie	Director of Field Telegraphs.
Feldw.	Feldwache	piquet.
Feldw.	Feldwebel	serjeant-major.
Fernerin	Inspektion der Fernsprech-Ersatz-Abteilungen	Inspectorate of telephone depôt detachments.
Fernsp. Abt.	Fernsprech-Abteilung	telephone detachment.
Fe.-Spr. Fe.-Spruch.	Fernspruch	telephone message.
Fest.	Festung (s-)	fortress.
Fest. E.B.K.	Festungs-Eisenbahn-Bau-Kompagnie	fortress railway construction company.
Fest.E. Betr. K.	Festungs-Eisenbahn-Betriebs-Kompagnie	fortress railway traffic company.
Feu.	Feuerleitungsstelle	fire control post.
F.E.W.	Feld-Eisenbahn-Wesen	field railway service.
Fowewa	Feldwetterwarte	field meteorological station.
Ffa F.Fl.Abt.	Feldflieger-Abteilung	reconnaissance flight (*obsolete term, now known as "Flieger-Abteilung"*).
F.Fr.	Feindliche Flammenwerfer	hostile *Flammenwerfer*.
F.Gr.	Feld-Granate	field gun high explosive (H.E.) shell.
F.H.	Feld-Haubitze	light field howitzer.

Abbreviation.	Signification.	English Equivalent.
F.H.M.K.	Feld-Haubitzen-Munitions-Kolonne	light field howitzer ammunition column.
Fhrp.	Fuhrpark	transport park.
Fhrw.	Fuhrwerk	vehicle, cart.
Fhrws.	Fuhrwesen	horsed transport service.
Fhrz.	Fahrzeug	vehicle; boat.
F.J.B.	Feld-Jäger-Bataillon	"Jäger" battalion.
F.K.	Feld-Kanone	field gun.
F.K.	Feld-Kompagnie	field company (*pioneers*).
Fk.	Funken-	wireless.
Fk.	Funker	wireless operator.
F.kl.Abt.	Funker-Klein-Abteilung	trench wireless detachment.
F.L.	Feld-Lazarett	field hospital.
Fl.	Fluss	river (*topog.*).
F.L.A.	Feld-Luftschiffer-Abteilung	balloon detachment.
Fl.Abt.	Flieger-Abteilung	reconnaissance flight (*aviation unit*).
Flak	Flug-Abwehr-Kanone	anti-aircraft gun.
Fl.A.K. auf Kraftw.	Flug-Abwehr-Kanone auf Kraftwagen	anti-aircraft gun on motor lorry.
Flakean	Flug-Abwehr-Kanonen-Ersatz-Abteilung	anti-aircraft "Ersatz" (depôt) detachment.
Flak Ers. Abt.	Flug-Abwehr-Kanonen-Ersatz-Abteilung	anti-aircraft "Ersatz" (depôt) detachment.
Flak Ers. Regt.	Flug-Abwehr-Kanonen-Ersatz-Regiment	anti-aircraft "Ersatz" regiment.
Flakgruko	Flug-Abwehr-Kanonen-Gruppen-Kommandeur	A. A. Group Commander.
Flakschule	Flug-Abwehr-Kanonen-Schule	anti-aircraft gun school.
Flak-Zug	Flug-Abwehr-Kanonen-Zug	anti-aircraft section.
Flamga	Flieger-Abwehr-Maschinengewehr (Abteilung)	anti-aircraft machine gun (detachment).
Flamak	Flug-Abwehr-Maschinen-Kanone (?)	anti-aircraft automatic gun (?).
Fla.M.G.	Flieger-Abwehr-Maschinen-Gewehr	anti-aircraft machine gun.
Fl.Br.	Fliegende Brücke	flying bridge.
Fldart.	Feld-Artillerie	field artillery.
Fldbäck. K.	Feld-Bäckerei-Kolonne	field bakery column.
Fldverw. Beh.	Feldverwaltungs-Behörden	field administrative authorities.
Fldw.	Feldwebel	serjeant-major.
Flg.	Flieger	airman; aeroplane, flying (*adjective*).
Fliehb.	Fliehbolzen	centrifugal bolt (*in fuze, etc.*).
Fl.Off.	Flieger-Offizier	flying officer.
Flugh.	Flughalle	hangar.
Fluma, Flu.M.A.	Flug-Melde-Abteilung	aircraft report detachment.
Fl.w., Fl.W.	Flammenwerfer	"*Flammenwerfer.*"
F.M.G.Z.	Feld-Maschinen-Gewehr-Zug	machine gun section.
Fnd.	Feind	enemy.
F.O.	Felddienst-Ordnung	Field Service Regulations.
F. Patr.	Feld-Patrone	field gun cartridge (*fixed ammunition*).

Abbreviation.	Signification.	English Equivalent.
Fp.	Fuhrpark	transport park.
Fp. 60/40	Füllpulver 60/40	Amatol 60/40, i.e. 60 per cent.
F.P. Amt. F.P.A	} Feld-Post-Amt	field post office.
Fp. 02	Füllpulver 02	1902 pattern explosive (T.N.T.).
Fp. D.O.	Feldpost-Dienst-Ordnung	Regulations for the Field Postal Service.
F. Pi. D.	Feld-Pionier-Dienst (aller Waffen)	Manual of Field Engineering for All Arms.
F.Pi.V.	Feldpioniervorschrift	Pioneer Field Service Regulations.
F.P. Exp. F.P. E.	} Feld-Post-Expedition	branch field post office.
Fpk.	Fuhrpark	transport park.
Fp. K. Fpk. K.	} Fuhr-Park-Kolonne	supply park.
F.P.M.	Friedens-Pulver-Magazin	peace time powder magazine.
F. P. Sek.	Feld-Post-Sektor	field post sector.
F. P. St. F. P. S.	} Feld-Post-Station	field post office.
F.P.W.	Feld-Post-Wesen	Field Postal Service.
F.P.W.	Fuhr-Park-Wagen	supply park vehicle.
franz.	französisch	French.
Fr.Bes.V.	Friedens-Besoldungs-Vorschrift	Pay Regulations (Peace).
F.R.D.	Feld-Rekruten-Depot	field recruit depôt.
Frhr.	Freiherr	Baron (*usually not translated*).
Fr.V.V.	Friedens-Verpflegungs-Vorschrift	Supply Regulations (Peace).
Fr. Wag.	Futterwagen	forage wagon.
F.S.	Feld-Schmiede	field forge.
F.Sch.A.	Feld-Schlächter-Abteilung	field butchers detachment.
F.Schr.Patr.	Feld-Schrapnel-Patrone	field gun shrapnel cartridge (*fixed ammunition*).
F.S.O.	Friedens-Sanitäts-Ordnung	Medical Regulations (Peace).
F. Sp.	feindliches Sperrfeuer	hostile barrage fire.
Fsp.	Fernsprech- (er)	telephone.
F. Spr.	Fernspruch	telephone message.
F.Spr.A.	Fernsprech-Abteilung	telephone detachment.
Fss.A. Fssa	} Fuss-Artillerie	foot artillery.
Fst.	Festung	fortress.
F.Stat.	Funken-Station	wireless station.
Fstg.	Festung	fortress.
Ft.	Funken-Telegraphie	wireless telegraphy (W/T).
Ft. Sperre	Funken-Telegraphie-Sperre!	Stop using wireless!
Fu.	Funker	wireless or wireless operator.
Fufa	Funker-Feld-Abteilung	field wireless detachment.
Fuhrp.	Fuhrpark	transport park.
Fuhrw.	Fuhrwerk	vehicle, cart, carriage.
Fukla		
Fu. Kl. Abt. Funkla	} Funker-Klein-Abteilung	trench wireless detachment.
Füs.	Füsilier	fusilier.
Funk. Abt.	Funker-Abteilung	wireless detachment.

Abbreviation.	Signification.	English Equivalent.
Funkeins...	Funker-Ersatz-Abteilung 1	No. 1 Wireless Depôt Detachment.
Funkla	Funker-Klein-Abteilung	trench wireless detachment.
Funk-st. ...	Funkenstation	wireless station.
Fu.spr. ... Fu.spruch	Funkspruch	wireless message.
Fuss-A. Fussart.	Fuss-Artillerie	foot artillery.
Fussa. S.S.	Fussartillerie-Schiess-Schule	Foot Artillery School of Gunnery.
Fuss. A.R.	Fuss-Artillerie-Regiment	foot artillery regiment.
Fuss. A.B.	Fuss-Artillerie-Bataillon	foot artillery battalion.
F.V.	Feldbefestigungsvorschriften	Field Fortification Regulations.
F.V.T.	Feld-Verpflegungs-Tabellen	Field Supply Tables.
Fvt. Fvtg. Fvtl.	Feuerverteilung	distribution of fire.
F.W.	Fliegerwarte	aeroplane observation post.
F.W. Fw.	Feldwache	piquet.
F.W.	Futterwagen	forage wagon.
F. W. St.	Feld-Wetter-Station	meteorological station.
f. 10 cm. K.	für 10 cm. Kanone	for 10-cm. gun.
F.Z. Fz.	Feldzeugmeisterei	Ordnance Department.

G.

G.	Garde	Guard.
G.	Garnison	garrison.
G.	Gas	gas.
G.	Gebirgs-	mountain (*adjective*).
G.	General	General.
G.	Geschütz	gun.
G.	Gewehr	rifle.
G.	Gouvernement	Government.
G.	Gramm	gramme.
G.	Grenadier	grenadier.
G.	Gross	great.
G.	Gruppe	Group.
G†.	Gerichtlich für tot erklärt	legally presumed to be dead (*casualty lists*).
g.	geheim	secret.
G.A.B.B.V.	Geschäfts-Anweisung für die Bahnbevollmächtigten	Regulations for (?)
Gard.	Garde	Guard.
Garn.	Garnison	garrison.
Gas.Kol.	Gas-Kolonne	gas column.
gb.	geboren	born.
Gb.	Gebirg	mountain.

Abbreviation.	Signification.	English Equivalent.
G.B.	Garnison-Bauordnung	Garrison Building Regulations.
Gbg.	Gebirgs-	mountain (*adjective*).
Gd.	Garde	Guard.
G.D.	Geschütz-Depot	gun depôt.
G.d.A.	General der Artillerie	General of Artillery.
Gde.	Garde	Guard.
G.d.I.	General der Infanterie	General of Infantry.
G.d.K.	General der Kavallerie	General of Cavalry.
G.d.Pi.	General der Pioniere	General of Pioneers.
G.E.	geübter Ersatz	trained drafts.
Geb.	Gebirgs-	mountain (*adjective*).
Geb. Kan. Abt.	Gebirgs-Kanonen-Abteilung	mountain gun detachment.
Gebr.	Gebrüder	Brothers.
gebr.	gebräuchlich	usual.
Geferna	Fernsprechabteilung bei einem Gruppen-(General-) Kommando	telephone detachment at a Group (Corps) Headquarters.
Gefgsch.	Gefangenschaft	captivity.
Gef. Ordnz.	Gefechts-Ordonnanz	orderly, runner.
Gefr.	Gefreiter	lance-corporal.
Gef. Std.	Gefechts-Stand	battle headquarters.
geh.	geheim	secret.
Geh.	Geheim	secret.
Geh.	Gehilfe	assistant.
Gekofern	Gruppen-Fernsprech-Kommando (Kommandeur) / General-Kommando-Fernsprech-Kommando (Kommandeur)	Group Telephone H.Q. (Commander). / Corps Telephone H.Q. (Commander).
Gekofunk	Gruppen-Funker-Kommando (Kommandeur) / General-Kommando-Funker-Kommando (Kommandeur)	Group Wireless H.Q. (Commander). / Corps Wireless H.Q. (Commander).
Gekofusta	Gruppen (General-Kommando) Funkenstation	Group (Corps) wireless station.
gel.	geladen	loaded.
gem.	gemäss / gemischt	according to. / mixed.
Gen. d. Pion.	General der Pioniere	Pioneer General.
Gen. Kdo.(s) Genkdo(s)	General-Kommando(s)	Army Corps Staff(s), Corps Headquarters.
Gen.-Lt. Genlt.	General-Leutnant	Lieutenant-General.
Gen. Maj.	General-Major	Major-General.
Gen. Ob.	General-Oberst	*not translated — usually commands an Army.*
Gen. St.	General-Stab	General Staff.
Gentel	General der Telegraphentruppen (*obsolete*)	Director of Signals.
Gesch.	Geschichte	history.
Gesch.	Geschütz / Geschoss	gun. / projectile.
Geschtl.	Geschichtlich	historically.
Gesetzl.	Gesetzlich	legal, legally.
Gew.	Gewehr	rifle.

Abbreviation.	Signification.	English Equivalent.
gez.	gezeichnet	signed.
	gezogen	rifled.
Gf.	Geschütz-Fabrik	gun factory.
	Geschoss-Fabrik	shell factory.
Gfgsch.	Gefangenschaft	captivity.
Gfm. / G.F.M.	General-Feld-Marschall	Field-Marshal.
G.F.P.	Geheime Feld-Polizei	secret police.
Gft.	Gefreiter	lance-corporal, acting bombardier.
Gftsaufklrg.	Gefechtsaufklärung	close reconnaissance.
Gfuk.-Station / G.Fuk.-Station	Grosse Funker-Station	large wireless station.
G.G.	Garnisons-Gebäudeordnung	Garrison Buildings Regulations.
G.G. / G.G.R.	Garde-Grenadier-Regiment	Guard Grenadier Regiment.
G.g.	Granate-Geschoss	high explosive (H.E.) shell.
G.Gr.	Gas-Granate	gas shell.
G.G.St.	Grosser General-Stab	the Great General Staff.
G.H.Q.	Grosses Haupt-Quartier	G.H.Q.
G.H.Qu.	Gruppen-Haupt-Quartier	Group (Corps) Headquarters.
G.J.D.	Garde-Infanterie-Division	Guard Infantry Division.
G.K.	Garde-Korps	Guard Corps.
G.K.	Gas-Kolonne	gas column.
G.K.	General-Kommando	Army Corps Staff, Corps Headquarters.
G.K.O.	General - Kommando - Ordnung (?)	Corps Order.
Gkofunk	General - Kommando - Funker-Kommando (Kommandeur)	Corps Wireless H.Q. (Commander).
G.K.V.	General - Kommando - Verordnung	Corps Order.
gl. l. W.M. Lanz	glatte leichte Wurf-Mine Lanz	light smooth bore Lanz *Minenwerfer* H.E. shell.
Glühl.	Glühlampe	incandescent lamp.
G.M. / G.Maj.	General-Major	Major-General.
G.M.G.K.	Gebirgs - Maschinen - Gewehr - Kompagnie	mountain machine gun company.
G.M.K.	Gebirgs - Munitions - Kolonne	mountain ammunition column.
G.M.W.K.	Gebirgs - Minenwerfer - Kompagnie	mountain *Minenwerfer* company.
G.O.	Gas-Offizier	gas officer.
G.O.	General-Oberst	*not translated—usually commands an Army.*
Gouv.	Gouvernement	Government.
G.P.	Geschütz-Park	gun park.
G.P.K.	Gewehr - Prüfungs - Kommission	Small Arms Committee.
G.R.	Grenadier-Regiment	grenadier regiment.
Gr.	Granate	high explosive (H.E.) shell.
Gr.	Gross (-er, -e, -es)	great.
Gr.	Gruppe	Group (Corps).
Grab. Kan Abt.	Graben - Kanonen - Abteilung	trench gun detachment.
Gr. Bag.	Grosse Bagage	baggage section of the train.
Gren.	Grenadier	grenadier.

Abbreviation.	Signification.	English Equivalent.
Grf. 88	Granatfüllung 88	1888 pattern explosive (picric acid).
Gr. Gen. Stab	Grosser General-Stab....	Great General Staff.
Gr. H. Qu.	Grosses Hauptquartier	General Headquarters.
G.R.H.Q.U.	Grosses Haupt-Quartier	G.H.Q.
Gr. H. Qu.	Gruppen-Hauptquartier	Army Group Headquarters.
Gr. Kr. Mun.	Grün-Kreuz-Munition	"green cross" gas shell.
Groftrupp	Grosser-Flammenwerfer-Trupp	large *Flammenwerfer* squad.
Gr.T.B.	Gruppen-Tages-Befehl	Group Orders of the day.
Gruferna	Gruppen - Fernsprech - Abteilung	Group telephone detachment.
Grufl	Gruppenführer der Flieger	Group Aviation Commander; Wing Commander.
Grufusta	Gruppen-Funker-Station	Group (Corps) wireless station.
Grukofern	Gruppen - Fernsprech - Kommando (Kommandeur)	Group Telephone H.Q. (Commander).
Grukonach	Gruppen - Nachrichten -Kommandeur	Group Signal Commander.
Gr. W.	Granatwerfer	"stick" bomb-thrower.
G.R.z.F.	Garde-Regiment zu Fuss	Foot Guards Regiment
Gr. Z.	Granat-Zünder	fuze for H.E. shell.
G.S.B.	Garde-Schützen-Bataillon	Guard Rifle Battalion.
G.S.L.	Gas-Schutz-Lager	Gas Defence Supply Depôt.
G.S.O.	Gas-Schutz-Offizier	anti-gas officer.
G.S.O. Pi.	Gruppen - Stabs - Offizier der Pioniere	Group Staff Officer for Pioneers.
G.S.U.	Gas-Schutz-Unteroffizier	anti-gas N.C.O.
Gtt. Br.	Gitter-Brücke	lattice girder bridge (*topog.*).
Gv.	Garnisonsverwendungsfähig	fit for garrison duty.
G.v.d.Art.	General von der Artillerie	Artillery General.
G.V.E.	Garnisonsverwendungsfähig im Etappengebiet	fit for duty on the L. of C.
G.V.F.	Garnisonsverwendungsfähig im Felde	fit for duty with regimental transport, &c.
G.V.G.	Garnisonsverwendungsfähig in einer Garnison	fit for garrison duty in a garrison.
G.V.H.	Garnisonsverwendungsfähig in der Heimat	fit for garrison duty in Germany.
G.V.O.	Gräber - Verwaltungs - Offizier	Graves Officer.
G.V.O.	Garnisons - Verwaltungs - Ordnung	Garrison Administration Regulations.
G.Z.	Granat-Zünder	percussion fuze for H.E. shell.
G.Z.	Güter-Zug	goods train.
G.z.F.	Garde-zu-Fuss	Foot Guards.

Abbreviation.	Signification.	English Equivalent.
	H.	
H.	Haubitze	howitzer.
H.	Haupt	chief, principal.
H.	Hauptmann	captain.
H.	Heeres-	Army (*adjective*).
H.	Hilfs-	auxiliary.
Haub.Gr.	Hauben-Granate	H.E. shell with false cap.
Hauptl.	Hauptleute	Captains.
Hauptm.	Hauptmann	Captain.
Hauwewa (heim)	Haupt-Wetterwarte (der Heimat)	chief meteorological observatory (in Germany).
H.d.K.	Hauptmann der Kraftfahrtruppen	Captain of the Mechanical Transport Troops.
Heeresgr.	Heeresgruppe'	Group of Armies.
H.Gr.	Haubitz-Granate	howitzer H.E. shell.
H.Gr.	Heeresgruppen-Kommando	H.Q. of a Group of Armies.
H.Lz.Z.	Hilfs-Lazarett-Zug	temporary *or* improvised hospital train.
Hp.	Halte-Punkt	stopping place (*railway; topog.*).
Hptm.	Hauptmann	Captain.
Hptl.	Hauptleute	Captains.
H.R.	Haupt-Richtung	main direction; zero line.
H.R.	Husaren-Regiment	hussar regiment.
H.Schr.	Haubitz-Schrapnel	howitzer shrapnel.
H.S.S.	Heeres - Sauerstoff - Schützgerät	military oxygen protective apparatus.
Hus.	Husaren	hussars.
H.W.L.	Haupt-Widerstands-Linie	main line of resistance.
H.W.St.	Hilfs-Weiterleitungs-Stelle	auxiliary forwarding station.
H.Z.	Haubitz-Zünder	howitzer fuze.
	I.	
I.	Infanterie	infantry.
I.	Ingenieur	engineer.
I.	Inspektion	Inspectorate (*or district, etc., under an inspector*).
i.A.	im Auftrag	"By order, "Signed for" (*above a signature on a document*).
I.B.	Infanterie-Bataillon	infantry battalion.
I.B.	Infanterie-Brigade	Infantry Brigade.
I.B.O.	Infanterie - Beobachtungs-Offizier	infantry observing officer.
I.D.	Infanterie-Division	infantry division.
I.d.E. } Ideis }	Inspektion des Eisenbahnwesens	Inspectorate of Railway Services.
Ifl	Infanterie-Flieger	infantry aeroplane, contact patrol.
i.J.	im Jahre	in the year.
Ika	Infanterie-Kampf-Artillerie	artillery detailed for the engagement of the enemy's infantry.
i. Kas. L.	in Kasematten-Lafette	on casemate mounting.
Ikraft	Inspektion des Kraftfahrwesens	Inspectorate of M.T. Services.

Abbreviation.	Signification.	English Equivalent.
i. Kst. L.	in Küsten-Lafette	on coast defence mounting.
I.L.R.	Infanterie-Leib-Regiment	Infantry Body Regiment.
Iluft	Inspektion der Luftschiffertruppen	Inspectorate of Airship Troops.
I.M.K.	Infanterie-Munitions-Kolonne	infantry ammunition column.
Ina	Nachrichtenmittel-Abteilung eines Infanterie-Regiments	infantry regimental signalling detachment.
Inf. Beob.	Infanterie-Beobachtung	infantry observation.
Inf. Geschütz	Infanterie-Geschütz	infantry gun, i.e. 7·62 cm. converted Russian field gun.
Int.	Intendant	Intendant.
Int.	Intendantur	
Int.	Intendanz	Intendance.
Intdr.	Intendantur	
I.O.v.Pl.	Infanterie-Offizier vom Platz	Fortress Infantry Officer.
i. P.L.	in Panzer-Lafette	on shielded mounting.
I.R.	Infanterie-Regiment	infantry regiment.
I.R.	Exerzierreglement für die Infanterie	Infantry Training (*drill book*).
i.R.L.	in Radlafette	on wheeled carriage.
I.Sch.V.	Infanterie-Schiess-Vorschrift	Infantry Musketry Regulations.
i.S.I.	in Schirm-Lafette	on carriage with overhead shield.
i.V.	in Vertretung	" By order," " Signed for " (*above a signature on document*).
Iwumba	Infanterie-Waffen- und Munitions-Beschaffungsamt	Infantry Section of the Munitions Department of the War Ministry.
Iz.	Innen-Zünder	internal fuze.

J.

J.	Jagd-	pursuit (*aviation*).
J.	Jäger	" Jäger."
J.	Infanterie	infantry.
J.	Inspektion	Inspectorate.
Jäg.	Jäger	" Jäger."
Jäg.z.Pf.	Jäger zu Pferde	" Jäger zu Pferde."
Jasta	Jagdstaffel	pursuit flight (*aviation unit*).
J.B.	Jäger-Bataillon	" Jäger " battalion.
J.D.	Infanterie-Division	infantry division.
J.d.E.	Inspektion des Eisenbahnwesens	Inspectorate of the Railway Services.
Jdegahei	Inspektion des Gasschutzdienstes für das Heimatgebiet	Inspectorate of Anti-gas Services (in Germany).

Abbreviation.	Signification.	English Equivalent.
Jdeis	Inspektion der Eisenbahntruppen	Inspectorate of Railway Troops.
Jdflieg	Inspektion der Fliegertruppen	Inspectorate of Flying Troops.
Jfl	Infanterie-Flieger	infantry aeroplane, contact patrol.
Jflak	Inspektion der Flugzeugabwehrkanonen	Inspectorate of Anti-aircraft Guns.
Jflakheim	Inspekteur der Flugzeugabwehrkanonen (Heimat)	Inspector of Anti-aircraft Guns (in Germany).
Jflakop	Inspektion der Flugzeugabwehrkanonen Operationsgebiet	Inspectorate of Anti-aircraft Guns in the area of operations.
Jkraft	Inspektion des Kraftfahrwesens	Inspectorate of Mechanical Transport.
Jluft	Inspektion der Luftschiffertruppen	Inspectorate of Airship Troops.
Jnach	Inspektion der Nachrichtentruppen	Inspectorate of the Signal Troops.
J.P.K.	Infanterie-Pionier-Kompagnie	infantry pioneer company.
J.R.	Infanterie-Regiment	infantry regiment.
J.St.	Jagdstaffel	pursuit flight.
J.z.Pf.	Jäger zu Pferde	" Jäger zu Pferde."

K.

Abbreviation.	Signification.	English Equivalent.
K.	Kaiserlich	imperial.
K.	Kampf	fighting, in line, battle.
K.	Kanone	gun.
K.	Kartätsche	case shot.
K.	Kavallerie	cavalry.
K.	Kolonne	column.
K.	Kommandant	Commandant.
K.	Kommandeur	Commander.
K.	Kommission	Commission.
K.	Kompagnie	company.
K.	Königlich	Royal.
K.	Korps	Corps.
K.	Kraftfahr-	motor (*adjective*).
K.	Kraftwagen-	M.T.
K.	Kriegs-	war.
K.	Kriegsgefangenen-	prisoners of war.
K.	Kürassier	cuirassier.
k.	klein	small.
k.	kurz *or* kürzer	short *or* shorter.
K.a.b.	Kriegsgefangenen-Arbeiter-Bataillon	prisoners of war labour battalion.
Kafunka	Kavallerie-Funker-Abteilung	cavalry wireless detachment.
Kagol / Kagohl	Kampf-Geschwader, Oberste Heeresleitung.	Bombing Squadron under General Headquarters.
Kan.	{ Kanone / Kanonier	gun. / gunner.
Karab.	Karabinier	carbineer.

Abbreviation.	Signification.	English Equivalent.
Kart.	Kartusche	cartridge (*gun or howitzer; it implies that it is not fixed ammunition*).
Kas.	Kaserne	barracks.
Kav.	Kavallerie	cavalry.
Kav. Fu. A.	Kavallerie-Funker-Abteilung	cavalry wireless detachment.
Kav. Div.	Kavallerie-Division	cavalry division.
K.B.	Königlich-Bayerisch.	Royal Bavarian.
K.Besold.V.	Kriegs-Besoldungs-Vorschrift	Pay Regulations (War time).
K.B.K.	Kampf-Bataillon-Kommandeur	Commander of the battalion in line.
K. Br. Tr.	Korps-Brücken-Train	Corps bridging train.
K.D.	Kaiserlich-Deutsch	Imperial German.
K.D.	Kavallerie-Division	cavalry division.
K.d.K. Kdr.d.Krftftr.	Kommandeur der Kraftfahr-Truppen (der Armee)	Commander of the Mechanical Transport Troops.
Kdo.	Kommando	command, word of command; party, detachment.
Kdo. Feldluft.	Kommandeur der Feldluftschiffer-Schule	Commander of the Balloon School.
Kdo. Lea	Kommandeur der Luftschiffer-Ersatz-Abteilungen	Commander of Airship Troops Depôts.
Kdo. L. Schule	Kommandeur der Luftschiffschule	Commander of the Airship School.
Kdo. L.V.A.	Kommandeur der Luftschiff-Versuchsanstalt	Commander of the Airship Experimental Establishment.
Kdo. Truhäg	Kommandeur der Luftschifftrupps, Luftschiffhäfen und Militär-Gasanstalten	Commander of Airship Sections, Airship Sheds and Military Gas Factories.
Kdo. Z.B.A.	Kommandeur der Luftschiffer-Zentral-Beschaffungs- und Abnahmestelle	Commander of the Central Depôt for the Supply and Delivery of Airship Material.
Kdr.	Kommandeur	Commander.
Kdr.d.Artillerie	Kommandeur der Artillerie	Artillery Commander.
Kdr.d.Min.	Kommandeur der Mineure	Commander of the Mining Troops.
Kdr. d. Mun. u. Tr.	Kommandeur der Munitionskolonnen und Trains	Commander of the Ammunition Columns and Trains.
Kdr. Munwes.	Kommandeur des Munitionswesens	Officer in charge of Ammunition Supply (Corps H.Q.).
Kdt. H. Qu. K.d.H.Qu.	Kommandant des Hauptquartiers	Camp Commandant.
Kdtr.	Kommandantur	Commandant's office.
K.E.O.	Kriegs-Etappen-Ordnung	Regulations for L. of C. Services.
Kest	Kampf-Einsitzer-Staffel	single-seater fighting flight.
K.F.	Kahnfähre	ferry by rowing boat (*topog.*).
K.F.	Kompagnie-Führer	company commander (*on trench maps, &c.*).
K.F.A.K.	Kaiserliches freiwilliges Automobil Korps	Imperial Volunteer Motor Corps.
K.f.b.Z.	Kriegsverwendungsfähig für besondere Zwecke	fit for active service in certain capacities. (*sometimes used of men classed in category " Garnisonsverwendungsfähig"*).

Abbreviation.	Signification.	English Equivalent.
K.Flak	Flugabwehrkanone auf Kraftwagen	anti-aircraft gun on motor lorry.
K.Fuk.-Station } Kfuk.-Station }	Kleine Funker-Station	small wireless station.
Kfw.	Kriegsfreiwilliger	war-volunteer.
Kg.	Kilogram	kilogramme.
K.Fu.16.	Kleine Funkerstation 16	1916 pattern small wireless station.
K.G.O.H.L.	Kampf-Geschwader, Oberste Heeresleitung	Bombing Squadron under General Headquarters.
K. Gr.	Kanonen-Granate	gun-(H.E.)shell.
Kgsfrw.	Kriegsfreiwilliger	war-volunteer.
Khf.	Kirchhof	churchyard (*topog.*).
K.H.Qu.	Korps-Hauptquartier	Corps Headquarters.
K.i.H.	Kanone in Haubitzlafette	"K.i.H." field gun (*new pattern 7·7-cm. field gun on howitzer carriage*).
Kino	Kinematograph	cinematograph.
K.i.R.L.	Kanone in Rad-Lafette	gun on wheeled carriage.
Kj.z.Pf.	Königsjäger zu Pferde	"Königsjäger zu Pferde" (*not translated*).
K.K.	Kavallerie-Korps	Cavalry Corps.
K.K.	Kraftwagenkolonne	M.T. column.
K. Kf. K.	Kaiserliches Kraftfahrkorps	Imperial Motor Corps.
Kl.	Klasse	class.
Kl.	Klein	small.
Kleiftrupp	Kleiner-Flammenwerfer-Trupp	small *Flammenwerfer* squad.
Kl.F.w.	Kleiner Flammenwerfer	small *Flammenwerfer*.
K. Ltg.	Kabel-Leitung	cable line.
K.M.	Kriegs-Magazin	war-magazine.
K.M.	Kriegs-Ministerium	War Ministry.
Km.	Kilometer	kilometre.
Kmdo.	Kommando	H.Q., staff; party, detachment.
Kmdr. Heim.Luft.	Kommandeur des Heimats-Luftschutzes	Commander of the Home Aerial Defences.
Kmdt.	Kommandant	Commandant.
Kmdtr.	Kommandantur	Commandant's office.
K.M.E.	Kriegsministeriumserlass	War Ministry Order.
K. Mun. } K. Munition }		"K"-ammunition (*armour-piercing ammunition for rifle*) or K-shell (*asphyxiating gas shell*).
K.M., Z. Ch.	Zentralstelle für Fragen der Chemie im Kriegs-Ministerium	Central Office for Chemical Questions in the Ministry of War.
K.O.	Kabinettsordre	Order of His Majesty in Council.
K.O.	Kalk-Ofen	lime kiln (*topog.*).
Kodeis	Kommandeur der Eisenbahn-Truppen	Commander of the Railway Troops.
Kodofea	Kommandeur der Flieger-Ersatz-Abteilungen	Commander of the Training Squadrons (Aviation Depôts).
Kofe	Kommandeur der Fernsprechtruppen	Commander of Telephone Troops (*at Army H.Q.*).

Abbreviation.	Signification.	English Equivalent.
Kofl	} Kommandeur der Flieger-Truppen	Commander of Aviation Troops (*with Corps, &c.*).
Koflieg		
Koflak	Kommandeur der Flug-Abwehr Kanonen	Commander of the Anti-aircraft Guns.
Kofu	} Kommandeur der Funkertruppen	Commander of Wireless Troops (*at Army H.Q.*).
Kofunk		
Kogen-Luft	Kommandierender General der Luftstreitkräfte	Commander of the Air Forces.
Kol.	Kolonne	column.
Koluft	Kommandeur der Luftstreitkräfte	Commander of the Air Forces (*at Army H.Q.*).
Komdrt.	Kommandiert	detached, detailed.
Komp.	Kompagnie	company.
Komtr.	} Kommandeur der Munitionskolonnen und Trains	Commander of the Ammunition Columns and Trains.
Ko.M.u.T.		
Komut		
Konab	Konstruktionsneuheiten-Abteilung	Inventions Section (of the Aviation Inspectorate).
Korp.	Korporalschaft	section (¼ *of a "Zug"*).
Kp.	Kompagnie	company.
Kp.	Kappe	cap (*of fuze, shell, etc.*).
Kpl.	} Korporalschaft	section (¼ *of a "Zug."*).
Kplschaft		
K.Pr.	Königlich-Preussisch	Royal Prussian.
Kps.	Korps	Corps.
K.R.	Kürassier-Regiment	cuirassier regiment.
Kr. (*in a postmark*)	Kreis	district.
Kr.	Kreuz	cross.
Kr.	Kriegs-	war (*adjective*).
Kr.	Krupp	Krupp (*trade mark*).
Krad	Kraftradfahrer	motor cyclist.
K. Rad. Abt.	Kraftrad(fahrer)-Abteilung	motor cyclist detachment.
Kraftfahr. Verb. Offizier	Kraftfahrtruppen - Verbindungs-Offizier	M.T. liaison officer.
Krfw.	Kraftwagen	motor lorry, motor car.
Krgs.Gef.Arb.Btl.	Kriegs-Gefangenen-Arbeiter-Bataillon	prisoners of war labour battalion.
Krktrg.	Krankenträger	stretcher bearers.
Kr.M.	Kriegs-Ministerium	War Ministry.
Krak. W.	} Krankenwagen	ambulance wagon.
Krnk.W.		
Krtw.	Kraftwagen	motor lorry, motor car.
Kr.W.Kol.	Kraft-Wagen-Kolonne	motor transport column.
K.S.	Königlich-Sächsisch	Royal Saxon.
K. Sig. 16	Kleines Signal-Gerät 16	small 1916 pattern lamp signalling apparatus.
K S.O.	Kriegssanitätsordnung	Field Medical Regulations.
Kst.	Küste (n)	coast (coast defence).
K.St.	Kraftwagen-Staffel	M.T. échelon.
Kst. H.	Küsten-Haubitze	coast defence howitzer.
Kst. K.	Küsten-Kanone	coast defence gun.
Kst. Mrs.	Küsten-Mörser	coast defence mortar.
K.St.O.H.L.	Kampfstaffel der Obersten Heeresleitung	Bombing Flight under G.H.Q.

Abbreviation.	Signification.	English Equivalent.
k.s.W.M.	kurze schwere Wurf-Mine	heavy *Minenwerfer* short H.E. shell.
Kt.	Kartätsche	case shot.
K.T.A.	Korps-Telegraphen-Abteilung	Corps telegraph detachment.
K.T.B.	Korps-Tages-Befehl	Corps Order of the Day.
K.Tel.A.	Korps-Telegraphen-Abteilung	Corps telegraph detachment.
K.T.K.	Kampf - Truppen - Kommandeur	Commander of the front line troops.
Kt.O.	Krankenträger-Ordnung	Stretcher Bearer Regulations.
Ktt. Br.	Kettenbrücke	suspension bridge (*topog.*).
Kür. R.	Kürassier-Regiment	cuirassier regiment.
K.V.	Kassen-Verwaltung	cashier's or paymaster's office financial administration.
K.V. / kv.	} Kriegsverwendungsfähig	fit for active service.
K.V.A.	Kriegs-Verpflegungs - Anordnungen	Instructions for Supply.
K.V.O.	Kraftfahrtruppen- Verbindungs-Offizier	M.T. liaison officer.
K.V.V.	Kriegs-Verpflegungs-Vorschrift	Field Supply Regulations.
K.W.	Königlich-Württembergisch	Royal Württemberg.
K.W.Flak.	Kraft-Wagen-Flak.	A.A. gun on motor lorry.
Kw.K.	Kraft-Wagen-Kolonne	mechanical transport column.
K.Z.	Kanonen-Zünder	gun fuze.
Kz.	Kopf-Zünder	nose fuze.
K. Zug	Kanonenmunitions-Zug	gun ammunition train.
kz. Bd. Z.	kurzer Boden-Zünder	short base fuze.
	L.	
L.	Lafette	gun carriage.
L.	Landsturm	Landsturm (*not translated*).
L.	Landwehr	Landwehr (*not translated*).
L.	Lang	long.
L.	Länger	longer.
L.	Lanz	"Lanz," a type of *Minenwerfer*.
L.	Lazarett	hospital.
L.	Lehr-	instructional.
L.	Leicht	light.
L.	Licht-	*usually* lamp.
L.	Links	left.
L.	Luft	air.
L.	Luftschiff (Marine-)	Naval airship.
l.	lang	long.
l.	leicht	light.
L/3·1, &c		Used in the nomenclature of Naval projectiles to indicate that the length is 3·1, &c., calibres.
L/40, &c.		Used in nomenclature of Naval guns to indicate that the length is 40, &c., calibres.
Ladekdo	Lade-Kommando	battery charging detachment (*wireless*).
Laf.	Lafette	gun carriage.

Abbreviation.	Signification.	English Equivalent.
Landw.	Landwehr	Landwehr (*not translated*).
Laz.	Lazarett	hospital.
l.B.	lange Brennlänge	long burning (*fuze*).
L.B.	Licht-Bild	photograph (*is also applied to an aeroplane photographic reconnaissance*).
L.B.E.B.	Landwehr-Brigade-Ersatz-Bataillon	Landwehr brigade Ersatz battalion.
Ldst.	Landsturm	Landsturm (*not translated*).
Ldst.E.B.K. ...	Landsturm-Eisenbahn-Bau-Kompagnie	Landsturm railway construction company.
Ldstm.	Landsturmmann	man of the Landsturm.
L.Dv.	Links-Nachbar-Division ...	neighbouring division on the left.
Ldw.	Landwehr	Landwehr (*not translated*).
Ldw.E.B.K. ...	Landwehr-Eisenbahn-Bau-Kompagnie	Landwehr railway construction company.
Ldw.Ers.Rgt. ...	Landwehr-Ersatz-Regiment ...	Landwehr Ersatz regiment.
L.E.		" L.E." (*a type of explosive bullet, see under* " *Munition*")
Lea ... ... L.E.A.	Luftschiffer-Ersatz-Abteilung	balloon depôt detachment.
Lebm. K. ...	Lebensmittelkisten	ration boxes.
Lebm. W. ...	Lebensmittelwagen	supply wagon.
L.E.Rgt. ...	Landwehr-Ersatz-Regiment ...	Landwehr Ersatz regiment.
l.f.	läusefrei	free of vermin.
lfd.	laufend	current.
l.F.H.	leichte Feld-Haubitze... ...	light field howitzer.
l.F.Stat.	leichte Funken-Station ...	light wireless station.
Lg.	Lang	long.
Lg.	Leuchtgeschoss	star shell.
lg. Bd. Z. ...	langer Boden-Zünder ...	long base fuze.
lg. Brlg.	lange Brennlänge	long burning (*fuze*).
l. gez.	leichte gezogene	light rifled.
l. gez. W.M. ...	leichte gezogene Wurfmine ...	light rifled *Minenwerfer* H.E. shell.
Lggr.	Langgranate	long shell.
Lg.Zdr.	Leuchtgeschoss-Zünder ...	fuze for star shell.
Lichts.Abt. ...	Lichtsignal-Abteilung ...	lamp signalling detachment.
Linkdtr.	Linienkommandantur ...	office of line commandant (*railway service*).
Li.Off.	Lichtsignal-Offizier	lamp signalling officer.
L.I.R.	Landwehr-Infanterie-Regiment	Landwehr infantry regiment.
Li.Sign.Off. ...	Lichtsignal-Offizier	lamp signalling officer.
L.K.Z.	Langer Kanonen-Zünder ...	long fuze for gun.
l.M.G.Tr. ...	leichter Maschinen-Gewehr-Trupp	light machine gun section.
l.M.K.	leichte Munitions-Kolonne ...	light ammunition column.
L.M.Tr.	Licht-Mess-Trupp	artillery observation section or " flash spotters."
L.M.W.	Lanz-Minenwerfer	*Lanz Minenwerfer* (*a kind of trench mortar*).
l.M.W.	leichter Minenwerfer	light *Minenwerfer* (*trench mortar*).
l.N.M.	leichte Nachrichten-Mine ...	light message shell.

Abbreviation.	Signification.	English Equivalent.
...	Lösung ...	relief; solution (*cipher*).
L.St.	Ladestelle	entraining station, loading platform (*topog.*).
l.s.W.M. ...	lange schwere Wurf-Mine	heavy *Minenwerfer* long H.E. shell.
Lt. lt.	} laut	according to.
Lt. Ltn.	} Leutnant	2nd Lieutenant.
Lubia (?) ...	Licht-Bild-Abteilung	Photographic Section (*Aviation Section of the Munitions Department*).
Luftsch. ...	Luftschiff	airship.
Luftsch. ...	Luftschiffer	aeronaut; man of an airship crew, *or* balloon section.
L.V.	Lautverstärker...	amplifier valve.
l.v.	leicht verwundet	slightly wounded.
L.V.A. ...	Luftschiff-Versuchs-Anstalt ...	Airship Experimental Establishment.
L.V.G.	Luft-Verkehrs-Gesellschaft ...	*A firm which manufactures aeroplanes known as L.V.G.*
l.W.M. ...	leichte Wurf-Mine	light *Minenwerfer* H.E. shell.
l.W.M.Zdr.	leichter Wurf-Mine-Zünder ...	fuze of light *Minenwerfer* shell.

M.

M.	Mühle ...	mill (*topog.*).
M.	Magazin	magazine.
	Mann ...	man.
	Marine ...	Navy; Naval.
M.	Mark ...	mark (*the coin*).
M.	Meter ...	metre.
M.	Militär- ...	military.
M.	Mine ...	mine; *Minenwerfer* shell.
M.	Ministerium ...	Ministry.
M.	Mittelsorts	medium quality.
M.	Modell ...	pattern, mark (*of a gun, etc.*).
M.	Mörser ...	mortar.
M.	Mühle ...	mill.
M.	Munitions- ...	ammunition.
M.	Muster ...	pattern.
m.	Meter ...	metre.
m.	mit ...	with.
m.	mittler (-er,-e,-es)	medium.
Mag.	Magazin	magazine, store, depôt.
Mag.Fp.K(ol).	Magazin-Fuhrparkkolonne	depôt supply column.
Maj.	Major ...	Major.
Mar.-K. ...	Marine-Korps ...	Naval Corps.
Masch. ...	Maschinen (gewehr) ...	machine gun (*on identity discs*).
Mascha ...	Maschinen-Amt	locomotive depôt.
Mat. ...	Material ...	material.
Matr. Art. Rgt. ...	Matrosen-Artillerie-Regiment	"Matrosen" Artillery Regiment.
M.B. ...	Militär-Brieftaube	military carrier pigeon.
M.D.B.W.	Militärische Benutzung der Wasserstrassen	Military Inland Water Transport Service.

Abbreviation.	Signification.	English Equivalent.
Mdlchb. ...	Mundlochbüchse	old pattern type of fuze.
Mdlchf. ...	Mundlochfutter	gaine (*of fuze*).
Mebau ...	Militär-Eisenbahn-Bauabteilung	military railway construction detachment.
Mebedo ...	Militär-Eisenbahn-Betriebs-Direktion-Dobrudscha	Military Railway Traffic Directorate, Dobrudsha.
M.E. Betr. Abt.	Militär-Eisenbahn-Betriebs-Abteilung	military railway traffic section.
Mebu ...	Mannschafts-Eisen-Beton-Unterstand	reinforced concrete dug-out (*machine-gun emplacement*).
M.E.D. ...	Militär-Eisenbahn-Direktion	Directorate of Military Railways.
M.E.u.B.W. ...	Militär-Erziehungs und Bildungswesen	Military Educational and Instructional Services.
M.E.V.A.	Militär-Eisenbahn-Verkehrs-Amt	military railway traffic office.
M.E.W. Abt. ...	Militär-Eisenbahn-Werkstätten-Abteilung	military railway workshops section.
M.F. ... Mf. ...	Mastfernrohr	giant periscope.
M.Fe.A. ...	Marine-Fernsprech-Abteilung	Naval telephone detachment.
M. Flak Zug. ...	3·7 cm. Flug-Abwehr-Maschinenkanonenzug	anti-aircraft gun section (3·7 cm. automatic guns).
M.Fuk.-Station Mfuk.-Station	Mittlere Funker-Station ...	medium wireless station.
M.G.A. ... M.G.Abt....	Maschinen-Gewehr-Abteilung	machine gun detachment.
M.G.D. ...	Militär-General-Direktion der Eisenbahnen	General Directorate of Military Railways.
m. gez. ...	mittlere gezogene	medium rifled.
M.G.K. M.G.Kp.	Maschinen-Gewehr-Kompagnie	machine gun company.
m. gl. ...	mittlere glatte	medium smooth bore.
M.G.L.K.	Maschinen-Gewehr-Lehr-Kursus (Kompagnie ?)	machine gun course (instructional company ?).
M.G.O. beim A.O.K.	Maschinengewehr-Offizier-beim Armee-Oberkommando	Machine Gun Officer at Army Headquarters.
M.G.O. b/St(abe)	Maschinen-Gewehr-Offizier-beim Stabe	regimental machine gun officer.
M.G.S.s.A.	Maschinen-Gewehr-Scharfschützen-Abteilung	machine gun marksman detachment.
M.G.S.s.K.	Maschinen-Gewehr-Scharfschützen-Kompagnie	machine gun marksman company.
M.G.S.s.T.	Maschinen-Gewehr-Scharfschützen-Trupp	machine gun marksman section (*obsolete*).
M.H. ...	Minen-Hülle	canister bomb.
M.H.Tr. ... M.Hu.Tr.	Meldehund-Trupp	messenger dog section.
Mi.	Minenwerfer	*Minenwerfer.*
Mil. San. Wes. ...	Militär-Sanitäts-Wesen ...	Army Medical Service.
Mil.-Url.-Zug	Militär-Urlauber-Zug	military leave train.
Min.	Mine (n)	mine or *Minenwerfer* shell.
Min. ...	Mineur (Kompagnie)	mining (company).
Min. ...	Minister...	Minister.
Min. ...	Ministerium	Ministry.

Abbreviation.	Signification.	English Equivalent.
Minenw. … Min.W. … Minw. …	Minenwerfer … … …	*Minenwerfer*.
Mi-Stelle …	Minenwerfer-Stelle …	*Minenwerfer* position.
Mi. W. K. …	Minenwerfer-Kompagnie	*Minenwerfer* company.
Mk. … …	Mark … … …	mark (*the coin*).
M.K. … …	Munitions-Kolonne …	ammunition column.
Mk. … …	Marschkolonne… …	column on the march.
m.K. … …	mit Kappe … …	with cap (*fuze*).
m.K. … …	mit Klappensicherung	with centrifugal safety device (*fuze*).
Mldg. … …	Meldung … …	report.
M.L.T. … …	Marine-Luftschiff-Trupp	Naval airship section.
mm. … …	Millimeter … …	millimetre.
m.M.W. … …	mittlerer Minenwerfer…	medium *Minenwerfer*.
m. Ozdg.… …	mit Oberzündung …	with overhead ignition (*pattern of 21 cm. mortar*).
mob. … …	mobil … … …	mobilized; mobile.
Mob. Et. Kdtur.	Mobile Etappen-Kommandantur	mobile L. of C. Commandant's office.
Morep-Komp. …	Motor-Reparatur-Kompagnie	motor repairs company (?).
m.P. … …	mit Panzerkopf … …	with armour-piercing head (*of shell*).
Mrs. … …	Mörser … … …	(21 cm.) mortar.
Mrs. Battr. …	Mörser-Batterie …	(21 cm.) mortar battery.
Mrs. m.Kr. …	Mörser mit Kraftwagen (?)	mortar with tractors (?).
M.S. … …	Melde-Sammelstelle …	report centre.
M. Sig. 16 …	Mittleres Signal-Gerät 16 …	medium 1916 pattern lamp signalling apparatus.
M.S.O. … …	Melde-Sammel-Offizier	intelligence officer (*at Corps or Divisional H.Q. for reconnaissance, observation, hostile activity, etc.*).
M.St.G.B. …	Militär-Straf-Gesetz-Buch …	Military Penal Code.
M.Str.G.O. …	Militär-Straf-Gesetz-Ordnung	Code of procedure for Military tribunals.
M.Str.V. …	Militär-Straf-Vollstreckungs-Vorschrift	Regulations for the carrying out of sentences of military tribunals.
M.S.W. … …	Militär-Sanitäts-Wesen …	Army Medical Service.
M.T. … …	Marschtag … … …	"marching day" (*in a withdrawal, e.g., to the Hindenburg Line*).
Mtl. K. … …	Mantel-Kanone … …	jacketed gun.
mtt. … …	mittels … … …	by means of.
Mun. … …	Munition … … …	ammunition.
Mun. Kol. n/A. …	Munitions-Kolonne neuer Art	new pattern ammunition column.
Mun. Trgt. …	Munitions-Tragetier …	ammunition pack animal.
Musk. … …	Musketier … …	private (*of the Active category in a line infantry regiment*).
… …	Militär-Urlanber-Zug …	military leave train.
M.V. … …	Mit Verzögerung …	with delay action (*fuze*).
m.v.F. … …	mit vorderem Führungsring …	with forward driving band (*shell*).

Abbreviation.	Signification.	English Equivalent.
m.V.u.K....	mit Verzögerung und Klappensicherung	with delay action and centrifugal safety device (*fuze*).
M.W.	Minenwerfer	*Minenwerfer*.
M.W.	Munitionswagen	ammunition wagon.
M.W.A.	Minenwerfer-Abteilung	*Minenwerfer* detachment.
M.W.B.	Militär-Wochen-Blatt...	Weekly Military Gazette.
M.W.G.	Melde-Wurf-Granate	message bomb *or* rocket.
M.W.K.	Minenwerfer-Kompagnie	*Minenwerfer* company.
M.W.Kp.(G)	Gebirgsminenwerfer-Kompagnie	mountain *Minenwerfer* company.
m.W.M.	mittlere Wurf-Mine	medium *Minenwerfer* H.E. shell.
M.W.O. b/Stabe	Minenwerfer-Offizier beim Stabe	regimental *Minenwerfer* officer.

N.

Abbreviation.	Signification.	English Equivalent.
N.	Nachmittag	afternoon.
N.	Nachrichten	Intelligence *or* signalling.
N.	Nacht	night.
N.	Nahkampf	close-range.
N.	Norden	North.
N.	Nummer	number.
n.	nach	" to " (*direction of road*).
n.	nördlich	north of, northerly
n/A.	neuer Art	new pattern.
N.A.	Nachrichten-Abteilung	regimental signalling detachment : intelligence section.
Nachh.	Nachhut	rearguard.
nachm.	nachmittags	in the afternoon, p.m.
Nachr.A.... Nachra	} Nachrichten-Abteilung	{ regimental signalling detachment ; intelligence section.
Nachrm.O.	Nachrichtenmittel-Offizier	regimental signalling officer.
Nahk. Battr.	Nahkampf-Batterie	close-range battery.
Namo Na.O.	} Nachrichtenmittel-Offizier	regimental signalling officer.
N.D.	Nachrichten-Dienst	Intelligence Service.
n.F.	neuer Form	of new shape.
N.G.	Nahkampf-Geschütz	close-range gun.
N.M.A.	Nachrichtenmittel-Abteilung	regimental signalling detachment.
nördl.	nördlich	north of, northerly.
N.M.O.	Nachrichten-Mittel-Offizier	regimental signalling officer.
N.O.	Nachrichten-Offizier	intelligence officer; signalling officer.
N.O.d. Regts.	Nachrichten-Offizier des Regiments	regimental signalling officer.
N.Z.II.	Nachrichten-Zug II	2nd battalion signalling section.

Abbreviation.	Signification.	English Equivalent.
	O.	
O.	Oberkommando	Headquarters Staff.
O.	Oberst	Colonel.
O.	Offizier	Officer.
O.	Ordnung	regulation; order.
O.	Orts-	local.
O.	Ortsfest	fixed.
O.	Ost	East.
O.	ohne	without.
o.	östlich	east of, easterly.
O.A.	Offizier-Aspirant	probationary or aspirant officer.
O./A. (in a postmark)	Ober-Amt	Head Office (*postal*).
o.Az.	ohne Aufschlagzündung	without percussion system (*fuze*).
Ob.	Oberst	Colonel.
Ob.	Oberstleutnant	Lieutenant-Colonel.
O.B.	Ortsbiwak	close billets.
Obbfhb.	Oberbefehlshaber	Commander-in-Chief.
Oberlt.	Oberleutnant	Lieutenant.
Oberost	Oberbefehlshaber Ost	C.-in-C. on the Eastern Front.
Oblt.	Oberleutnant	Lieutenant.
Obost	Oberbefehlshaber Ost	C. in C. on the Eastern Front.
Ob. Ost	Oberkommando Ost	
Obstlt.	Oberstleutnant	Lieutenant-Colonel.
Ob. West	Oberkommando West	C. in C. on the Western Front.
O.d.K.	Oberkommando der Küstenverteidigung	Coast Defence Headquarters.
Offz.	Offizier	officer.
Off. Stellv.	Offizier-Stellvertreter	acting officer (*but usually not translated*).
O-Flak	Ortsfeste - Flug - Abwehr - Kanone	fixed anti-aircraft gun.
O. Flak-Battr.	7·7 and 7·62 cm. Ortsfeste-Flug-Abwehr-Kanonen-Batterie	fixed anti-aircraft battery (7·7 and 7·62 cm. guns).
O. Flak-Zug.	7·62 cm. Ortsfeste-Flug-Abwehr-Kanonen-Zug	fixed anti-aircraft section (7.62 cm. guns).
O.H.L.	Oberste Heeresleitung	General Headquarters, Commander-in-Chief, Higher Command.
O.K.	Ortskommandant	Town Major.
O.Kr.	Orts-Krankenstube	medical inspection room.
Olt.	Oberleutnant	Lieutenant.
O-Punkt	Null-Punkt	aiming point, reference point.
O.Q.	Oberquartiermeister	*see page* 109.
Ortskdt.	Ortskommandant	Town Major.
östl.	östlich	east of, easterly.
O.U.	Orts-Unterkunft	(*ordinary*) billets.
O.V.	Ohne Verzögerung	without delay action, direct action (*fuze*).
O.v.N.	Offizier vom Nachrichtendienst	information officer (*at Brigade H.Q.*).

Abbreviation.	Signification.	English Equivalent.
	P.	
P.	Park	park.
P.	Patrone	cartridge.
P.	Personen-	ordinary (*of a train*).
P.	Pferd	horse.
P.	Pionier-	pioneer.
P.	Post	Post (*Office, etc.*).
P.	Posten	sentry.
P.	Proviant-	supply (*food*).
P.	Pulver-	powder (*usually black powder*).
Patr.	Patrone	cartridge (*in the case of a gun, only when it is fixed ammunition*).
Patr. W.	Patronenwagen	small arms ammunition wagon.
P.B.	Pionier-Bataillon	pioneer battalion.
P.Bl.Tr.	Pionier-Belagerungs-Train	pioneer siege train.
P.B.S.T.	Panzer-Beobachtungs-Turm	armoured observation turret.
Pf. D.	Pferdedepot	remount depôt.
Pfflb.	Pferdefeldbahn	(40 *cm. gauge*) trench tramway (*animal traction*).
Pf.L.	Pferde-Lazarett	veterinary hospital.
Pf.W.	Pferde-Wärter	groom.
Pf.W.	Pferde-Wechsel	stage (*change-of-horses*).
P.H.D.	Pionier-Haupt-Depot	pioneer main depôt.
Pi. (B., Kp., &c.) Pion. (B., Kp., &c.)	Pionier (-Bataillon,-Kompagnie, &c.)	pioneer (battalion, company, &c.).
Piko	Pionier-Kommandeur	pioneer commander.
Piwumba	Pionier Waffen-und Munitions-Beschaffungsamt	Pioneer Section of the Munitions Department of the War Ministry.
Pk. W.	Packwagen	baggage wagon.
Pl. W.	Planwagen	ladder-sided wagon.
P.M.	Pulver-Magazin	powder magazine.
Pont.	Ponton	pontoon.
p.p.	*praemissis praemittendis*	&c., &c.
Prov.	Proviant	supply.
Prov. Amt.	Proviant-Amt	supply depôt.
Pr. K.	Proviant-Kolonne	supply column.
P.S.	Pferde-Stärke	horsepower, H.P.
P.S.-Gr.	Panzer-Stahl-Granate	steel armour-piercing shell.
P.U.	Planübergang	level crossing.
Puw	Prüf-Anstalt und Werft	testing workshops (*for aeroplanes*).
P.V.	Pontonier-Vorschrift	Pontoon Bridging Regulations.
P.W.	Proviant-Wagen	supply wagon.
P.W.	Pack-Wagen	baggage wagon.
P.Z.	Personen-Zug	ordinary passenger train.
P.Z.D.	Pionier-Zwischendepot	pioneer intermediate dump *or* depôt.

Abbreviation.	Signification.	English Equivalent.

Q.

Q.	Quartier	quarters.
q.	quadrat	square.
qm.	Quadratmeter	square metre.
Q.M.		
Qu.	Quartier	quarters.

R.

R.	Regiments-	regiment(al).
R.	Reitend-	horse, mounted.
R.	Reiter	horseman, cavalry man.
R.	Rekruten-	recruit (*adjective*).
R.	Reserve-	Reserve.
R.	Riesen	giant.
r.	reitende	horse (*e.g., artillery*).
R.A.	Regiments-Arzt	regimental medical officer.
Radf.	Radfahrer	cyclist.
R.A.K.	Reserve-Armee-Korps	Reserve (Army) Corps.
R.B.	Regiments-Befehl	regimental order.
r. Bttr.	reitende Batterie	horse artillery battery.
R.D.	Rekruten-Depot	recruit depôt.
Rdf.	Radfahrer	cyclist.
Rea	Riesen-Ersatz-Abteilung	giant aeroplane training depôt.
R.E. B.K.	Reserve - Eisenbahn - Bau - Kompagnie	Reserve railway construction company.
Reg.	Regiment	regiment.
Rekodeis	Regiments-Kommandeur der Eisenbahn-Truppen	Regimental Commander of the Railway Troops.
Rekr.	Rekruten-	recruit (*adjective*).
Res.	Reserve	Reserve.
Res. Eisb. Bau-Komp.	Reserve - Eisenbahn - Bau - Kompagnie	Reserve railway construction company.
Rev. K.	Revolver-Kanone	revolver-gun.
R.F.A.	Reitende Feld-Artillerie	horse artillery.
Rfla		
R. Fliegerabteilung	Riesen-Flugzeug-Abteilung	giant aeroplane flight.
R.G.O.	Regiments-Gas-Offizier	regimental gas officer.
R.G.St.	Regiments-Gefechts-Stand	regimental battle headquarters.
Rgt.	Regiment	regiment.
Rgt.z.F.	Regiment zu Fuss	dismounted cavalry regiment.

Abbreviation.	Signification.	English Equivalent.
R.I.R.	Reserve-Infanterie-Regiment	Reserve infantry regiment.
Rittm.	Rittmeister	Captain (*of cavalry or train*).
R.K.	Ring-Kanone	gun with chase rings.
R.K.	Revolver-Kanone	revolver gun.
R.K.O.	Regiments-Kampf-Ordnung (?)	regimental operation order.
R.K.O	Regiments - Kommando - Ordnung (?)	regimental order.
R.P.	Relais-Posten	relay post.
R.P.K.	Reserve - Pionier - Kompagnie	Reserve pioneer company.
R.Q.	Reise-Quartier	march billet.
R.S.K.	Reserve- Sanitäts - Kompagnie	Reserve bearer company.
R.St.	Regiments-Stab	regimental staff.
R.T.K.	Reserve - Truppen - Kommandeur	commander of the troops in reserve.
Rttm.	Rittmeister	Captain (*cavalry*).
R.U. (3)	Reserve - Ulanen - Regiment(3)	(3rd.) Reserve "Ulanen" Regiment.
R.U.	Reserve-Unterstand	reserve dug-out.
R.W.	Reparatur-Werkstätte	repair workshop.

S.

S.	Sanitäts-	medical.
S.	Schiessschule	School of Musketry *or* Gunnery.
S.	Schrapnel	shrapnel.
S.	Schütze(n)	rifleman, *or* riflemen.
S.	Seite	page.
S.	Signal	signal.
S.	Soldat(en)	soldier(s), private(s).
S.	Station	station.
s.	schwer	heavy.
s.	südlich	south of, southerly.
s.	siehe	see, *vide*.
s.A.d. Feldh.	schwere Artillerie des Feldheeres	Heavy Artillery of the Field Army.
San.	Sanitäts-	medical.
San. K.	Sanitäts-Kompagnie	medical *or* bearer company.
San. K.A. Sanka	} Sanitäts- Kraftwagen - Abteilung	motor ambulance section.
Sanko San. Ko.	} Sanitäts-Kompagnie...	medical *or* bearer company.
Sas.	Sandsack	sand bag.
S.B.	Soldatenbrief	soldier's letter.
Sch.	Scheune	barn (*topog.*).
Sch.	Schrapnel	shrapnel.

Abbreviation.	Signification.	English Equivalent.
Sch.	Schuss	round, shot.
Sch.	Schütze	rifleman.
Schäf.	Schäferei	sheep farm (*topog.*).
Scheinw. Zg.	Scheinwerferzug	searchlight section.
Sch. Grab. Kan.	Schützen-Graben-Kanone	trench-gun.
Schl.	Schlächterei	slaughter house.
Schnee. Batl.	Schneeschuhläufer-Bataillon	Skiers Battalion (*identity discs*).
Schnellf.	Schnellfeuer	rapid fire.
Schr.	Schrapnel	shrapnel.
Schusta	Schutzstaffel	protective flight (*aviation unit*).
Schwefla (-Batterie)	schwere flachbahn (-Batterie)	heavy flat trajectory (battery).
Schwf.	Scheinwerfer	searchlight.
Schw. R.R.	Schweres Reiter-Regiment	heavy cavalry regiment (*Bavarian or Saxon.*)
schw. v.	schwer verwundet	severely wounded.
Schzzgdep.	Schanzzeugdepot	engineer dump.
S.E.	Seine Exzellenz	His Excellency (*Corps Commanders, etc.*).
Seilabt.	Seilbahn-Abteilung	aerial railway detachment.
Seiltrupp	Seilbahn-Betriebs-Trupp	aerial railway traffic section.
Sek.	Sekunden	seconds.
Sekt.	Sektion	section.
selbst.	selbständig	independent.
S.F.	Scheren-Fernrohr	stereo-telescope.
s.F.H.	schwere Feld-Haubitze	heavy field howitzer.
s.F.H. 02 (&c.)	schwere Feld-Haubitze 02 (&c.)	1902 (&c.) pattern heavy field howitzer.
s.F.H.M.W.	schwere Feld - Haubitze Munitions-Wagen	ammunition wagon for heavy field howitzer.
S.F.K.	Schnell-Feuer-Kanone	quickfiring (Q.F.) gun.
s.F.St.	schwere Funkenstation	heavy wireless station.
Si.	Signalisation	signalling.
Si. Spruch	Signalspruch	signal message.
S.K.	Sanitäts-Kompagnie	medical *or* bearer company.
S.K.	Sanitäts-Kolonne	ambulance column.
S.K.	Schnelllade-Kanone	quick-firing (Q.F.) gun.
S.Ko.	Sanitäts-Kompagnie	medical *or* bearer company.
S.L.	Schirm-Lafette	overhead shield (*of gun*).
S.L.	Schütte-Lanz	a type of German airship.
S.m.K.-Munition	Spitz-Munition mit Kern	armour-piercing ammunition (*rifle and machine gun*).
S.M.Tr.	Schall-Mess-Trupp	sound ranging detachment.
S-Munition		" S " ammunition (*see under* "*Munition*").
Sp.	Spitze	point; head of an advanced guard.
sp.	spännig (*e.g.*, 1 spännig, 4 spännig)	1-horsed, 4-horsed.
Span. Reit.	Spanische Reiter	" knife rests " (*entanglements*).
Sprgr.	Spreng-Granate	high explosive (H.E.) shell (naval).
Spgr.m.K.	Sprenggranatenzünder mit Klappensicherung	fuze for (naval) H.E. shell with centrifugal safety device.
S.R.	Schützen-Regiment	" Schützen " regiment.
S.St.	Sammel-station	collecting station.

Abbreviation.	Signification.	English Equivalent.
S.s. Trupp	Scharfschützen-Trupp	(machine gun) marksman section (*obsolete*).
Stbr.	Steinbruch	quarry (*topog.*).
St.	Stab	staff, H.Q.
St.	Stellung	position.
St.	Stück	piece; unit; copy.
St. Abt.	Sturm-Abteilung	assault detachment.
ständ.	ständig	permanent.
Stat.	Station	station.
Stautrains	Kommandeur der Staffel und des Trains	Commander of Trains and Train Echelons.
Stck.	Stück	piece; unit; copy.
Stellv.	Stellvertretend	acting, deputy.
Stffstb.	Staffelstab	divisional train échelon.
Stk. V.	Stellungskriegsverwendungsfähig	fit for employment in trench warfare.
Stllg.	Stellung	position.
Stllvtr.	Stellvertreter	acting, representative.
St.N.	Stärke-Nachweisung	list *or* statement showing strength *or* establishment.
Stoeis	Stabsoffizier der Eisenbahntruppen zu besonderer Verwendung	Staff Officer for the Special Service Railway Troops.
Stofelda	Stabs-Offizier der Feld-Artillerie	Staff Officer for Field Artillery.
Stofl	Stabs-Offizier der Flieger-Truppen	Staff Officer for Aviation (*at Army H.Q.*).
St.O.Flak	Stabs-Offizier der Flug-Abwehr-Kanonen	Staff Officer for Anti-aircraft Guns.
St.O.Flu.M.	Stabsoffizier des Flugmeldedienstes im Heimatgebiet	Staff Officer of the Aircraft Reporting Service in Germany.
St.O.Fussa	Stabs-Offizier der Fuss-Artillerie	Staff Officer for Foot Artillery.
St.O.Gas Stogas	Stabsoffizier für Gas (des A.O.K.)	Army Gas Officer.
Stokraft	Stabsoffizier der Kraftwagentruppen zu besonderer Verwendung	Staff Officer for Special Service Motor Transport Troops.
Stoluft	Stabs-Offizier der Luftschiffer-Truppen	Staff Officer for Air Services.
Stoluftheim	Stabsoffizier der Luftschiffertruppen in der Heimat	Staff Officer for Airship Troops in Germany.
Stomag	Stabsoffizier der Maschinengewehr-Truppen beim A.O.K.	Staff Officer for Machine Gun Troops at Army H.Q.
St.O.M.G.	Stabs-Offizier der Maschinen-Gewehr-Truppen	Staff Officer for Machine Guns.
Stopi	Stabs-Offizier der Pioniere	Staff Officer for Pioneers (*Corps H.Q.*).
Sto. Sta	Stabsoffizier der Starkstrom-Abteilung	Staff-Officer for Electric Power Detachment.
Stotel	Stabsoffizier der Telegraphentruppen	Staff Officer for the Telegraph Troops.
Stotrain	Stabsoffizier des Trains beim A.O.K.	Staff Officer for "Train" Troops at Army Headquarters.
Stoverm	Stabs-Offizier des Vermessungs-Wesens	Staff Officer for Survey.

Abbreviation.	Signification.	English Equivalent.
St. Qu.	Stabsquartier	Headquarters.
St. Str. Abt. (Komp.)	Starkstrom-Abteilung (Kompagnie)	electric power detachment (company).
Str.	Strasse	street, road.
Str.B.K.	Strassen-Bau-Kompagnie	roadmaking company.
S.Tr.O.	See-Transport-Ordnung	Regulations for Movements by Sea.
St.St(ab)	Staffelstab	divisional train échelon.
Stuka	Sturm-Panzer-Kraftwagen-Abteilung	tank detachment.
südl.	südlich	south of, southerly.
s.W.M.	schwere Wurf-Mine	heavy *Minenwerfer* H.E. shell.
S.Z.	Scheinwerfer-Zug	searchlight section.

T.

Abbreviation.	Signification.	English Equivalent.
T.	Tagesbefehl	Order of the Day, daily orders.
T.	Telegraph	telegraph.
T.	Telefon	telephone.
T.	Train	Train (*not translated*).
T.	Truppen	troops.
t.	Tonne	metric ton (2,205 *lbs.*).
Tafern	Technische Abteilung der Fernsprechtruppen	Technical Section of the Telephone Troops.
Tafunk	Technische Abteilung der Funkertruppen	Technical Section of the Wireless Troops.
Tb.	Taube	pigeon.
Tel.	Telegraph	telegraph.
Tel. Abt. / Telegr. Abt.	Telegraphen-Abteilung	telegraph detachment.
Teleins (zwei, usw.)	Fernsprech-Ersatz-Abteilung 1, usw.	1st (2nd, etc.) Telephone Depôt Detachment.
Tewumba	Telegraphen Waffen-und Munitions-Beschaffungsamt	Telegraph Section of the Munitions Department of the War Ministry.
Tgt.	Tragetier	draught animal.
T.H.	Turm-Haubitze	howitzer in turret.
T.I.W.	Train-Instandsetzungs-Werkstatt	repairing workshop of the Train.
T.K.	Turm-Kanone	gun in turret.
T-Munition		T-shell (*lachrymatory gas shell*).
T.N.A.	Truppen-Nachrichten-Abteilung	regimental signalling detachment.
Tpp.	Trupp	section, party, squad.
Tr.	Train	Train (*not translated*).
Tr.	Trupp	section, party, squad.
Tragt.	Tragetier	draught animal.
Träg. Kol.	Träger-Kolonne	column of carriers.
transf.	transformiert	converted (*ammunition*).
Tr.F.	Train-Fahrer	Train driver.
Trgw.	Tragweite	range; span (*of a bridge*).
Tr. Hdw.	Train-Handwerker	Train artisan.
Trig. P.	Trigonometrischer Punkt	trigonometrical point (*topog.*).
Tr. Ub. Pl.	Truppen-Übungs-Platz	training ground.
T.V.	Technische Vorschrift	technical regulations.
T.V.P.	Truppen-Verband-Platz	regimental aid post.

Abbreviation.	Signification.	English Equivalent.
	U.	
U.	Ulan	"Ulan" (lancer).
U.	Unterkunft	accommodation, quarters.
U.	Unteroffizier	non-commissioned officer.
U.	Unterrichts-	instructional.
U.	Unterstand	dug-out.
u.	um	about, around.
u.	und	and.
u.	unter	under.
u.	urschriftlich	autographic, in original.
u.a.	unter andern	amongst others.
U.A.K.	Unter-Abschnitts-Kommandeur	sub-sector commander.
u.A.w.g.	um Antwort wird gebeten	reply requested.
Üb.	Übungs-	practice.
überw.	überwiesen	allotted.
Übgr.	Übungsgranate	practice shell.
Üb. Ldg	Übungs-Ladung	practice charge.
Üb. Pl.	Übungs-Platz	training ground.
Übpl.	Überplanmässig	surplus to establishment.
Übs.	Übersetzung	translation.
Uffs.	Unteroffiziers	non-commissioned officers (see "Unteroffizier").
Ul.	Ulan	"Ulan" (lancer).
Ul. R.	Ulanen-Regiment	"Ulanen" regiment (lancer regiment).
umg.	umgeändert / umgearbeitet	converted (ammunition).
Untffz. / U.O.	Unteroffizier	non-commissioned officer (see "Unteroffizier").
U.O.	Unterrichts-Offizier	education officer.
U.P.	Unteroffizierposten	an outpost commanded by a non-commissioned officer.
U.R.	unter Rückerbitten	Please return (appears on orders).
U.S.A.	Unterwasser-Schneide-Abteilung	river detachment.
U. St.	Unterstand	dug-out.
Uffz. / U. Offz.	Unteroffizier	non-commissioned officer: also "under-officer," which is a special rank of N.C.O. corresponding to our corporal.
u.U.	unter Umständen	in certain circumstances.
U.U.	Unterirdischer Unterstand	underground shelter.
U.V.	Unteroffizier-Vorschule	Non-commissioned Officers' Preparatory School.
	V.	
V.	Vedette	vedette.
V.	Verbindungs-	communication, liaison.
V.	Verkehrs-	traffic, communication.
V.	Vernehmungs-	see Vernehmungs-Offizier.
V.	Verordnung	order, instructions.
V.	Verpflegungs-	supply (food).

Abbreviation.	Signification.	English Equivalent.
V.	Versuchs-	experimental.
V.	Verwaltungs-	administration.
V.	Verwendungsfähig	fit for duty in.
V.	Vorposten	outpost.
V.	Vorschrift	regulations.
v.	verwundet	wounded.
v.	vide	see.
v.	von	from.
V.A.	Vermessungs-Abteilung	survey section.
Vadeis	Versuchsabteilung des Eisenbahn-Ersatz-Parks	Experimental Section of the Railway Depôt Park.
Vauwumba	Waffen - und Munitions - Beschaffungsamt Verwaltung	Munitions Department Administration.
Vb.G.	Verbindungs-Graben	communication trench.
V.d.F.H.	Verpflegung des Feldheeres	supply of the Field Army.
Verf. } Verfg. }	Verfügung	disposal; order.
Verk.O.	Verkehrs-Offizier	traffic officer.
Verm. Abtlg.	Vermessungs-Abteilung	survey section.
Verpfl.	Verpflegung	supply (*food*).
Vers.	Versuchs-	experimental.
Vers.K.	Versuchs-Kanone	experimental gun.
Vers. Kdo. Flak	Versuchskommando für Flugabwehr-Kanonen	Anti-aircraft Gun Experimental Detachment.
verst.	verstanden	understood.
verst.	verstärkt	strengthened.
Vert.	Verteidigung	defence.
Verw.	Verwaltung	administration.
Verw.	Verwundet(er)	wounded.
Vfg.	Verfügung	disposal; order.
Vfldw. } Vfw. } Vfwbl. }	Vizefeldwebel	vice-serjeant-major.
V.G.U.	verlesen, genehmigt, unterschrieben	noted, approved, signed.
v.H.	von Hundert	per cent.
v.J.	vom Jahre	of the year.
v.J.	vorigen Jahres	last year.
V.K.	Verkürzte Kammerhülse	shortened central tube (*of shrapnel*).
V.K.	Vorposten-Kompagnie	outpost company.
V.K.G.	Verkehrsgraben	supervision *or* lateral communication trench.
V.L.	Vereins-Lazarett	auxiliary hospital.
v.M.	vorigen Monats	last month, ult.
v.m.	vormittags	in the morning, a.m.
V.O.	Verbindungs-Offizier	liaison officer.
V.O.	Vernehmungs-Offizier	intelligence officer at Corps H.Q. (*for the examination of prisoners*).
Vorh.	Vorhut	advanced guard.
Vorl.	Vorlage	flash reducer (*in propelling charge*).
vorm.	vormittags	in the morning, a.m.
Vorp. Komp.	Vorposten-Kompagnie	outpost company.
Vorst.	Vorstecker	safety pin (*of fuze*).

Abbreviation.	Signification.	English Equivalent.
V.O.v.Pl.	Verkehrs-Offizier vom Platz	fortress communication officer.
V.P.	Vorposten	outpost.
Vpfl.O.	Verpflegungs-Offizier	supply officer.
V.P.K.	Verkehrstechnische-Prüfungs-Kommission	Technical Examining Committee of the Communication Service.
Vpl.	Verpflegung	supply (*food*).
v.Pl.	vom Platz	of the fortress.
V.s.d.A.O.K.	von seiten des Armee-Oberkommandos	On behalf of the Army Commander.
V.s.d. stv.G.K.	von seiten des Stellvertretenden General-Kommandos	For the Corps District Commander.
Vrst. / Vst.	Vorstecker	safety pin (*of fuze*).
V.S.d.	Von Seiten des...	For .... (*above signature*).
v.T.	vom Tage	of the day.
V.W.	Vorrats-Wagen	store wagon.
Vw.	Vorwerk	farm, manor (*topog.*).
Vzfeldw.	Vizefeldwebel	vice-serjeant-major.
Vz. Wm.	Vizewachtmeister	vice-serjeant-major (*mounted troops*).

W.

W.	Wache	guard, sentry.
W.	Waffen	arms.
W.	Wagen	cart, railway carriage.
W.	Warte	station post.
W.	Wasser	water.
W.	Werft	shipyard.
W.	Werkstatt	workshop.
W.	Westen	west.
W.	Württembergisch	Württemberg
w.	wende	turn over.
w.	westlich	west of, westerly.
Wachtm.	Wachtmeister	serjeant-major (*of cavalry, field artillery*).
W.B.K.	Wasser-Bau-Kompagnie	water supply construction company.
W.Betr.K.	Wasser-Betriebs-Kompagnie	water supply company (?).
Wehrm.	Wehrmann (Landwehrmann)	Landwehrman.
Werkst.	Werkstätte	workshop.
westl.	westlich	west of, westerly.
Wewa (a.L.)	Wetterwarte (am Luftschiffhafen)	meteorological station (at airship base).
W.F.	Wagen-Fähre	ferry for wagons (*topog.*).
W. Flak. Battr. (Zug)	Flug-Abwehr-Kanonen-Batterie (Zug) auf Wagen	anti-aircraft battery (section) mounted on wagons.
W.Gr.	Wurfgranate	trench mortar bomb (*fired from "Granatwerfer"*).
Wk.V.	Winker-Verbindung	flag signalling communication.
W.M.	Wurf-Mine	*Minenwerfer* H.E. shell.
Wohlf. O.	Wohlfahrts-Offizier	"welfare" officer.
W.P.	Wachposten	sentry.

Abbreviation.	Signification.	English Equivalent.
W.S.O.	Waffen-Sammel-Offizier	Officer in charge of the salving of arms, salvage officer.
Wth.	Wacht-Turm	watch tower (*topog.*).
W.U.	Wohn-Unterstand	living dug-out.
Wumba	Waffen- und Munitions-Beschaffungs-Amt	Munitions Department of the War Ministry.
W.W.	Windewagen	winch wagon (*balloon equipment*).
W.W.	Windwarte	wind observation post.

Z.

Abbreviation.	Signification.	English Equivalent.
Z.	Zeit	time.
Z.	Ziffer	paragraph; cipher; numeral.
Z.	Zug	platoon, section; train.
Z.	Zünder	fuze.
z.	zu	to, at, for.
Z.A.B.	Zivil-Arbeiter-Bataillon	civilian labour battalion.
Z.A.K.	Zentral-Abnahme-Kommission	Central Commission (for taking over aeroplanes from the factory).
z.B.	zum Beispiel	for example.
z.b.V.	zu besonderer Verwendung	for special employment.
z.D.	zur Disposition	on half pay (*of officers*).
Zdg.	Zündung	fuze.
Zdldg. Zdlg.	Zündladung	exploder (*in a shell*).
Zdr.	Zünder	fuze, detonator.
Zetwumba	Zentral Waffen- und Munitions-Beschaffungsamt	Central Munitions Department.
Zf.	Ziffer	paragraph; cipher; numeral.
z.F.	zu Fuss	Foot (*Guards*).
Zg.	Zug	platoon, section; train.
Zgf.	Zugführer	platoon commander.
Zgl.	Ziegelei	brick-field (*topog.*).
Zif. Ziff.	Ziffer	paragraph; cipher; numeral.
Ziv. Arb. Btl.	Zivil-Arbeiter-Bataillon	civilian labour battalion.
Zlmstr.	Zahlmeister	paymaster.
Z.m.W.M.	Zünder mittlerer Wurf-Mine	fuze of medium *Minenwerfer*.
Z.-Schlüssel	Zünder-Schlüssel	fuze key.
Z.s.W.M.	Zünder schwerer Wurf-Mine	fuze of heavy *Minenwerfer*.
Z.s.u.m.W.M.	Zünder schwerer und mittlerer Wurf-Mine	fuze of heavy and medium *Minenwerfer*.
z.T.	zum Teil	partly.
Ztg. Kru.	zeitig kriegsunbrauchbar	temporarily unfit.
Z.U.	zeitlich untauglich	temporarily unfit.
zuget.	zugeteilt	allotted to.
zugew.	zugewiesen	allotted; detailed.
Zugf.	Zugführer	platoon commande
Zugpf.	Zugpferd	draught horse.
z.Z.	zur Zeit	at present.

Abbreviations not ordinarily found in documents, but sometimes employed in telephone and wireless messages.

Abbreviation.	Signification.	English Equivalent.
AB.	abgeschlagen	repulsed.
DLT.	Drahtlose Telegraphie	wireless telegraphy.
DR.	Drahtverhau	"wire," wire entanglement.
E....	Eigene Truppen	our troops.
EA.	Eigene Artillerie	our artillery.
EB.	erbeten	requested.
EDG.	Etat der Gewehrmunition	statement showing quantity of rifle ammunition available.
EF.	Einzelfeuer	independent fire.
EF.	erforderlichen Falls	if necessary.
EFR.	Eigener Flammenwerfer	our *Flammenwerfer*.
EGMIN....	Eigenes Gasminenfeuer	our *Minenwerfer* gas shell fire.
EI.	Eigene Infanterie	our infantry.
EI.—VW.	EigeneInfanterie geht vorwärts	our infantry is advancing.
EMG.	Eigenes M.G. Feuer	our machine gun fire.
EMIN.	Eigenes Minenfeuer	our *Minenwerfer* fire.
ESP.	Eigenes Sperrfeuer	our barrage fire.
FA.	feindliche Artillerie	hostile artillery.
FBT.	feuerbereit	ready to open fire.
FFR.	feindliche Flammenwerfer	hostile *Flammenwerfer*.
FGMIN....	feindliches Gasminenfeuer	hostile *Minenwerfer* gas shell fire.
FI	feindliche Infanterie	hostile infantry.
FMG.	feindliches Maschingewehr-Feuer	hostile machine gun fire.
FMGF.	feindliches Maschinengewehr-Feuer	hostile machine gun fire.
FMIN.	feindliches Minenfeuer	hostile *Minenwerfer* fire.
FSP.	feindliches Sperrfeuer	hostile barrage fire.
FST.	feindliche Stellung	the enemy's position.
FU.	Feuerüberlegenheit anstreben	"Try to silence the enemy's fire."
FV.	Feuer vereinigen	"Concentrate your fire."
FVT.	Feuer verteilen	"Distribute your fire."
G.	durch das eigene Gewehr-(Maschinengewehr-)feuer gefährdet	endangered by our own rifle machine gun fire.
GF.	gewöhnliches Feuer	normal rate of fire.
GGR.	Gasgranate	gas shell.
GLW.	Geländewinkel	angle of sight.
GMIN.	Gas-Mine	*Minenwerfer* gas shell.
GT.	Granate	high explosive (H.E.) shell.
GW.	Gerätewagen	pioneer store wagon.
GW.	Granat-Zünder	fuze for H.E. shell.
GZ.	Geschütz	gun.

Abbreviation.	Signification.	English Equivalent.
HB.	Haubitzbatterie	howitzer battery.
HDGR. VW.	Handgranaten vorwärts!	Bring up hand grenades!
I. MUN. VW.	Infanterie-Munition vorwärts!	Bring up small arms ammunition!
KODR.	Kommandantur	Commandant's office.
LW.	Lebensmittelwagen	supply wagon.
M.	Trommelfeuer	intense bombardment.
MIN. VW.	Minen vorwärts!	Bring up trench mortar ammunition!
MQ.	Marschquartier	billet on the line of march.
OB.	Orts-Biwak	close billets.
OQ.	Orts-Quartier	billet.
PW.	Packwagen	baggage wagon.
RP.	Relaisposten —	relay posts.
SA.	Schwere Artillerie	heavy artillery.
SA.	Sandsäoke	sand bags.
SKO.	Sanitätskompagnie	medical *or* bearer company.
TZ.	Tagesziel	day target, target of the day(?).
ZP.	Zielpunkt	objective.
ZP. NR—G.	Zielpunkt Nr.—genommen	Objective No. — captured.

www.ingramcontent.com/pod-product-compliance
Lightning Source LLC
Chambersburg PA
CBHW070534090426
42735CB00013B/2978